THE DISARMERS

By the same author

A FUTURE FOR THE FREE CHURCHES?

THE DISARMERS

A Study in Protest

by P.

CHRISTOPHER DRIVER

HODDER AND STOUGHTON

Copyright © 1964 by Christopher Driver

First printed 1964

Printed in Great Britain
for Hodder and Stoughton Ltd.,
St. Paul's House, Warwick Lane, London, E.C.4
by Richard Clay and Company, Ltd.,
Bungay, Suffolk

For

CATHARINE and PENELOPE

and for

their children's children

"A Japanese flowering cherry planted in Christchurch Park, Ipswich, on Good Friday, was found cut down yesterday. A clump of rhubarb was in its place.

"The tree had been planted by the local branch of CND as a peace symbol to mark the dropping of the atomic bombs on Nagasaki and Hiroshima."

(The *Guardian*, April 7, 1964)

THIS is not a history—nor even an obituary—of the Campaign for Nuclear Disarmament, although the activities of this organisation figure largely in the text, and the recent resignation of its Chairman clearly closes a period. It is a book about a nation's developing response to the possession of weapons too destructive to be rationally used. It is a book about the Absurd. Behind the black-and-white symbol of anti-nuclear protest gathered hundreds of thousands of people, especially young people, for whom this cause often became a substitute for religion, commanding the same loyalties, exhibiting the same fundamentalisms, and arousing the same resentments. The Campaign was accustomed to the language of hysteria, employed against it by bishops and cabinet ministers, and on its behalf by canons and philosophers. So it was that for every nuclear disarmer who planted a Nagasaki cherry-tree as a symbol of international reconciliation there was, figuratively speaking, a "patriot" to chop it down and substitute a clump of rhubarb. So it was that to make up for a largely hostile and contemptuous press the disarmers on occasion thought of inscribing their message in seaside rock and of attaching it to hydrogen-filled balloons ... Yet the Campaign for Nuclear Disarmament itself was no sudden creation. The child of a gradually accumulated sense of crisis, it expressed the pent-up fears and emotions of a decade. It was like yet unlike the peace movements which preceded it in this century of wars, and it will no doubt have successors, though the exact line of succession may be as hard to determine as its ancestry has been.

In writing this book, I have received extensive help from an embarrassingly large number of people. It is not possible to mention them all, and indeed, since my main sources have been documentary, it would give the wrong impression. But I am especially grateful to: Richard Exley and David V. Edwards, for letting me read and draw extensively upon their academic theses on different aspects of the Campaign (see bibliography); Hugh Brock, until this year editor of *Peace News*, and his staff; and David Hoggett, librarian of the Commonweal Trust.

I am grateful to the publishers of the following books for permission to quote passages:

Bruno Bettelheim *The Informed Heart* (Thames & Hudson); Bertolt Brecht *Life of Galileo*, translated by Desmond Vesey (Methuen and Suhrkamp Verlag); Jane Buxton and Margaret Turner *Gate Fever* (Cresset Press); Martin Harrison, *Trade Unions and the Labour Party* (Allen & Unwin); Herman Kahn *On Thermonuclear War* (Oxford University Press and Princeton

University Press); Charles Morgan *The Burning Glass* (Macmillan); David Mercer *The Generations* (Calder); J. A. T. Robinson *On Being the Church in the World* (SCM Press); Bertrand Russell *Power* (Allen & Unwin); C. P. Snow *Science and Government* (Oxford University Press); John Strachey *The Prevention of War* (Macmillan); Clara Urquhart (ed.) *A Matter of Life* (Cape).

Among the many people with whom I have usefully conversed are: Sir Joseph Simpson, Canon L. John Collins, Dr John Burton, Pat Arrowsmith, David Boulton, George Clark, Peggy Duff, David L. Edwards, John Gittings, Richard Gott, Trevor Hatton, Jeremy Isaacs, Brian Lapping, Vera Leff, Peter Moule, Michael Randle, Bruce Reid, Ralph Schoenman, Gene Sharp, John Slater, Jean Stead, John Vincent, and Oliver Walston. Valuable letters have been sent or documents lent by, among others: Gerald Bailey, Peter Brown, Peter Cadogan, Ianthe Carswell, J. Russell Cleaver, Judith Cook, Howard Davies, Tony Dickie, Jacquetta Hawkes, Terence Heelas, Cyril Hughes, Eric Jacobs, Hugh Jenkins, Denis Knight, Kenneth Leech, Alan Litherland, Guy Metcalf, Werner Pelz, Charles Radcliffe, Bob Radford, Colin Smart, and Richard Storey. I am also indebted to the Gallup Poll for permission to quote from their survey findings.

For the errors, misinterpretations, and prejudices which this book no doubt contains, these people are in no way responsible, but it could hardly have been written without their help. Even more is this true of the editor of The *Guardian*, Alastair Hetherington, who gave me leave of absence at a critical period; the paper's librarians in Manchester and London, Frank Singleton and Kenneth Murphy; and my wife, who suffered much and complained no more than was reasonable.

CHRISTOPHER DRIVER

Highgate, April 1964

CONTENTS

CHAPTER ONE

GESTATION OF A CAMPAIGN: 1943-57

"When the devil was real to people, he destroyed hapless victims just as the bomb does. Those burned at the stakes because they or their fellow men believed in the devil died no imaginary death; they were as dead as the victims of atomic warfare. The prophecy of the world coming to an end in the year A.D. 1000 was not only as widespread, but led to more suicides, percentage-wise, than our fear of atomic bombs destroying the world. In a religious age, men believed and feared out of religious knowledge: namely, the 1,000th anniversary of Christ's birth. In a scientific age, man fears on the basis of scientific knowledge: the atomic bomb."

Bruno Bettelheim,
The Informed Heart (Thames & Hudson, 1961), p. 54

THE first atomic bomb to be dropped in anger exploded over Hiroshima on the morning of August 8, 1945. On the evening of January 15, 1958, the Campaign for Nuclear Disarmament had its birth registered in Canon John Collins' study at Number Two, Amen Court, near St Paul's. On the time-scale of post-war history, 13 years are an extraordinarily long gestation period. The British are by temperament a conscience-struck people, quickly stirred by national or international outrages. Why did it take so long?

Without a detailed analysis of British social and political history since the war no definite answer to this question could be given. In this chapter I only offer certain pointers. Meanwhile, it should be noted that the first public protest against the manufacture and use of nuclear weapons was voiced in Britain not in 1958, not in 1945, but in 1943, two-and-a-half years before the first successful atomic bomb was exploded at Alamogordo, New Mexico, and only one month after Fermi and his fellow scientists at the University of Chicago had achieved the world's first self-sustaining chain reaction.

There are probably not more than a dozen people in the country who remember the occasion. It never entered the knowledge of the peace movement as a whole, and I owe its rediscovery to Mr Cyril Hughes, of Penmaenmawr, who on a Sunday afternoon in January 1943 took the chair at an ILP meeting, attended by 20 or 30 local supporters, in a dingy Co-op hall in St Helens. The speaker was Mr Bob Edwards, then an official of the Chemical Workers Union and now Labour MP for Bilston. I have been unable to discover any contemporary record of what was said, but later in the year Mr Edwards published through the ILP a pamphlet which contains the words:

"In Germany, the USA, and to a lesser degree in Britain thousands of leading scientists are concentrating in an effort to solve the problem of the effective use of atomic power as a destructive weapon in the present or future wars . . .

"The search for Uranium 235, from which this power is derived, opens up the possibilities of such devastating frightfulness and destruction that human imagination could not fully grasp the actuality from the use of a single bomb produced from uranium atomic energy. According to the scientists who are conducting this research, one pound of this substance would have a destructive power equal to a thousand of the largest bombs so far used in the present conflict. One small bomb exploded in the centre of London, Berlin, Tokio, or New York would literally destroy the whole city."*

Not surprisingly, Mr Edwards had considerable trouble with the Censor before his pamphlet appeared, and both he and Mr Hughes say that the spoken version at St Helens was more detailed and definite. He had reached his conclusions, he says, by putting two and two together from remarks dropped by acquaintances in the American chemical industry about, for example, the sweeping up of uranium dust in the mines of Colorado. When he published his pamphlet it was refuted by an ICI scientist, who patiently explained that it would be quite impossible to use atomic fission for military purposes.

Mr Edwards, a Spanish Civil War veteran whose international career includes meetings with Roosevelt, Stalin, and Trotsky, forgot about his pamphlet and turned to fresh causes. Whether it was through his agency or not, knowledge of the forthcoming weapon was fairly widespread in the Forces early in 1945—a friend who was called up at that time remembers being told about it by a sergeant at his training camp. But neither before nor after Hiroshima was the British peace movement in a condition to take a strong and popular line about nuclear weapons. The reasons for this deserve a brief examination, for even today, fifty years after the outbreak of the First World War, the anti-Bomb movements can still exhibit survivors of the 1914 No Conscription Fellowship.

Active pacifism has a long and on the whole honourable history in Britain. Since the mid-17th century it has been a feature of the radical branch of English religious Dissent, represented chiefly in the Society of Friends. Over the past 150 years it has undergone, like other originally religious inspirations, a gradual though still far from complete secularisation. Even some of the techniques used by nuclear disarmers in the 1950s can be paralleled from the 1850s. The international group which marched from San Francisco to Moscow in 1961 had their counterpart in the group of Quakers who travelled by sledge to Moscow in an attempt to stop the Crimean War. (*The Times* of the day—*semper idem*—wrote a supercilious leader.) By 1914, when war became total, evoking total enthusiasm from the majority of the population and total rejection from a few, the Quakers had two other strands of protest with which to intertwine: the Suffragettes and the ILP. The No Conscription Fellowship of 1914 was formed as the result of a letter in the *Labour Leader* signed by a young Socialist called Fenner Brockway. The Fellowship declared that in the event of conscription being introduced, its members would refuse to bear arms. When

* *War on the People* (Independent Labour Party, 1943), p. 26.

13

conscription came, in 1916, the Fellowship held its first convention, attended by 2,000 young men of whom most were officially "deemed to be enlisted". In all during the 1914–18 war, 6,261 men refused to obey the Military Service Act and were arrested.

The treatment they were accorded brought lasting shame on to the Government of the day, the military authorities, and not least the public itself. The Government set out to smash the Fellowship, which was provided—like the Direct Action Committee in 1959—with shadow officials to take over their duties as soon as the originals were arrested. Eight members of the National Committee were fined a total of £800 for publishing a leaflet, *Repeal the Act*, and the Hon. Bertrand Russell (as he then was) was imprisoned after writing a leaflet describing the victimisation of a conscientious objector. Both in military and in civil custody, the victimisation of conscientious objectors reached an extraordinary pitch. Of the 6,261 arrested, 71 died in prison or after release on medical grounds, and many others were permanently scarred in mind or body by their experiences. The imposition of solitary confinement, bread-and-water punishment, and the silence rule were commonplace. Many had sentences of death passed upon them by courts martial, commuted—after a long judicial pause—to penal servitude. On one occasion the pause lasted so long that there was time for the Army to convey the men to France to be shot at the front as an example. Just in time, a telegram to Professor Gilbert Murray enabled Professor Murray's brother-in-law, Mr Geoffrey Howard, to secure an interview with the Prime Minister, who forbade the executions.

The organic link between the No Conscription Fellowship and the radical wing of the Campaign for Nuclear Disarmament is symbolised in the person of J. Allen Skinner, who spent eighteen months in Wormwood Scrubs and Wandsworth Gaol during 1916 and 1917. A Post Office clerk who had never lost a day's work through illness, Mr Skinner contracted surgical TB in the knee and elbow—persistently diagnosed as rheumatism by the prison doctors—and underwent several operations after the war. He subsequently became editor of *Peace News*, and a sponsor of the Emergency Committee for Direct Action against Nuclear War when it was formed in 1957. When he was taken to Brixton Prison in 1960 after a Direct Action Committee demonstration he was able to tell the Governor that he had done time in British prisons 43 years previously. With feeling, the Governor replied: "That must have been a terrible experience." Mr Skinner still had to protect his paralysed left arm and elbow joint with a sling when he took part in the Ministry of Defence sit-down in 1961. The leader of that sit-down, Lord Russell, had been a speaker at the 1919 rally which wound up the No Conscription Fellowship.

The Fellowship, he said then, "has been completely victorious in its stand for freedom not to kill or to take part in killing . . . in winning this victory you have won an even greater victory; you have won a victory for the sense of human worth."*

After 1919 the impetus of the Fellowship, under Clifford Allen's leadership, was carried over into the No More War Movement, later merged with the Peace Pledge Union under Canon Dick Sheppard and George Lansbury. By 1939 the PPU had secured from 136,000 people a signature to the declaration: "I renounce war and will never sanction another."

In the Peace Ballot (an entirely separate affair, conducted in 1934–5 under the auspices of the League of Nations Union) $11\frac{1}{2}$ million people cast votes on a series of questions which included: "Do you consider that, if a nation insists on attacking another, the other nations should combine to compel it to stop by (a) economic and non-military measures (b) if necessary, military measures?" Only 6 p.c. of the respondents answered no to both these questions, but 20 p.c. rejected the military measures. While there is, in fact, no reason whatsoever to interpret the Peace Ballot as a vote for Appeasement—it was, rather, a vote for collective resistance to aggression and was attacked as such by the Conservative ministers and newspapers who later supported Munich—it certainly represented a change from the mindless war-fever of 1914; and the 20 p.c. who rejected military sanctions should be compared with the very similar proportion of the population which was found by opinion polls to be in sympathy with the CND's case between 1958 and 1964.†

Both the ILP and the whole internationalist strain of the British Labour Party lost ground after 1918, partly because domestic political power was by then within the Labour movement's reach, but partly, perhaps, because it had been an article of faith with pre-1914 British Socialists that the German trade unions would halt the Kaiser in his tracks by industrial action, and it had been a notable disillusionment when they voted war credits instead. The first post-war leaders of the Labour Party, Ramsay Macdonald and George Lansbury, were both pacifists. But by the mid-thirties, Macdonald was anathema to all Socialists and Lansbury had been compelled by Ernest Bevin to resign. From that moment on, there was still room for pacifists within the Labour Party, but not at the top. If support for collective security, and recognition that "Fascism means war", had been as widespread on the Right as it was on the Left, the history of the thirties might have been different.

But after 1945 it was not this aspect of the inter-war years

* The foregoing account is taken from Hugh Brock, *The Century of Total War* (*Peace News* pamphlet). † See p. 98 *et seq.*

which was most generally remembered. The peace movements as a whole, with the rest of the population, accepted what can now be seen to be a guilt-induced myth: the myth that the religious and humanitarian reaction to the Somme and Passchendaele, expressed in the activities of the Peace Pledge Union, had itself been a major contributory cause of the Second World War.* Not a few of those who had signed the Peace Pledge changed their minds when war came, regarding the conflict as inevitable and the cause as just. At the end of the war, what with news of the fate suffered by European Jewry and speedy disillusionment with Soviet Russia, the peace movements were further demoralised. In 1946 Middleton Murry, who had edited *Peace News* right through the war, abandoned pacifism and resigned.

In other respects also the decade which followed 1945 bore little resemblance to the decade which followed 1918. After the Second World War the opinion-forming classes of Britain had lost their faith in political utopias. Despite the shorter casualty lists, the second war's tentacles had reached farther down into the national life than the first's. The task of physical and social reconstruction looked more formidable. As for Hiroshima and Nagasaki, they were a long way away, and the revolutionary implications of nuclear power were, despite the initial shock, hardly understood at all. In December 1945, when the British public was asked by the Gallup Poll what changes it expected to be brought about by the splitting of the atom, only 4 p.c. of the respondents mentioned changes in military techniques and international relations. Moreover, in an idealistic fling, Britain had elected a Labour Government. For the first time, Socialist supporters of peace movements found themselves caught up in the nation's business as units in a huge Parliamentary majority. Later, in Opposition, the forces of dissent became stronger again, and the names of Labour MPs appear more frequently in the columns of *Peace News*. But in the years after 1945 there was almost always too much else to do.

Nor was the outer circle of Labour MPs allowed access to decisions with which they might have disagreed. In June 1947 Mr Raymond Blackburn, MP, assured a pacifist audience that no British atomic bomb was being made or could be made for several years, and in October 1952, when the first British A-bomb was tested, the Prime Minister (Mr Churchill) drily expressed envy of his predecessor, who had managed to get the £100 million which it had cost tucked away in the Supply Estimates without Parliament noticing. Mr R. H. S. Crossman,

* It naturally suits modern Conservatives, especially ex-Appeasers, to keep this belief alive. For a useful shot at debunking it: cf. *Who was for Munich?*, a pamphlet by the University Group on Defence Policy (Peter Eaton, 1959).

MP, recently even asserted that the decision to make the bomb, which was unobtrusively announced to Parliament by Lord Alexander in May 1948, was taken by Mr Attlee without consulting the Cabinet as a whole. This was later denied on Lord Attlee's behalf by Mr G. R. Strauss, who was Minister of Supply at the time, and who states that the decision was taken in the Defence Sub-Committee of the Cabinet and circulated to Cabinet members.*

It is just possible that had the effects and strategic implications of nuclear weapons become generally known in Britain immediately after Hiroshima, the impression produced on the public mind would have been deep enough to outlast later distractions. But they were not. Certainly, some of Middleton Murry's snap judgements were acute:

"The power of the atom bomb allied to the robot weapon is a possibility that comes immediately to the layman's mind,"†

and:

"It is quite idle to suppose that the secret can be kept. Within ten years the atomic bomb, probably in a far more destructive form, will be available as a weapon to every major power."‡

But thanks to the effects of American censorship in occupied Japan, the precise effects of atomic weapons on their victims was not widely known until much later. John Hersey's *Hiroshima*,§ the first full description, was not published until the autumn of 1946, and for two years after the end of the war, the main public debate on atomic weapons, such as it was, centred round the problem of international control (the Baruch Plan was published in January 1947) and round the recriminations of the physicists over the manner in which the decision to drop the bomb was taken. As early as September 1945 Professor M. E. Oliphant, Professor of Physics at Birmingham University and a member of the British technical committee of scientists on atomic bomb development, expressed the widely held scientific belief that "this weapon could have been used against Japan very effectively without dropping it on a city".

In 1946 the McMahon Atomic Energy Act, which prohibited American scientists from imparting atomic secrets to their British counterparts, imposed a further curfew on free discussion in the scientific world, and the British public showed little disposition to inquire whether the Government was going it alone, and if so with what success. Nor were some of the men subsequently

* Cf. *Encounter*, April 1963, p. 26, and correspondence in the June and August numbers. † *Peace News*, August 10, 1945. ‡ *Ibid.*, September 28, 1945. § Penguin, 1946.

prominent in the CND at this period united in their views. In May 1947 Mr Kingsley Martin, editor of the *New Statesman*, argued in his "Londoner's Diary" that "if an atomic war came, these vulnerable islands would be completely destroyed in the clash between the hemispheres", and continued: "Our only hope is that by atomic neutrality we should avoid provoking either side to destroy us either as an arsenal or as a base." But at the same period Lord Russell advocated using the threat of preventive war to compel the Soviet Union to accept the Baruch Plan for the internationalisation of atomic energy.

In view of the strictures later to be passed by members of CND on the behaviour of the churches, it is surprising to find that in the late forties, ecclesiastical assemblies and reports constituted a major forum for public discussion of atomic weapons.* The discussions were admittedly inconclusive, and to the pacifists profoundly unsatisfactory. But in 1948–9 the pacifists were gathering their forces for what then seemed a more pressing challenge—the fight to prevent conscription being reintroduced in Britain. True, there was a Caxton Hall meeting on atomic weapons in April 1948, addressed by Vera Brittain, Alex Wood, and Ritchie Calder (later Vice-Chairman of CND); and in October 1949, after the establishment of NATO and the agreement to accept American air-bases on British soil, a similar group which also included Benjamin Britten, Augustus John, and Henry Usborne (then a Labour MP) issued a letter urging the Government not to make or borrow atomic bombs, to withdraw American bases, and to open atomic research centres to any country's inspection. But by this time, well-informed persons were already announcing that atomic weapons were *vieux jeu*. The previous month Mr Brock Chisholm, Director General of the World Health Organisation, told the World Union of Peace Organisations:

"The atomic bomb is obsolete. It is child's play compared to biological weapons. There is a product in existence† which if spread extensively can kill on contact or if breathed in. It can kill all living beings within six hours and leave the area safe for troops to occupy within the twelve hours it takes to disappear."‡

In one sphere only during this period were the future lines of CND policy discernible. This was over Civil Defence. Then as now, the Government thought it necessary to go through the motions of organising recruiting campaigns and persuading the

* Cf. Chapter 7. † Presumably one of the nerve gases was being referred to. In Washington the Finletter Report, *Survival in the Air Age*, published in January 1948, had already emphasised the vast destructive potential of biological weapons. ‡ *Peace News*, September 16, 1949.

public that what was widely assumed to be indefensible could in fact be defended. Professor Kathleen Lonsdale, a pacifist who is also a nuclear physicist, persistently accused the Home Office of lacking candour:

"At Hiroshima, 27 out of 33 fire stations were gutted and three-quarters of the fire fighting personnel put out of action. At the same time, fires broke out all over the city. A quarter of a million people were killed or injured, but so were 90 p.c. of the doctors and 75 p.c. of the nurses. Every hospital but one was wrecked, every power and railway station, every telegraph and telephone exchange destroyed.

"The Home Office inspectorate for Civil Defence are paid to do their job by us and of course they do it as well as they can. If war were unthinkable, they would have to find other jobs. Part of their job is to create an atmosphere of security."

Similar opinions were expressed in Parliament during Civil Defence debates, and *Peace News* returned to the attack in the autumn of 1949, when the annual Civil Defence recruiting campaign was launched. It published photographs (rarely seen in British publications) of bodies being cremated in the streets for want of people to bury them after the Allies' conventional raid on Dresden in 1945. Nor were pacifists the only people to make what might be regarded as alarmist statements. In a House of Lords debate on Civil Defence in November 1949 Lord Trenchard, a former Air Chief Marshal, said that atomic bombing could kill 10 million people in a week and 20 million in a month. He added: "A nation which lost that amount of manpower in such a short period could not exist."

There was little sign that Lord Trenchard's appreciation of the situation had penetrated to the people's elected representatives. On July 24, 1950, the House of Commons debated Civil Defence for the first time for two years. Mr Stephen McAdden, a Conservative, slated Mr S. O. Davies, a Labour pacifist, for asking the Prime Minister to inform the people that there is no means of protecting them against atom bombs. "If such nonsense is to be found in the heads of Members of Parliament, it is no wonder that such ideas are gaining a certain amount of ground among the people of the country." Seven years later a Conservative Minister of Defence in his annual White Paper was to say: "It must be frankly recognised that there is at present no means of providing adequate protection for the people of this country against the consequences of an attack with nuclear weapons." Nor were Labour Members, in 1950, conspicuously wiser. The House was treated to Mrs Bessie Braddock's experiences of the black-out in wartime Liverpool:

"One noticed a slight chink of light that could be seen round the top and the side of a window or an inability to cover the area between the top of the curtain and the top of the window. These are small but important matters ... It might be suggested to local authorities that, in the building of new houses there should be, between the top of the window and the top of the curtain, a covering pelmet of wood under which the curtain could go so that there would be no possibility of light escaping from the top of the window and down the side."*

Another Labour Member, Mr Arthur Lewis, wondered whether it would be practicable to have a system of balloon barrage round the coast, "those balloons perhaps being treated with radioactivity to affect incoming planes. I am no expert, but I still wonder if that would be possible. If it is not, could they be electrified so as to emit an electrical ray to prevent the bombers coming in?" A year later a United States Congressional Committee asked Robert Oppenheimer: "Is there any defence against this weapon?" "Certainly," he replied. "And that is ...?" "Peace."

As the Labour Government's life wound fretfully to its close public anxiety began to stir. The stirrings were masked by the other contemporary anxieties of war resisters and Left-wing Labour MPs. Beset from without by the Korean War, which broke out in June 1950, and from within by the quarrels over the pace of rearmament, Mr Attlee's Government could hardly have been expected to notice such a tiny straw in the wind as the Peace Pledge Union's establishment of a new Non-Violence Commission to study and discuss the possibility of direct action to seek withdrawal of American forces, stoppage of the manufacture of atomic weapons in Britain, withdrawal of Britain from NATO, and disbandment of the British Armed Forces.

However, on January 31, 1950, President Truman announced that he had directed the Atomic Energy Commission to continue its work on all forms of atomic energy weapons, including the so-called hydrogen or super-bomb. The decision, for a time finely balanced, was clinched by the defection of Klaus Fuchs from Britain to the Russians. In the spring of that year the new weapon—which had arrived before the scale of its comparatively tiny predecessors had been fully appreciated by the British public—evoked sporadic protests. In March the Bishop of Birmingham (Dr Barnes) said that Britain should give a lead to the world by refusing to make H-bombs, and a Bexhill vicar started a fast. In April, 100 Cambridge scientists petitioned the Government on the same lines. In August, 3,000 attended an Hiro-

* Hansard, July 24th, 1950.

shima Day commemoration in Trafalgar Square, organised jointly by several peace societies; and Dr Donald Soper, who told the Methodist Conference that he would rather see the country overrun by Communism than the world plunged into another world war, announced that of the 600 letters he subsequently received, only 10 were critical. The pacifists also returned to the attack on Civil Defence. The PPU sold 45,000 copies of a leaflet by a young biologist, Dr Alex Comfort, entitled *Civil Defence: what you should do now*. A Conservative MP who regarded the leaflet as subversive asked a question in the House about it, and Dr Comfort's reply was printed in the *News Chronicle*. The peace movements were plucking up their courage again, and in January 1951, *Peace News* reviewed *Christianity and the War Crisis*, by an up-and-coming cleric, John Collins, and an established publisher, Victor Gollancz. "Is it revolutionary enough?" asked "T.R.D." "Has it got that prophetic vision which takes it out of the flow of pious sentiment and gives it that dramatic quality which something *really* new and revolutionary would have? Many readers may feel that it stops short of the vital step."*

In 1951 the first piece in the CND jigsaw pattern fell into place. The Conservatives were returned at the General Election held in October. While in Opposition, the Conservatives had naturally supported the tough line which Mr Attlee took with his own Left wing, even while exploiting the Labour Party's divisions politically. At the same time, they were by no means as rigid as they later appeared, when in power themselves. It was Mr Churchill who warned the House in February 1951:

"We must not forget that by creating the atomic bases in East Anglia we have made ourselves the target and perhaps the bull's eye of a Soviet attack."†

And it was Lord Hinchingbrooke, a Conservative MP and a High Tory democrat, who said a month later:

"I believe that people who say that police restraint should be put on any groups or factions or parties who might oppose a government's warlike purpose are dangerously wrong."‡

In October 1951 Britain had a new Government, and in February 1952 a new monarch. The first official communiqué from 10 Downing Street in Queen Elizabeth's reign announced that Britain proposed to explode an atomic bomb of her own. On both sides in Parliament the desire to preserve British inde-

* *Peace News*, January 12, 1951.   † Hansard, February 15, 1951, col. 632.
‡ *Peace News*, March 12, 1951.

pendence from Washington was strong, though it was not shared by the *Manchester Guardian*, which commented:

"It is more than a little odd that we must waste millions of pounds in order to impress our best ally and odder still that we must build a bomb in order to explode the McCarran Act."*

And by this time, the PPU's Non-Violence Commission had borne fruit. Serious study of non-violent resistance in the pacifist movement dated back to 1940, when the threat of imminent invasion made the problem "existential" in ways that it had not been in 1916. The Commission's terms of reference, drawn up in 1949, contained the seeds of the Aldermaston March and the Direct Action demonstrations at the Norfolk rocket bases. Members were to examine:

"The place of non-violence in pacifist faith or philosophy, its day to day and emergency methods, relationship between them, appropriate types of self-discipline and public demonstration.

"The basic pattern of a non-violent economy for Britain having regard to the rights and needs of all other peoples, with some indication of what can be done by individual or small group example in present circumstances.

"The aims and methods of a non-violent foreign policy for Britain, with some indication of suitable individual or small group demonstrations practicable in present conditions."

Contact was established with two parallel groups in the United States: the Congress of Racial Equality, whose sit-in techniques were later to become the most successful example of mass non-violent action so far seen in the West; and Peacemakers, a pacifist group whose missile-base projects anticipated those of the British Direct Action Committee. Against this background, the British Non-Violence Commission met on December 12, 1951, to talk about "the danger of the British public getting more and more used to the fact that the American Air Force was occupying this country, and that atomic weapons were actually now manufactured on British soil". They discussed a programme for direct action which they termed "Operation Gandhi", with the ambitious aims of effecting:

The withdrawal of American forces at present in this country.
The stopping of the manufacture of atomic weapons in Britain.
The withdrawal of Britain from the North Atlantic Treaty Organisation.
The disbanding of the British Armed Forces.

* February 18, 1952.

Participants in the programme would have to be willing "to face imprisonment, loss of income, and other hardships". Seven possible places for a sit-down were discussed: Grosvenor Square, Whitehall, Fleet Street, the House of Commons, a Labour Exchange on National Service Registration Day, Harwell, and the USAAF HQ at Ruislip. In the event, an invitation was issued to a sit-down outside the War Office on January 11, 1952, and 11 people responded. A few others agreed to distribute leaflets and to report on the reactions of the police and the public. After some argument, it was decided to inform the police and the press beforehand of what was intended. (This puzzled the police. As one constable pointed out in the lorry which took the demonstrators to Cannon Row after their arrest, they could have had fifteen minutes clear time to display their posters if the police had not already been in position. The officer then had the principles of non-violent action explained to him. It was an unfamiliar subject, but by the end of the decade, there can have been few members of the Metropolitan Force who were not expert in it.)

Arrests were made after the group had sat down and been pulled to their feet twice, and had sat down for the third time. They were all fined 30s. at Bow Street, and a statement of their motives was then handed to the press at the Friends Meeting House in St Martin's Lane. It concluded: "If this demonstration brings new support for non-violent resistance we shall hope to organise others."

The sower had sown his seed, and though most of it withered on the stony flags of Whitehall, some brought forth fruit literally an Hundredfold. An 18-year-old conscientious objector at the London CO Tribunal asked the *Peace News* reporter to put him in touch with the new group. This was Michael Randle, who as Secretary of the Committee of 100 organised the Ministry of Defence sit-down in February 1961, and was later gaoled for eighteen months, along with five colleagues, for his share in organising the Wethersfield demonstration in December of the same year. In May 1952 he wrote to a member of Operation Gandhi:*

"I think the only thing all of us have in common is a belief in the 'negative' side of Gandhi's teaching, his method of resistance. But should this deter us from going on? After all, it is war we are opposing, not social legislation, as Gandhi often was, and we do give people a constructive alternative to war . . .

"We are such a small group that the most effective way of upsetting evil war preparations is to make a direct appeal to those actively engaged in such work, to undermine their morale."

* Cf. Hugh Brock, *op. cit.*

One of the Whitehall group's "observers" was a former Army sergeant, David Hoggett, who had become a pacifist in 1948, been court-martialled and imprisoned. He was later crippled by polio and given the UN Nansen Award for his work with International Voluntary Service for Peace, and his enthusiasm for the Gandhian demonstration communicated itself to his cousin April Carter, then a 13-year-old schoolgirl. She later became the Secretary and resident philosopher of the Direct Action Committee Against Nuclear War.

The announcement that Britain was to test her own atomic bomb helped to keep Operation Gandhi alive. Jack Salkind, a pacifist whose hobby was bus timetables, came across a route which went from Reading to a place called Aere. Hugh Brock, editor of *Peace News*, who was a member of the group, took the bus from Reading to the far side of the village of Aldermaston, and found the Atomic Energy Research Establishment. He reported that 50 people would be needed for an effective act of civil disobedience. The group could not mobilise 50 for a sit-down, but 30 demonstrators went from London by coach to distribute leaflets and show posters to the workers pouring out of the site. They were sympathetically received. But publicity was negligible. The group then turned its attention to the American Air Force. Michael Randle and Hugh Brock went to Mildenhall to tell the police and the Americans that they proposed to hold a demonstration, and on Saturday, June 28, when Dorothy Morton and Constance Jones lay down on the asphalt of the main gateway to the Mildenhall base, the USAAF was prepared for a major emergency. Guards with sten guns or walkie-talkie radios lined the perimeter, and all traffic had been diverted. However, no one was arrested.

This was, effectively, the first of the "false starts" which led up to the founding of CND. Operation Gandhi changed its name to the Non-Violent Resistance Group, discussed, and occasionally demonstrated. But for a year there was virtual quiet on the anti-nuclear front.

However, in October 1952 Britain tested her atomic bomb in the Monte Bello Islands. The following month, the Americans exploded the first H-bomb—far more powerful than the experts had expected—at Bikini Atoll, and in August 1953 the Soviet Union also demonstrated her hydrogen capacity. Moreover, strategists, though not yet the public and politicians as a whole, were beginning to acknowledge the military implications of these events. Chester Wilmot wrote in the *Observer*:* "There is no direct defence against the long-range rocket ... The extent of the transformation in Britain's strategic position has not

* October 25, 1953.

24

yet been reflected in either the pattern of her defence spending or the composition of her military forces." At the same time, the sheer vulnerability of Britain and the moral implications of her defence policy were being more widely recognised. The speeches of Mr R. H. S. Crossman, then a Labour backbencher, are often a sound guide to what progressive public opinion will be a few months later—even if he is by then sometimes discovered to have changed his mind. And in March 1954, during a debate on the Air Estimates, Mr Crossman replied to his own party's defence spokesman, John Strachey, who had urged the building up of a British A-bomber force in order to strengthen Britain's bargaining position *vis-à-vis* the United States. (This remains the main plank of the Conservative case for the British independent deterrent.) Mr Crossman said:

"In 1940 we thought it absolutely inhuman and a violation of every democratic right to bomb the centre of an unprotected city. Then we started preparing to do it ourselves. We started systematic plans for what we called dehousing, which meant deliberately not bombing military targets but systematically destroying working class areas in German towns. That was the policy of Bomber Command. It was absolutely inhuman, and it culminated in Dresden when, quite deliberately, knowing that refugees were in the town, the bombing took place . . .

"This strategic air force epitomises the philosophy of total destruction, which was expressed by the hon. Gentleman who said the point of a war is killing people. But the point of a war is to win with the minimum casualties. Agreed that the Americans will use the atomic bomb. Of course they will. If they are going to use it, and if it is admitted that, in spite of the money we spend, a lot of Russian atomic bombers will get through to Britain, and if we fully support the Americans on this, how can it be justified to have no passive defence for our people at all? . . . That seems to me to be either the rankest inhumanity or bluff . . .

"In my view we should not have a costly passive defence. I think that decision is quite right. But I do not think we should have costly strategic bombers either. We should think in terms of NATO and save our gold. We should think in terms of balanced land and air forces in Europe. We should give up this delusion about strategic bombers. It is demoralising Western democracy."*

The stage was set for the second false start, and it came in April, both at Westminster and among the pacifist protagonists of Direct Action. A hundred MPs signed a motion urging that no further H-tests should take place, and calling for a Five

* Hansard, March 4, 1954, cols. 1541–52.

Power Conference. The city of Coventry (Mr Crossman is MP for Coventry East) voted by 32 to 14 to decline its statutory obligation to provide Civil Defence for its citizens. In New York Professor Lewis Mumford caused some stir by an appeal published in the *New York Times*, arguing that "submission to Communist totalitarianism would still be far wiser than the final destruction of civilisation". *Peace News* published a letter from a Hull reader suggesting that some pacifists should hire a fishing boat and sail out, claiming the freedom of the seas, into the area where the next H-bomb explosion was planned. There was a Commons debate on April 5, and on April 7, 300 delegates from Church, peace, and labour organisations met six Labour MPs at the House of Commons, and gave birth to the Hydrogen Bomb National Campaign. The Revd. Dr Donald Soper—pacifist, Socialist, Methodist—was in the chair, and Canon L. John Collins, of St Paul's Cathedral, who was also present, emphasised that the Campaign was a moral issue.

Unfortunately, the Campaign was not nearly moral enough for the pacifists. The sole object of the Campaign was to collect millions of signatures on a petition whose wording was identical with Mr Attlee's motion in Parliament, asking for a disarmament conference to be convened and for the United Nations to be strengthened. Even before the initial mass meeting in the Albert Hall on April 30, discontent was openly expressed. *Peace News* called the enterprise ill-fated and its sponsors disingenuous. The PPU discouraged pacifists from taking part. *Tribune* suggested that the Government should use the American need for air-bases in Britain as a diplomatic weapon to force American agreement on a joint nuclear policy. Mr Ted Hill, General Secretary of the Boilermakers Union, told his members in his monthly circular that the H-bomb issue could only be settled by the workers themselves "stopping the wheels of industry" until "Sir Winston Churchill and his gang" paid heed to the protests.

The mass rally was advertised by a West End poster parade led by six Labour MPs. As the procession passed the Ministry of Housing and Local Government, Mr Harold Macmillan came down the steps, shook hands with Mr Fenner Brockway, and said: "I'm glad to see you true to your cause." It was probably both the first and the last time that Mr Macmillan made a personal appearance at an anti-nuclear demonstration. He must have thought it an innocuous affair. Of the Labour MPs who sponsored the Campaign one, Mr Anthony Wedgwood Benn, claims never to have been a unilateralist. Disorganised if not demoralised, the Campaign Committee struggled on until the end of the year, eventually claiming a million signatures to its petition. At the closing rally in the Kingsway Hall Mr Anthony

Greenwood, MP, later a Vice-President of CND, said that at least the Campaign had brought together people of all parties and denominations. But since the terms of the petition were anyway acceptable to the Government, this was hardly surprising.

The Hydrogen Bomb National Campaign is little remembered, and it is an index of its obscurity that a year or two later, when anti-nuclear agitation sprang up spontaneously in various parts of the country, most people felt that they were starting something fresh—as indeed, in a sense, they were. Only in the universities, where there were several active and radically-inclined Labour Clubs, did the Campaign achieve much. In Oxford 1,140 undergraduates signed a petition of their own which referred to the "moral responsibility of Britain in her key position in world politics", and in May a Third Camp conference, convened at Ruskin College, started a hare which was later reincarnated in CND literature: the proposal that Britain should, as a logical consequence of abandoning nuclear weapons, disengage from the Great Power struggle and join up with any other powers prepared to pursue a "positive neutralism". A friendly observer of this particular conference says that it was notable for the attendance of "people who wanted to live in trees and abandon all recognised political methods".

The trouble was that even in the Labour Party at that time the British Bomb was only beginning to become a live issue. The first Hydrogen Bomb debate took place in the House of Commons on April 5, 1954. During it Mr Churchill was able to express "astonishment" that a two-month-old speech by the Chairman of the Joint Congressional Atomic Energy Committee, describing the effects of the H-bomb, had barely been noticed by British newspapers and opinion. The debate itself was remarkable mainly for bemused speeches from the back benches and an involved quarrel between Mr Attlee and the Prime Minister over the circumstances in which Britain had been given or denied access to American nuclear secrets. In fact, although the temper of the Labour Party was then more anti-American than it became after the death of Mr John Foster Dulles, possession of the Bomb was popularly attributed by British Socialists to the West as a whole rather than to America or Britain in particular. Sharp distinctions between the American and British deterrents were not drawn, and it was over German rearmament, not the Bomb, that Aneurin Bevan in April resigned from the Shadow Cabinet. In this respect, the National Campaign came a year too soon. A belated obituary of it was contributed by the present Political Correspondent of the *New Statesman*, then President of the Oxford Union:

"For the trumpet call 'Ban the Bomb' to be effective," wrote Mr Anthony Howard, "it must mean two things. First that a thermonuclear disarmament agreement is worth it even if it leaves conventional weapons untouched; and secondly that if an international agreement proves impossible then this country should not hesitate to announce that it at any rate will never make use of thermonuclear horrifics . . . That certainly is the position which I—and I think many other ordinary members— would like to see the Labour Party adopting."*

By this time (less than three months, as it was to turn out, before a General Election) the Labour Party was in serious trouble. In February the annual Defence White Paper had announced for the first time that Britain intended to manufacture her own H-bomb. Two Labour MPs, R. H. S. Crossman and George Wigg, published in the *New Statesman* a far-sighted analysis of the meaning of the Bomb for British strategy. On March 2, Aneurin Bevan, speaking from the back benches, brusquely challenged his own leader in the House of Commons to say whether the official Labour amendment in the Defence debate agreed with the Government's policy, which seemed to commit Britain to using the H-bomb "at once, in the beginning of any sort of hostilities". Seventy Labour MPs abstained from voting in the debate, and Mr Gaitskell and Mr Morrison attempted to have Mr Bevan expelled from the Party. Then on March 10 Sir Richard Acland, Labour MP for Gravesend, resigned his seat and announced his intention of contesting the consequent by-election on the H-bomb issue. "I have sinned," he told the House. "I should have protested, or protested much more vigorously, not merely against the H-bomb today, but against the A-bomb and the strategic bomber force in each year this matter has come forward since the war." In a letter to *The Times*, Mr Howard spoke for his generation by acclaiming Sir Richard's decision as "the most significant private political action since the war. It reveals to some of us what we had previously doubted, that both integrity and intelligence can exist in politics today."

Had Sir Richard been allowed to fight his by-election, the result might quite conceivably have brought forward by three years the founding of a popular mass movement against nuclear weapons. Sir Richard, after all, had already been the leader of one political party—the Commonwealth Party, to which he belonged between leaving the Liberal Party in 1941 and joining the Labour Party in 1947. But Sir Richard, a devout Anglican and humanitarian who was known by his schoolmates at Rugby as "the little Sinn Feiner" because of his loathing for the Black

* *Peace News*, April 7, 1955.

28

and Tans, saw his gesture swallowed up in Mr Churchill's resignation and the May General Election. He fought a brave, virtually one-man campaign in a seat where the splitting of the Labour
vote was almost bound to let the Tory in. He showed little knots
of giggling children and silent adults an exhibition of Hiroshima
photographs. From friendly journalists he drew some neatly-
turned phrases. Harry Boardman of *The Guardian*:

"He is never provoked, never angry. If the electors were to
stone him he would mildly invite them to consider whether they
were not imposing an unnecessary burden on the police."

But local Labour officials accused him of "deserting the team
on Cup Final Day", and V. S. Pritchett in the *New Statesman*,
describing the strange mixture of envy and suspicion which
formed their attitude to Acland, unconsciously anticipated the
agonies of later years:

"People know that Labour's strength is collective spirit, not
romantic singularity, but that Acland expresses something which
the Labour Party once had, but has lost."*

Labour lost the seat, Sir Richard saved his deposit, and
another Anglican—Peter Kirk, son of a famous Bishop of Oxford
—was elected for Gravesend.

After the 1955 Election the defeated Left temporarily lost its
stomach for protest. It was a time for sowing rather than reap-
ing. In July Lord Russell called a press conference and circulated a resolution against the H-bomb signed by ten famous
scientists, including Max Born (Robert Oppenheimer's teacher)
and Albert Einstein of the United States, L. Infield of Poland,
and Hideki Yukawa of Japan. The statement, which was sent to
heads of States, called for an international conference of scientists from East and West and from uncommitted nations.
Subsequently, the American millionaire Cyrus Eaton placed his
estate at Pugwash, Nova Scotia, at the disposal of the Congress
and donated funds. The first Pugwash Conference did not take
place until July 1957. It was attended by three scientists from
the USSR, among others, and according to *I. F. Stone's Weekly*
not a single American newspaper published the communiqué
issued afterwards—a circumstance which may perhaps have
contributed to the extreme sensitivity since shown by Lord
Russell to real or fancied neglect by the press.

Also during 1955 there were signs that the slightly synthetic,
Westminster-based National Campaign possessed, or might have
possessed, much more spontaneous local counterparts. In the
early spring the Revd. Werner Pelz of Lostock, near Bolton, a

* *New Statesman*, May 21, 1955.

refugee from Hitler now widely recognised as one of the most original minds in the Church of England, wrote with his wife letters to one or two local and national papers asking that a movement should be founded against "H-bomb politics". The letter put them in touch with the Toldas Group, a pre-existing pacifist society in Liverpool. The Pelz's had hundreds of letters and, in their own words, "saw groups and cells spring up in most cities from Edinburgh to Bournemouth, and saw them die because we refused to let them turn themselves into mass movements. We did write at that time to most of those who were to feature as the leaders of the intrepid CND—which we ourselves joined in due course with a slightly heavy heart—but none deigned us worthy of a reply."*

The literature circulated by the Pelz's at the time covered so many of the subjects that have since become fashionable in progressive circles (a British Peace Corps, industrial machinery for under-developed countries, and the planning of housing estates and flats on a communal basis) that it is hardly surprising that they were less successful than their more single-minded successors in establishing a simple, short-term campaign to ban the Bomb.

But for such a campaign to be launched an externally introduced catalyst was necessary, and at the beginning of 1956 none was in sight. It seemed more like a testimony to the remoteness than to the urgency of the war problem when in February 1956 the Third Programme broadcast a mediaeval disputation on the morality of nuclear weapons. The disputation was organised by the National Peace Council (an umbrella body sheltering several peace organisations), with Fr Ian Hislop defending nuclear war and Fr Lawrence Bright opposing him. A sample of the dialogue:

Bright: The genetic effects caused by radiation are without assignable limits.

Hislop: If the damage caused is predictable, then the limits are assignable; if unpredictable, the use of nuclear weapons is irresponsible. But the only prediction that can be made is that nuclear weapons produce unpredictable genetic damage.

Bright: If the number of casualties can be calculated, they are predictable. But at the time of operation its victims will not be born. They cannot be said to share in the guilt for which they suffer.

Different aspects of nuclear weapons have worried people more at different periods, and in 1956/7 it was predominantly the tests which caused alarm. De-Stalinisation was in progress after Mr Khruschev's 56th Congress speech, and there seemed less prospect of the weapons being let off in anger. But the Pope's

* In a letter to the author.

Christmas message called for an end to experiments with nuclear weapons, and on January 14 the *Daily Telegraph*, rarely much perturbed by any action of a Conservative Government, said in a leader on the British and American H-tests scheduled for the spring: "Scientists are sharply divided about the genetic effects of radiation . . . We should all be relieved for many reasons if the volume of explosions could everywhere be curtailed."

These doubts were reinforced in June by the publication of a report by the British Atomic Hazards Committee entitled *The Hazards to Man of Nuclear and Allied Radiations** which officially confirmed the danger to young children contained in the strontium-laden dust of hydrogen bomb explosions. Members of the Toldas Group, including Professor Coulson, Professor Lonsdale, Ruth Fry, and Laurence Housman, wrote a letter which was published in many newspapers, asking people who shared their desire for "a revolutionary change of outlook" to communicate with them. There were 600 replies, many of them indicating a desire for "some sort of national campaign" against the H-bomb. The Secretary of the Toldas Group (now "Peacemakers"), Mr Alan Litherland, estimates that as a result some 50,000 individual letters to MPs were sent over the following few months.

But national movements, though they may originate outside London, need a metropolitan base if they are to last, and unknown to the Toldas Group, just such a base was in course of being established. In March 1955 a Socialist doctor's wife in Golders Green, Mrs Vera Leff, mentioned to her local Women's Co-operative Guild the problem of the radiation risk from H-bomb tests. Women's Co-operative Guilds being what they are, it is probable that little would have happened but for another of the Guild's members, a retired civil servant called Gertrude Fishwick. Miss Fishwick was a member of the Anglican Pacifist Fellowship and the Finchley Labour Party. She was also, significantly, an ex-Suffragette, and if any single person can be said to have triggered off the chain reaction which ended in CND it is Miss Fishwick, who died exhausted by her efforts two days before the Central Hall meeting which launched CND in February 1958. She ran the Golders Green Committee for the Abolition of Nuclear Weapons virtually single-handed, visiting vicars, distributing posters, and circulating background information on disarmament negotiations. The title was soon changed to ". . . Committee for the Abolition of Nuclear Weapon Tests" in an attempt to find a basis which most people could accept. Quite swiftly in this closely knit, intellectually and politically active part of London, the circle was widened. Other groups

* HMSO.

were founded in Willesden, Finchley, and Hampstead. Mr Arthur Goss, proprietor of the *Hampstead and Highgate Express*, and Clerk to the Middlesex Quarterly Meeting Peace Committee of the Society of Friends, became Chairman of the Hampstead Committee against Nuclear Weapon Tests, and later of the National Committee. (Later still, when CND was formed, he joined its Executive.) The Hampstead group organised film shows and asked the proprietor of the Hampstead Everyman Cinema to show *Children of Hiroshima*. He refused, and one snowy night the group had the pleasure of seeing queues outside the Town Hall, where they were showing the film themselves.

For the peace-minded, the years 1955–7 were extremely active ones. There were several cross-fertilisations. A famous broadcast by Lord Russell at Christmas 1954, brooding on the H-bomb's threat to mankind, sparked off an editorial in the *Friend* and drove many Quakers, hitherto stuck in their traditional "peace testimony", to the conclusion that nuclear weapons were something different, demanding fresh action. And in February 1957 the clumsily titled National Committee for the Abolition of Nuclear Weapon Tests (hereafter called the NCANWT) was formed, with Dr Sheila Jones, a Hampstead physicist and social scientist, and Mrs Ianthe Carswell as joint secretaries. They took over from Miss Fishwick who, Mrs Carswell records, "lost all her hair through worry about the lack of concern on the part of the public and said (not intending it to be funny) that if only she had lost her hair at Hiroshima it would impress people and help the campaign".

The strength of the feelings that were being aroused is attested by the campaign's continuance without interruption through the autumn of 1956 to the spring of 1957. For in November 1956 the British invaded Suez and the Russians suppressed the Hungarian revolution. Mobilising relief for Hungary and demonstrations for Suez occupied the entire energies of the Left, pacifist and non-pacifist alike. *Peace News*, like most other papers, contained little else for weeks on end, and when at the year's end it posed "Great Questions for 1957" nuclear weapons did not figure among them.

But amid the leaping emigration figures and the reports that 50 p.c. of University reservists would refuse recall to the colours, it could be seen that nothing—political alignments, attitudes to authority, acceptance of war as a political last resort—could ever be quite the same again. And when the immediate fury over Suez had died down and the Tory Party had ceremonially sacrificed its scapegoat, the sap began to rise in burgeoning popular movement for nuclear disarmament. In January Professor P. M. S. Blackett, the leading military scientist of the Labour Party, published his *Atomic Weapons and East–West Relations,** in which he wrote: "I think we should act as if atomic and hydrogen bombs have abolished total war." At the other end of the Labour spectrum, Dr Donald Soper talked to *Peace News*† about his new campaign with united pacifist organisations for British disarmament:

"Most people who can read the signs of the times would agree that we are watching the end of an era and the beginning of a new one . . . We have confined ourselves too naïvely to public meetings. There is a kind of direct action which, I believe, can have profitable results. I am sure we must get out on to the streets more often."

The Sunday Times reported that NATO's Senior Civil Emergency Planning Committee was operating on the "moderate" hypothesis that an H-bomb attack on Britain would kill at least a million people outright, and that people would have to fend for themselves, since the mass destruction would prevent social organisation. A motion was signed by 101 MPs expressing the belief that "violence can never solve the problems of modern society, and any nation attempting to impose its will on any other nation by armed force can only endanger peace and freedom".

The NCANWT was lent a Fleet Street office by the National Peace Council, and after appeals for support published in the *News Chronicle* and the *Observer* a thousand letters arrived in a week. The time for the British test explosion on Christmas Island was drawing near, and Mr Tom Driberg, MP, publicised "a startling and exciting suggestion" that had just been revived: it called for "several boatloads of people to refuse to recognise the validity of the closing of waters in the area to shipping and to dare the British authorities to carry out the tests with them in the neighbourhood".‡ (In 1954 the fall-out from the first American hydrogen bomb test had killed one member of the crew of the Japanese fishing smack *Lucky Dragon*, which had strayed into the area, and this event, quite apart from Hiroshima and Nagasaki, ensured strong Japanese resentment against the British Government's decision, and equally strong support for the proposed "suicide voyage".) Immediately a Quaker couple from Malvern, Harold and Sheila Steele, volunteered to go. On March 5 the Prime Minister told Mr William Warbey in the House of Commons that "the present and foreseeable hazards, including genetic effects from external radiation due to fall-out from test explosions of nuclear weapons fired at present rates and in

---

* Cambridge University Press, 1956. † January 18, 1957. ‡ *Reynolds News*, February 17, 1957.

33

present proportions of the different kinds, are considered to be negligible".* He therefore declined to postpone the forthcoming Christmas Island hydrogen bomb test series. This statement was coolly received by British biologists, and the Liberal Party—which some shrewd Conservative observers have always regarded as a weathercock by which to judge the movement of public opinion—fired off an alternative scientific opinion at the Prime Minister. Another weathercock, the British Council of Churches, decided by 39 votes to 32 at its quarterly Council meeting to oppose the tests (against the advice of its Chairman, the Archbishop of Canterbury).

In the next two months four more pieces of the CND jigsaw fell into place.

1. In April the Minister of Defence, Mr Duncan Sandys, published the annual Defence White Paper.† On this occasion the Minister had written the White Paper himself, for it contained what the author described as "the biggest change in military policy ever made in normal times". It reduced the Defence Estimates from £1,600 million for 1956/7 to £1,483 million for 1957/8, and promised to end national service in 1960, provided that voluntary recruiting produced the 375,000 men the Regular Forces required. At the same time, Mr Sandys spelt out to the nation what this policy implied:

"It must be frankly recognised that there is at present no means of providing adequate protection for the people of this country against the consequences of an attack with nuclear weapons. Though, in the event of war, the fighter aircraft of the RAF would unquestionably take a heavy toll of enemy bombers, a proportion would inevitably get through. Even if it were only a dozen, they could with megaton bombs inflict widespread devastation (para 12).

"Pending international agreement, the only existing safeguard against major aggression is the power to threaten retaliation with nuclear weapons (para 14).

"The free world today is mainly dependent for its protection upon the nuclear capacity of the United States. While Britain cannot by comparison make more than a modest contribution, there is a wide measure of agreement that she must possess an appreciable element of nuclear deterrent power of her own. British atomic bombs are already in steady production and the RAF holds a substantial number of them. A British megaton weapon has now been developed. This will shortly be tested and thereafter a stock will be manufactured (para 15)."

The reduction of expenditure and the ending of National

* Hansard, March 5, 1957, col. 178.   † Cmnd. 124.

34

Service put the Labour Party in a difficult position—it could hardly attack either. Moreover, the general thesis of the White Paper was not distasteful to the Labour leadership. In a characteristically frank broadcast, Mr George Brown (then Labour Defence spokesman) said that Britain's vital interests were not always the same as America's vital interests, and that the threat to bring the deterrent into play "must exist here as well as in America . . . I hope it is not a situation in which we use the H-bomb, but I can well imagine a situation where we want to use it as a threat."

Much more surprisingly, even pacifist opinion was at first not unfriendly to Mr Sandys. Dazzled by the prospect of an end to conscription, Mr Stuart Morris, the General Secretary of the PPU, though naturally opposed to the document as a whole, wrote in *Peace News* of a "spirit of realism . . . drastic reappraisal . . . goes a long way to justify many of the assertions made by pacifists in recent years".* Comments like these left precisely the opening that the CND needed. With all their faults, the emerging leaders of the anti-nuclear movement were more imaginative than the Labour Party and quicker in the uptake than the PPU. It did not take them long to see that Mr Sandys' was a doctrine in which despair and callousness were equally compounded.

2. The Emergency Committee for Direct Action against Nuclear War was set up at the beginning of April. Its sponsors included several Quakers (Horace Alexander, Ruth Fry, Laurence Housman), an Earl (Russell), a Goon (Spike Milligan), and an Anarchist biologist (Alex Comfort). Its declared objects were to raise funds for the Steeles to get to the Pacific, to co-operate with similar Japanese and American organisations, and "to provide a basis for further Direct Action in future so long as it may be necessary". Harold Steele's journey, though it amply paid for itself in terms of worldwide publicity obtained for anti-nuclear protest, failed to achieve its original object. He left London by air on May 9, but on arrival in Tokyo was told that the Christmas Island test had already taken place. Efforts to secure a Japanese boat for the protest voyage had failed. He stayed on in Tokyo some weeks to address meetings.

But the Direct Action Committee, as it afterwards became, had another role to play. From 1957 until 1961 (when it was merged into the Committee of 100) the DAC was the heart and soul, or the thorn in the flesh—according to taste—of CND. On November 23, 1957, the Committee met at the YMCA in Great Russell Street to welcome Harold Steele, who had returned from Japan, and to discuss further projects. Hugh

* *Peace News*, April 12, 1957.

Brock, a tall, vital man of radical views and a faintly boyish air, who was imprisoned in 1941–2 as a conscientious objector, suggested a march to Aldermaston, the atomic weapons plant which he had visited a decade previously. The idea was accepted, though Steele thought it rather small beer, and Brock approached the NCANWT, which he knew contained a sub-group of Direct Action enthusiasts. These included Pat Arrowsmith, a Cambridge history graduate and trained social worker later described by *The Times* as "a brisk young woman". After a meeting on December 12, when the would-be Aldermastonians were joined by Frank Allaun, MP, and Walter Wolfgang, organiser of the reformed Labour Hydrogen Bomb Campaign Committee, Pat Arrowsmith volunteered to put off looking for a new job until after Christmas, and organise the March instead.

3. The idea for a March to Aldermaston had not been Hugh Brock's own. Laurence Brown had suggested it to him in May, after they had both watched one of the early NCANWT demonstrations: 2,000 women with black sashes and flags walking on a pouring wet Sunday from Hyde Park to Trafalgar Square. The organiser of this demonstration was Mrs Peggy Duff, Chairman of St Pancras Housing Committee, former organiser of Save Europe Now and the National Campaign for the Abolition of Capital Punishment. Mrs Duff leapt to the minds of Mrs Carswell and Mrs Jones when it became impossible for them to continue as secretaries of the NCANWT without paid help. CND might well not have lasted six months had it not inherited Mrs Duff from the NCANWT. Many Campaign supporters later doubted whether St Pancras politics were the best preparation for the delicate and ambitious aims which CND had set itself, but the immediate need in the anti-nuclear business was to run an office and bang people's heads together. Mrs Duff approached these tasks with vigour.

4. In late April Commander Sir Stephen King-Hall, a retired naval officer and former Independent National MP, who had since 1936 published an individual and widely read *Newsletter*, issued a number calling for a Royal Commission to study the possibilities of unarmed resistance as a national policy, since armed defence was no longer sufficient to protect the British way of life. Probably for the first time in the nation's history not everyone was prepared to dismiss the notion as totally absurd. Sir Stephen was not a pacifist, and though he inevitably failed to secure his Royal Commission, the non-pacifist Left was sympathetic. "An inquiry," thought the *Manchester Guardian*, "at any rate seems a cheap precaution, though not one which a Government could readily take. It would be less embarrassing if it were organised by non-official bodies." Sir Stephen's

expanded proposals, published as a book* just before the first Aldermaston March in 1958, greatly encouraged the Campaign. The stage was almost set, and already the nuclear protesters were attracting to themselves the tribute of hostile criticism. On April 29 the Foreign Secretary, Mr Selwyn Lloyd, using the unusual platform of a broadcast in the BBC's *Woman's Hour*, said that a good deal of the agitation against British H-tests came from Communist sources which wanted to prevent Britain from emerging as the third nuclear power. This observation evoked hundreds of letters, a quick repudiation by the NCANWT, and the feline comment from Mrs Barbara Castle, MP, that "Selwyn must have thought he was talking on *Children's Hour*". In fact, the Communist Party's relation to the Campaign for Nuclear Disarmament has always been at once hesitant and complex, and at this date was virtually non-existent. The British Communist Party is not a flexible instrument, capable of creating ground-swells of opinion, and in the early months of 1957 even its normal competence at infiltrating established movements had deserted it.

Again, on May 8 in the House of Lords, Lord Cherwell took a similar line to Mr Lloyd. Lord Cherwell, whose scientific reputation had not at that date been publicly assaulted by Sir Charles Snow, denounced the protesters as "hysterical people" and added:

"This sort of thing has become particularly obnoxious since universally respected figures such as the Pope and Dr Schweitzer have been persuaded to intervene. How they can allow themselves to be taken in by the inaccurate propaganda of the friends of Russia is hard to understand ... The number of gamma rays we get from radioactive materials in the walls of our houses is 50 times greater than the amount to which we are exposed by the nuclear tests. If the protagonists of stopping the tests had any logic in their being, they ought to tell us all to go and live in tents."

At the beginning of September the NCANWT announced 24 new sponsors, including a rich crop of artists and writers: Henry Moore, E. M. Forster, Edith Evans, Rose Macaulay, Ben Nicolson. The Labour H-Bomb Campaign held a big rally in Trafalgar Square. By this time, in all probability, nothing could have stopped the emergence of a substantial and long-lived campaign against nuclear weapons. But four further events in the autumn of 1957 acted as final precipitants.

The first event was political. On September 30 the Labour Party Conference opened at Brighton. Out of 127 resolutions

* *Defence in the Nuclear Age* (Gollancz).

37

from local parties and trade unions on the subject of nuclear weapons, 60 were broadly speaking unilateralist, and a composite resolution was drafted pledging that the next Labour Government would refuse to test, manufacture, or use nuclear weapons, attempting thereby to give a lead towards disarmament. Aneurin Bevan, the unquestioned leader of the Left in the Labour Party, was also at this time the Party's Shadow spokesman on foreign affairs. He tried unsuccessfully in private to have the terms of the resolution moderated. In one of his spells of rebellious exile from the Shadow Cabinet, Mr Bevan might well have been found moving such a resolution. In the debate on October 3 he had no choice but to ask the delegates to reject it, and characteristically he did so with a forcefulness of phrase that recalled Ernest Bevin's excoriation of the pacifist George Lansbury in 1935. Unilateralism, Mr Bevan said, "is not statesmanship—it is emotional spasm". Borrowing a phrase which Sam Watson, the miners' leader, had used in committee he asked delegates not to renounce the Bomb and send a British Foreign Secretary "naked into the international conference chamber". The Left mourned, as one of them put it, "the loss of a great leader", and the weight of the anti-nuclear campaign as a result shifted temporarily away from the political battlefield. The unilateralist resolution was lost by 5,836,000 votes to 781,000.

The second event was technological. On the day the Labour Party Conference ended the Russians launched the first sputnik, and jolted American confidence of an unassailable lead in weaponry.

The remaining two events were literary. In November Professor George F. Kennan, United States Ambassador in Moscow from 1952 to 1953, was delivering the Reith Lectures under the title *Russia, the Atom, and the West*.* These broadcast lectures were to many people their first indication that even at this diplomatic level in the United States there existed a considered alternative to the policy of "brinkmanship" and "massive retaliation" which characterised the Dulles era at the State Department. Kennan questioned, for example, the usefulness of the "so-called tactical atomic weapon" and asked "What sort of a life is it to which these devotees of the weapons race would see us condemned?" He also complained that "efforts towards composition of major political differences between the Russians and ourselves have been practically abandoned". Determined and united nations with militia-type forces could, he thought, well suffice to deter Russia from aggression in Europe.

By coincidence, Kennan's lectures had been immediately preceded by an article which J. B. Priestley, still the most artful

* OUP., 1958.

mood-catcher of them all, had published in the *New Statesman*.*
It was called "Britain and the Nuclear Bombs", and described
the frustrations and discontents of nuclear-age man:

"The British of these times, so frequently hiding behind masks
of sour, cheap cynicism, often seem to be waiting for something
better than party squabbles and appeals to their narrow self-
interest, something great and noble in its intention that would
make them feel good again. And this might well be a declaration
to the world that after a certain date one power able to engage in
nuclear warfare will reject the evil thing for ever."

After this, the birth of CND was only a matter of midwifery
and committee work.

* February 2, 1957.

CHAPTER TWO

AMEN COURT TO ALDERMASTON

"I seem to get much less trouble here than most people in their schools—sexual intercourse, I mean, and all that— simply because I sometimes wear my suit with the badge of the Campaign for Nuclear Disarmament." *Headmaster.*

"You need to get out of yourself, have an urge to express yourself, you gotta prove you're alive and not dead inside in this age of mass culture—for some people it's speed, for some it's religion, for me it's CND." *Pupil.*

Reported by Uwe Kitzinger,
Third Programme, and *Listener*, May 16, 1963

LATE in November 1957 some of the midwives of CND met at the home of Kingsley Martin, then editor of the *New Statesman*. The occasion for the party was the presence of George Kennan. Apart from Kennan, those present included Lord Russell, whose Open Letter to Mr Khrushchev, and the reply, were published by Martin on November 23 and December 21; J. B. Priestley and his archaeologist wife Jacquetta Hawkes; and Professor P. M. S. Blackett, who brought with him Denis Healey, a Right-of-Centre Labour MP with a special interest in defence and foreign affairs. At this conversation not the tests merely but the Bomb itself was the problem discussed, and some—though clearly not all—of the guests began to see virtue in a campaign for the abolition of nuclear weapons. Not all the subsequent leaders of CND had originally taken this position. Lord Russell, for example, had in July told the NCANWT that he would be prepared to sponsor a campaign against tests, but not one for the prohibition of atomic weapons. "Suspicion," he had argued, "would continue, and war become more probable."

Lord Russell was not the only link which the Kingsley Martin group had with the NCANWT, to which the group now turned. (Kingsley Martin had already unloaded on to Arthur Goss' organisation some of the huge correspondence which Priestley's *New Statesman* article had generated. The chief go-between was Mrs Peggy Duff, the Secretary of the NCANWT, who knew Martin, and also knew very clearly what sort of organisation she wanted to emerge from the meeting of the NCANWT's eminent sponsors, which was now planned for January 1958. Another link, equally important, was the Collins family. Canon Collins, like Kingsley Martin and J. B. Priestley, had been on the executive committee of the National Campaign for the Abolition of Capital Punishment, which Peggy Duff had organised. His wife Diana was a sponsor of the NCANWT, about which her husband was lukewarm: "I thought it silly not to test the bombs if you had them."

On the evening of January 15, 1958, a highly distinguished group of some 50 persons, ranging from Sir Julian Huxley to Dame Rose Macaulay, assembled in Canon Collins' capacious study at Number Two, Amen Court, a few minutes walk from either Fleet Street or St Paul's. The venue chosen neatly symbolised what was happening. The "prima donnas of the campaigning business", as the Canon himself later called them, were beginning to sing in harmony. The NCANWT Executive, confident in the possession of a successful history, an office in Fleet

Street, three paid staff and a bank balance of £450, thought that they could effectively press their own views on the function and composition of the new campaign. They were mistaken. Kingsley Martin remained in the chair, despite the effort of the NCANWT people to get a less obviously "political" figure like Ritchie Calder. There is little doubt that the composition of the new Executive had been effectively decided beforehand among the Martin–Priestley group, and when it was all over Canon Collins was the Chairman of CND. He was selected, according to Mrs Duff, for his "campaigning experience". This he certainly possessed. Ever since the end of the war he had been running things, from relief for starving Europe to the South African Treason Trial Fund. In 1946 he had set up, with the publisher Victor Gollancz (whose non-appearance on the CND Executive was something of a surprise to connoisseurs of British peace movements), an organisation called Christian Action, which soon became established as a highly personal but effective religio-humanitarian pressure group and fund-raising agency. The Canon's history of cause promotion dated back to his days as a chaplain of Bomber Command during the war, when he was able to lure Sir Stafford Cripps down to talk to the men about God and the RAF. He possessed flair and energy, and his canonry of St Paul's, given him by Mr Attlee later, did not engage his full talents. Indeed, it might have been wiser to make him a bishop, for he needed to have his "own show". Dedication and diplomacy, quick footwork in committee and plain speaking in the pulpit, were neatly balanced in his character. He was more than a match for his followers when they proved troublesome, at least until they ganged up against him in 1960, but he had no intellectual gift for persuading those who would have had to be persuaded if the Campaign were to achieve any tangible success, and he also had a considerable negative talent for irritating both colleagues and opponents. By the time he resigned from the Chairmanship in April 1964, his name had become a household word, and it was reported from at least one school that any boy surnamed Collins was automatically nicknamed "Canon".

The rest of the first Executive consisted of:
Ritchie Calder (Vice-Chairman); James Cameron; Howard Davies; Michael Foot; Arthur Goss; Kingsley Martin; J. B. Priestley; Professor J. Rotblat; Mrs Sheila Jones; and Mrs Peggy Duff (Organising Secretary).

During the first year, Mrs Jones and Professor Rotblat resigned. There were eight co-options: Lord Wilmot (who became Treasurer but later resigned and was replaced by Ted Bedford); Sir Richard Acland; Frank Beswick, MP; Jacquetta

43

Hawkes; Benn Levy; Lord Simon of Wythenshawe (who later resigned); and A. J. P. Taylor.

Of the nineteen names, thirteen were in *Who's Who*—a marked contrast to the membership of the Direct Action Committee and the NCANWT. Four were professional journalists, and of the others, almost all were occasional or habitual contributors to newspapers and journals. Most were aged between 45 and 65. Ten at least had been publicly identified with the Labour Party (even if, in some cases, chiefly as Labour rebels); and there were few who could not present a history of association with a variety of social causes: Christian Action, Peace with China, Victory for Socialism, UNA, Save Europe Now, and the National Campaign for the Abolition of Capital Punishment. Only two (Canon Collins and Arthur Goss) were pacifists, and the committee was subsequently cautious about adding pacifists to its number. The same two, with Sir Richard Acland, were the only members generally known to be church-going (or go-to-meeting) Christians.

The NCANWT yielded the primacy gracefully, to the greater glory of the Cause. Canon Collins later remarked to me that it had been the only occasion in his experience that a voluntary organisation had voluntarily folded up and transferred its funds to a new one. Of the NCANWT's 33 sponsors, 28 became sponsors of CND and Lord Russell became its President. Of the NCANWT Executive, on the other hand, only two—Sheila Jones and Arthur Goss—were put on the CND Executive, and considerable pains were later taken to exclude another NCANWT Executive member who also belonged to a suspect organisation, Science for Peace. Within a few months, Sheila Jones left the CND Executive and joined the Direct Action Committee. Locally, 114 of the 115 groups which had sprung up in support of the NCANWT transferred their loyalties to the new campaign. The NCANWT's platform was acceptable to the Labour and Liberal Parties, most trade unions, the British Council of Churches, and the United Nations Association. CND's was not. This ease of assimilation was surprising, and boded trouble. If the local groups had by and large been revealed as more radical than the NCANWT itself, might they not one day prove too radical for the CND Executive?

This possibility was emphasised by the composition of CND's second administrative tier, the Co-ordinating Committee, which consisted of Executive appointees, representatives of co-operating organisations and regional bodies, as well as a number of politicians and trade unionists, such as Stephen Swingler and Frank Allaun (both Labour MPs), Ernie Roberts of the AEU, and John Lapthorne of the *Universities and Left Review*. The Co-ordinating Committee was the place where CND tried to keep open its lines of communication with the wayward and wary Direct Action Committee, whose representative (usually April Carter or Pat Arrowsmith) sometimes consented to be co-ordinated, sometimes not. The regional delegates also included a high proportion of pacifists, such as Austin Underwood from Amesbury and Donald Pennington, a Manchester University lecturer; and also a non-political, non-pacifist member of the Direct Action Committee, Michael Howard (not to be confused with the strategist of the same name).

The Campaign also possessed at this period 38 sponsors. The list speaks for itself. The virtual omission of MPs was deliberate: the heavy preponderance of artists over scientists surprising. In addition to Earl Russell, the sponsors were:

John Arlott, Dame Peggy Ashcroft, the Bishop of Birmingham (Dr J. L. Wilson), Lord Boyd Orr, Benjamin Britten, Viscount Chaplin, Count Michael de la Bedoyère, Bob Edwards, MP, Dame Edith Evans, E. M. Forster, A. S. Frere, Gerald Gardiner, QC, Victor Gollancz, Dayan Dr, Dr I. Grunfield, Barbara Hepworth, Patrick Heron, the Revd. Trevor Huddleston, CR, Sir Julian Huxley, Edward Hyams, Doris Lessing, the Bishop of Llandaff (Dr Glyn Simon), Sir Compton Mackenzie, the Very Revd. George MacLeod, Miles Malleson, Denis Matthews, Sir Francis Meynell, Henry Moore, John Napper, Ben Nicholson, Sir Herbert Read, Flora Robson, Michael Tippett, Vicky, Professor C. H. Waddington, and Professor Barbara Wootton. Professor J. Rotblat, Lord Simon of Wythen-shawe, and Lord Wilmot became sponsors after leaving the Executive. Later, after protests at the 1959 National Conference that the list of sponsors was insufficiently representative, other names were added.

The first task of the new Executive was to publicise itself, and arrange an inaugural meeting. Considering the concentration of journalistic talent assembled on the Campaign's Executive, the newspaper space accorded to the opening press conference on January 30 was meagre: nine inches in the *Manchester Guardian*, 51 inches in—ominously—the *Daily Worker*, and not much else except in the Left-wing and pacifist weeklies. Canon Collins declared that the aim of the new organisation was "a sharp, virile, and successful campaign to rid Britain of dependence on nuclear weapons, if need be by unilateral action". The policy statement distributed declared that as a first step towards a general disarmament agreement, Britain should press for top level negotiation to end nuclear tests, and the establishment of new missile bases, establish neutral nuclear-free zones, end manufacture and stockpiling of all nuclear weapons, and prevent the diffusion of nuclear weapons to other nations. In order to underline the sincerity of her own initiative, Britain should be prepared to announce that, pending negotiations, she would suspend patrol flights of aeroplanes equipped with nuclear weapons, make no further nuclear tests, suspend establishment of missile bases on her territory, and refuse to provide any other country with nuclear weapons.

Answering questions from the press, the Canon said that with the help of the feeling which already existed in the country they were determined to create a climate of opinion which the political parties would have to follow. Asked whether the Campaign advocated passive resistance if the nation were invaded, he declared this a hypothetical issue: getting rid of nuclear armaments was a likely way to save Britain from occupation. (Sir Stephen King-Hall, the apostle of non-violent resistance, was not on the Campaign's Executive, though he spoke at the inaugural meeting.) J. B. Priestley said that the Campaign aimed at the withdrawal of US troops, and Canon Collins put in: "I agree with you that this is the logical conclusion." Ritchie Calder said that one of the things they wanted to do was to give Britain back her authority in the world. "Do you mean moral authority?" he was asked. "Yes."

The Central Hall, Westminster, and four adjoining overflow halls, were booked for the inaugural meeting, with ticketed admission, on February 17. It was this meeting, as we shall see, which effectively fixed the Campaign as a campaign for *unilateral* nuclear disarmament, and it was very soon followed by the breaking of the tenuous thread which up to that time had bound together the United Nations Association and the CND. Immediately after the Central Hall meeting, delegates of organisations associated with CND met at St Pancras Town Hall and criticised the ambiguities of the original policy statement. Two officers of the United Nations Association in particular, David Ennals (the Secretary) and Howard Davies (the Hon. Treasurer), were highly sympathetic to CND, and Mr Davies had been co-opted to the Campaign's Executive. With the leaders of the three political parties as its Presidents, UNA was going as far as it dared in supporting unilateral suspension by Britain of nuclear patrol flights, tests, and missile base construction. At the St Pancras Town Hall meeting it was agreed that a clarificatory policy should be prepared for private use by the Campaign administration. A few days later both delegates and newspapers received a revised CND policy statement which made it quite clear that CND was for unilateral nuclear disarmament. At least one CND sponsor resigned, the UNA officers felt angry and disillusioned, and Lord Hailsham, then Chairman of the Conservative Party, made a speech pointedly suggesting that Conservatives should take a more active part in the work of the United Nations Association. On March 12 the Director General of UNA, Mr Charles Judd, noted that:

"There are many points that are common to the policy statements of the Campaign for Nuclear Disarmament and of UNA, there are major points in the policy of the CND which UNA cannot support, and there are proposals not mentioned by the CND for which UNA believes it is urgently necessary to win the widest possible measure of public support."

(These last proposals included a nuclear-free zone in Europe, international inspection and control of disarmament, and a UN Peace Force.)

The revised CND policy ran:

"We shall seek to persuade British people that Britain must:

"(a) Renounce unconditionally the use or production of nuclear weapons and refuse to allow their use by others in her defence.

"(b) Use her utmost endeavour to bring about negotiations at all levels for agreement to end the armaments race and to lead to a general disarmament convention.

"(c) Invite the co-operation of other nations, particularly non-nuclear powers, in her renunciation of nuclear weapons.

"Realising the need for action on particular issues, pending success in its major objectives, Britain must:

"(a) Halt the patrol flights of planes equipped with nuclear weapons.

"(b) Make no further tests of nuclear weapons.

"(c) Not proceed with the agreement for the establishment of missile bases on her territory.

"(d) Refuse to provide nuclear weapons for any other country."

The evolution of its main policy was not the only problem which confronted the Campaign Executive at this time. It was also necessary to decide what to do about the Direct Action Committee and its Aldermaston March. The question was raised at the Executive's second meeting, on January 28.

According to Canon Collins, it was he who persuaded the Executive to agree to the Aldermaston March Committee's request for support, and also to the inclusion of civil disobedience on the Executive's list of possibilities to be discussed. Certainly the minuted resolution, that the Executive should "give its blessing to the Emergency Committee's plans, and should publicise them, but should make it clear that at this stage of the Campaign they could not be very closely involved", has an unmistakable ring of the Canon's phraseological fox-trotting. After the Central Hall rally, the Executive discussed the position again and agreed —unilaterally, it seems—that "ad hoc bodies such as the Direct Action and the Labour H-Bomb Campaign Committee should have the same status as the local Groups and Committees, and that the Campaign would support their activities, and help as far as possible, but could take no direct responsibility for the organisations". Help extended to meeting over £300 of the Direct Action Committee's expenses, but this was aid not entirely without strings. The largest single grant was agreed at an Executive meeting after the success of the Aldermaston March. It had become imperative to bring the enterprise and if possible its sponsors under official CND control, and at the same meeting it was decided to ask Pat Arrowsmith, then Organising Secretary of the Aldermaston March Committee, to be the Assistant Secretary of CND; and at the same time to set up an Advisory Group for Direct Action, with which the Direct Action Committee should be invited to merge. Other organisations interested in this type of activity should be invited to send delegates. This was turned down by the DAC, and the CND then resolved to go ahead with an Advisory Committee for Co-ordination and Action. The DAC attended the first meeting as observers, and were able to watch the Co-ordinating Committee agreeing that the "March on London", then being organised by Direct Action, should be "a Campaign March". Michael Howard (who had been chief marshal of the first Aldermaston March) should continue to be responsible for organisation, but the Chairman of CND and the Campaign Office should be responsible for "the general policy of the March, press and financial responsibilities". The DAC did not return to the Co-ordinating Committee again until they did so as full members at the end of the year, though on particular projects and publications co-operation continued.

The fact was that even at this early date the DAC put little reliance upon the CND Executive as a body, and least of all upon Canon Collins. "As for C.C.," wrote one of the DAC's leaders to a friend in September 1960, while the Committee of 100 was being formed, "I've never known a time when he wasn't politicking to do down d.a. projects, and naturally he has been intervening like mad. I think we hope for the best and aim at 'democratic' elections to CND Exec. next February. Must confess I am much too cynical to set much store by good will intermediary missions."

From the DAC's point of view, this diagnosis is perhaps borne out by Canon Collins' own correspondence. On June 4, 1958, he wrote to a fellow member of the CND Executive:

"I'm still struggling with direct action enthusiasts and enthusiastic groups of extremists of all types! But I think we're slowing down dissidence and gradually getting things on an even keel."

But looking at the situation from Canon Collins' own point of view, it is hard to see how he could have acted differently. His campaign, though broadly based, depended heavily for its emotional drive on a core of radical activists whose own views and projects commanded a far narrower range of support. The Canon was only following a basic principle of politics in attempting to moderate the zeal and fissiparous tendencies of the activists and at the same time ensure that they continued to contribute their vitality to the main Campaign. Nor did he have far to look for a large-scale model on which to base his behaviour. Any leader of the Labour Party is confronted with precisely the same problem. During five of the CND's six and a half years of existence, Mr Gaitskell led the Labour Party, and it is arguable that his comparative inflexibility as a leader contributed to the Party's chronically schismatic state during most of this period. Canon Collins more closely resembled Mr Wilson in his recognition of what his own Left wing had to offer, and in his careful avoidance of show-downs. His difference from Mr Wilson—and this was perhaps the secret of his failure to get on with the DAC—was that his machinations—his "politicking"—were more transparent and his own personality more obtrusive.

But personalities apart, there was a great gulf between the DAC and the CND Executive: a gulf not merely of tactics and ideology but of age, background, and political experience. In the course of 1958 the Committee's members included:

April Carter, who had worked in the Foreign Office and given up an Oxford scholarship to become Secretary of Direct Action; Pat Arrowsmith (Field Organiser), who had lost a job as a mental hospital nurse for organising a petition against nuclear weapons; Michael Randle (Chairman), at this time a reporter on *Peace News*; Hugh Brock; Dr Alex Comfort; Frances Edwards, an Oxford housewife; (Col.) Michael Howard, a former refugee administrator and officer of the Crusade for World Government; Sheila Jones; Francis Jude; the Revd. Michael Scott, now director of the Africa Bureau and then well known for his advocacy of S.W. Africa's cause at the United Nations; Allen Skinner; Harold and Sheila Steele; and Will Warren, an Oxford

Quaker, who lost his job as a printer's reader through his commitments with Direct Action.

All the officers were in their early twenties. Most of the members were pacifists, and six of these Quakers.

The sponsors of the DAC were:

Horace Alexander; Frank Allaun, MP; John Berger; Dr Alex Comfort; Professor Charles Coulson; Arthur Goss; Doris Lessing; Ben Levy; Wolf Mankowitz; Ethel Mannin; Dr Martin Niemöller; Lord Boyd Orr; Lord Russell; the Revd. Dr Donald Soper; Michael Tippett; Philip Toynbee.

This list was later extended and internationalised to include: Lindsay Anderson; Claude Bourdet (France); John Braine; Hugh Brock; Constance Cummings; Hon. K. A. Gbedemah (Ghana); Ammon Hennacy (US); Homer Jack (US); Dr Winifred de Kok; Pierre Martin (France); George Melly; Spike Milligan; A. J. Muste (US); Jayaprakash Narayan (India); John Osborne; Dr Linus Pauling (US); E. C. Quaye (Ghana); Sir Herbert Read; Archbishop Roberts; Ernie Roberts; Bayard Rustin (US); Sydney Silverman, MP.

Since this list included the President of the CND, another of CND's sponsors, three members of its Executive and other CND leaders; and since Sheila Jones transferred from the CND Executive to the DAC during the year, it is hardly surprising that occasions for friction, as well as opportunities for co-operation, from time to time arose. Co-operation was in fact often achieved, and recognised by the movement as a whole: thus, DAC relied on the support of many local CND groups up and down the country; and the Nuclear Disarmament Newsreel Committee, which made some films of Direct Action demonstrations, split the profits between the CND and the DAC. But it became clear by the end of the year (when the DAC's first sit-down demonstrations took place) that there was a crucial difference of approach. For the most part the members of the DAC were people of exceptionally pure motives, at least at the conscious level. They were initially more interested in individual conversion than in crowd manipulation. Unlike the CND Executive, and unlike some of their successors in the Committee of 100, into which the DAC was eventually merged, many DAC members were not particularly interested in the local and national publicity which their actions evoked, except in so far as it helped to make converts to Gandhi's ideas on non-violent action. It has been a long Quaker tradition in England to do good and take stands by stealth.

The logic of their philosophy also made them comparatively indifferent to the effect of their actions upon other members of the main Campaign, and even upon the Campaign's own short-term success or failure. After all, part of the case which they were arguing to scientists at Aldermaston and missile workers at Stevenage was that a man should do what his conscience told him was right, without paying too much attention to its possible effect in the world of systems, or even in his own domestic circle.

A characteristic figure was Pat Arrowsmith. "I never felt we were bound to win, only bound to try," she has said.* Born in 1930, a graduate of Cheltenham Ladies College and Newnham, she has spent a large part of her life taking stands, first against various forms of racial intolerance, then against the Bomb. Her maternal grandparents were stoned to death as missionaries in China. Her family, Evangelical Anglican on one side, Plymouth Brethren on the other, had her baptised by two bishops. Like many similarly brought up people of her generation, she secularised her parents' vocation, becoming a trained social worker and working on racial reconciliation projects in Chicago before taking a job in an English mental hospital. She was sacked in 1957, after a long battle with the matron over a petition against tests which she circulated in the hospital canteen. She wrote to Harold Steele offering to go with him to the Pacific to be blown up by the British H-bomb. They met "in a dark church during a thunderstorm and had a gloomy conversation about getting irradiated". Since then she has remained, paid or—often enough —unpaid, with the anti-Bomb movements. Practical, level-headed, but deeply engaged, she has served five prison sentences, and was again imprisoned after the Committee of 100 demonstrations at Easter 1964. She was artificially fed in Greenock Prison after she had gone on hunger strike against the fact that only work available for the other inmates of the prison was sewing sandbags for Civil Defence. Out of prison, she has organised marches and sit-downs, and spent months in dreary lodgings trying to get workers to "black" military contracts and cargoes.

Appeal to the people

The public, of course, knew little either of the politicking in Amen Court or the philosophising in Blackstock Road, N.4, where the Aldermaston March Committee had its headquarters in the early months of 1958. But from February on, the anti-nuclear public itself began to impose its imprint on the parent organisations, and the imprint was deep.

The size of this public surprised the organisers from the beginning, and continued to do so. For the inaugural meeting on February 17 5,000 people filled the Central Hall, Westminster, and three overflow meetings—a large crowd for a winter night in Central London. The audiences were observed to applaud

* The *Observer*, May 13, 1962.

most enthusiastically those speakers who put an uncompromising moral case against Britain's possession or use of nuclear weapons. They were assisted in this line by the 1958 Defence White Paper, just published,* which spelt out even more brutally than its predecessor what British defence policy now was:

"The democratic Western nations will never start a war against Russia. But it must be well understood that, if Russia were to launch a major attack on them, even with conventional forces only, they would have to hit back with strategic nuclear weapons. In fact, the strategy of NATO is based on the frank recognition that a full scale Soviet attack could not be repelled without resort to a massive nuclear bombardment of the sources of power in Russia."

With a straight face, the document went on to say three paragraphs later:

"It must be recognised that, however, carefully the balance of armaments is held, or thought to be held, there always remains a possibility that some unforeseen circumstance or miscalculation might spark off a world-wide catastrophe."

The platform had been chosen to accommodate all tastes. The speakers were Lord Russell, who thought it an "even chance" whether any human beings would exist in 40 years' time; Canon Collins, who accused the Archbishop of Canterbury of "thinking that it is fear that makes the world go round"; Sir Stephen King-Hall, who began by telling his audience that not all of them had been to staff college and went on to suggest that £800 million could be cut from the Defence estimates and 100,000 young Russians invited to see for themselves what Britain was like; Mr J. B. Priestley, who said that Washington civil servants were instructed what form to fill in after a H-bomb attack and where to take it; Mr Michael Foot, who said that Britain had given rocket bases to America at the December NATO meeting and received nothing of substance in return; and Mr A. J. P. Taylor. It was Mr Taylor whose moral passion and demagogic art made the most lasting impression on the audience. One Right-wing Labour MP present has subsequently confessed that he almost got up and walked out when Mr Taylor recalled how the Suffragettes had never allowed a Cabinet Minister to speak without rising at the back of the hall to cry "Votes for Women". The audience should do the same when today's Cabinet Ministers spoke at meetings, Mr Taylor suggested, but instead of "Votes for Women" they should cry "Murderers". Another electric effect was achieved by Mr Taylor's outlining the effects

* Cmnd. 363.

52

of an H-bomb explosion—so many miles of total destruction, so many miles of partial destruction, so many miles of uncontrollable fires, so many miles of lethal fall-out—by his pacing about in silence and then inquiring squeakily: "Is there anyone here who would want to do this to another human being?" A complete hush—the Empire Loyalists had already been ejected. "Then why are we making the damned thing?"—thunderous applause.

The meeting ended with an appeal for funds by Canon Collins. It raised £1,750, but struck the first false note for one member of the audience, a visiting Russian woman biologist, who had been taken along by her British host to learn about British democratic institutions. When she understood what Canon Collins was on about—this took some time, in view of his circumlocutory style—she observed: "That I do not like. It is wrong that there should be an appeal for money. In my country the Government would provide funds for a good cause like this."

At the end of the meeting the audience felt flat, and demanded action. Against the wishes of the platform, about 1,000 went in procession to Downing Street, where they shouted "Ban the Bomb" and even, reminiscently, "Eden must go" (Eden having gone twelve months previously). It was an orderly and good-humoured crowd until the Metropolitan Police, rather rattled, brought dogs and began making arrests; Wayland and Elizabeth Young subsequently claimed to have heard a policeman telling a demonstrator: "If there's any trouble it's your lot and their stupid ideas causing it." There was even an incipient sit-down, with Doris Lessing and others complaining of physical ill-treatment. An enduring feature of the Campaign had been delineated early.

The pattern of the Central Hall meeting (though not of its aftermath) was repeated all over the country. There were 270 public meetings under CND auspices in the Campaign's first year, and £10,000 was raised by these and other means. The Campaign in Manchester was particularly well founded. Led by the Bishop (Dr W. D. L. Greer) and the late Lord Simon of Wythenshawe, the industrialist and social benefactor, whose house in Didsbury was the Executive's meeting-place, it drew packed audiences in both city and university, and has throughout retained the traditionally autonomous posture of Manchester organisations towards their metropolitan counterparts. The adherence of so many Manchester notabilities may even have assisted the then *Manchester Guardian* to make a quicker assessment than most of its contemporaries of the Campaign's general significance. (The *Guardian* was already opposing British manufacture of her own thermo-nuclear weapons, and though never persuaded by the Campaign's unilateralist case, began during 1958 to press on a rather unwilling Mr Gaitskell the idea of a "non-nuclear club.")

The Times, by contrast, gave the Campaign great offence by failing to report the Central Hall meeting. The paper later compounded the offence by writing a leader about the demonstrations in Downing Street and the misbehaviour of the police without mentioning what had preceded the demonstrations. Later, however, Printing House Square apologised for an "inadvertent" omission and a consolatory report was published in the Educational Supplement. Similar Fleet Street neglect (as Campaigners saw it) befell the 800 "Women Against the Bomb" who met at Church House in June to hear Dr Antoinette Pirie say that after a nuclear war children would have to be conceived by AID, from sperm previously collected, to ensure one set of uncontaminated genes; Miss Amabel Williams-Ellis advise them to join Civil Defence in order to "make a bit of a bang" by resigning; and Dr Winifred de Kok say: "You should not listen to arguments at all, but follow your feelings. Every woman knows that a deformed baby is a tragedy which she would not wish on any other woman." A letter from a Hiroshima widow, and a specially written poem, were read; and this "inspiring occasion", as *Peace News* called it, raised £700. Miss Hawkes, in a letter published in several papers, thought that "it could well start a women's movement against Britain's nuclear armaments at least as powerful as the movement for women's suffrage . . . It seems that so long as we women are trivial, we are assured of space in the press: when we are deeply serious over a matter of life and death we are ignored." What was being ignored, however, was the Campaign as an organisation rather than nuclear disarmament as a subject. *The Times* alone published 65 letters on the subject between February 27 and March 27.*

All this amounted to something, in the way of pressure on the pulses of political power, especially since the Labour Party's own "Plan for Peace" meetings were being very poorly attended. But sociologically, it did not amount to anything very new, and in June Mr A. J. P. Taylor complained in the *New Statesman* that the public meetings consisted chiefly of the converted, that appeals were to the emotions rather than to the intellect, and that there were too few nuclear physicists on the platforms. But public meetings were not all. Within two months of the Central Hall meeting, the Campaign's image was fixed, socially and visually, for the duration. On Good Friday, April 4, some 4,000 people set off from Trafalgar Square in the general direction of

* Reprinted as *The Nuclear Dilemma*, with a leading article, The Times Publishing Co., 1958.

Aldermaston; and a 46-year-old American negro, Bayard Rustin, who was later to organise the Civil Rights "March of 100,000" on Washington in 1963, kept saying in a daze to his companion: "All these young people, it's unbelievable . . ."

"Walk for a weekend, a day, or an hour," said the Direct Action Committee's leaflet, welcoming to the first Aldermaston March "all who are opposed on any ground to nuclear weapons, whether possessed by the British, American, or Russian Governments". In its optimistic moments, the Committee expected to get 300 people. It was the coldest Good Friday for 41 years, and the wettest Easter holiday since 1900. But numbers never fell below 540, and between 5,000 and 10,000 people marched the last mile to Falcon Field, Aldermaston, in absolute silence. Few of them had any other bed at night than the floor of a school or a church hall. Bayard Rustin's remark about young people became truer in subsequent years than it was in 1958, when the March, small as it was, constituted a more complete cross-section of ages, if not of classes. Audience reaction was good: most onlookers seemed to nurse an admiring curiosity about the motives of the people who behaved so oddly in such terrible weather. The police in Slough restrained a group of youths who were proposing to throw tomatoes. Other spectators handed out their own tomatoes—or eggs or bananas—to the passing walkers. A young woman danced at her window, holding a baby; a clergyman was heard to shout from his vicarage: "Where do you think you're going—your policy will take us to Siberia."

The press, by and large, was respectful, conscious that nothing quite like this had been seen in Britain before:

"The marchers were mainly middle-class and professional people. They were the sort of people who would normally spend Easter listening to a Beethoven concert on the Home Service, pouring dry sherry from a decanter for the neighbours, painting Picasso designs on hardboiled eggs, attempting the literary competitions in the weekly papers, or going to church with the children. Instead they were walking through the streets in their old clothes. They were behaving entirely against the normal tradition of their class, their neighbourhood, and their upbringing . . . The quiet suburbanites were on the march."

(*Daily Mail*, Alan Brien, April 8, 1958.)

"The young brother and sister, farouche yet open-faced, he from his public school, she from Oxford—a sort of Quaker Sebastian and Viola . . .

"What he wanted, an electronic engineer on the march told me, was that 'my boy should be able to grow up and teach the Russians to play cricket' . . .

"On the grass of Kensington Gardens lay sprawled a young man reading from *Further Studies in a Dying Culture*. Obvious Communists were few—if any ... An Oxford undergraduate complained of 'all this guff about Britain giving a moral lead'. He admits the truth of 'the moral stuff'—but what we want to know is what political action we can take to change the Government's policy even by little—and nobody here has said a thing about that."

(The *Guardian*, April 8, 1958.)

Of notabilities there were plenty. Five Labour MPs (Fenner Brockway, Frank Allaun, Michael Foot, Ian Mikardo, Stephen Swingler). Doris Lessing, Christopher Logue, Kenneth Tynan— "a skeletal young man with a face like an aristocratic rocking horse", was the description chosen for him by a fellow theatre critic reporting the March. There was even the darling of the Chelsea set, Miss Suna Portman, escorted by the embryo satirist Christopher Booker. But the gossip columnists had not realised that the March was going to turn out to be a social occasion, and the pair were overlooked. Nor, indeed, was this essentially a march of notabilities. You might find yourself beside a famous actor, an undergraduate, a professor's wife or a retired merchant seaman: they were all alike after four days rain. There were speeches, of course, in fact dozens of them at start, finish, and halting points, ending with a long oration from Dr Martin Niemöller in the dank field at Aldermaston. The true-blue McWhirter brothers, one of them later Conservative candidate for Orpington, came to jeer, and had their car dented by impatient spectators. Austin Underwood arrived at the head of the car convoy from the West of England, chanting: "England arise, the long dark night is over."

What did it all mean to the participants? The descriptions which follow are taken from what is probably the only existing diary of the first Aldermaston, written by Denis Knight, Secretary of the Film and TV Committee for Nuclear Disarmament, for his family "newspaper": Mr Knight was with his sons, Christopher aged 15 and Kevin aged 13.

"The approach and entry into Reading were the gayest part of the whole walk. It was a succession of

> *"Oh, when the saints, Oh, when the saints*
> *Oh when the saints go marching in!*
> *Oh Lord, I want to be in that number*
> *When the saints go marching in!"*

and

> *"It's a long, long way to Aldermaston*
> *It's a long way to go!"*

56

and

"Men and women, stand together
Do not heed the men of war
Make your minds up now or never
Ban the bomb for evermore."

"All these songs, the variations on old songs and new, the invention of new slogans, and the fun of trying to make them catch on all up and down the column, together with the thought of the approaching town and the knowledge that it was our last night on the march, all helped to quicken the pace and increase the feeling of gaiety and expectancy. In the centre of Reading is a wide and long market street, St Mary's Butts, and this was now packed with people who had turned out to see the fun. It was about half past five as we entered this square at a very fast pace, with every instrument that could play playing, all mixed up with groups shouting or singing. Above our heads the bells of St Mary's were clanging wildly (we heard later that the Vicar was giving his bell-ringers an extra practice) and the marchers, accompanied by occasional police on foot or in cars, were cheering and counter-cheering in turn as they filed past one another until gradually the centre of the square was packed tight, though the column of marchers still entering seemed never to be coming to an end.

"Finally after the last marcher (and police car) had been cheered, the Salvation Army appeared in full marching order and musical blast. For us, the next thing to do was to find somewhere to sleep; and as Pat Arrowsmith was trying to get all children into beds in private houses, I was able to get the name of Mr and Mrs Harold Casey who were among those who had offered their homes to marchers. We found Harold at home with his three young children, his wife being in Reading helping with feeding and sleeping arrangements. Harold gave us a wonderful supper and did everything possible to make us comfortable. Denis then left the boys in front of the fire and went down to the meeting in the Town Hall 'Against Nuclear Weapons' sponsored by the Reading Labour Party . . .

"Shortly after leaving Burghfield, the fields began to wear an aspect less green and pleasant, as we entered a tract of sandy heath that grew nothing well but gorse and fir. 'Radioactive country,' said Christopher . . . Between the regiments of sour and drab fir, planted up to the very edges of the road, there was moving forward a great mass of men, women, and children, four or five or six abreast, in a procession that was probably the longest that English roads have seen these centuries on foot, and was certainly the most purposeful. Its purpose was significant

57

not only for England, but for every other country East and West, because it became clearer with every yard walked that this was more than an old-fashioned peace demonstration, more than a spiritual hunger march. It was felt, as we walked almost in silence through these menacing and monotonous woods, that this was above all a civilising mission, a march away from fear towards normality, towards human standards, towards the real people in the nursery rhyme whose houses are over the hill but not so far away that we will not get there by candlelight, whose hands are set to the plough and the making of things."

This sense of participation in a modern Canterbury Tale, common to the primal innocence of that year's long marches, was captured on film by the documentary *March to Aldermaston*, made by Lindsay Anderson with the help of £100, 15,000 feet of assorted lengths of other people's spare film, and the free help of 80 technicians and some of the best known names in entertainment: Anthony Asquith, Miles Malleson, Ted Willis, Spike Milligan. The *New Statesman*'s critic wrote: "I shall never forget the shot from a graveyard with the marchers beyond and a grim ballad accompaniment to the guitar, 'I dreamt that the bomb had fallen, and a million people were dead', and the cross-cutting stills at the end to contrast the horror of Hiroshima with the live sea of faces in an Aldermaston field." The *Financial Times* added: "It squashes the idea that the music and dancing which enlivened the march showed some kind of immaturity. As the commentator says, 'It's no good being against death if you don't know how to enjoy life when you've got it.'"

Finally, as a visual adhesive to bind the March and later the whole Campaign together, there was the famous nuclear disarmament symbol, probably the most powerful, memorable, and adaptable image ever devised for a secular cause. The designer, Gerald Holtom, is a professional artist who does decorative work in schools for the Ministry of Education. He brought the design —unsolicited—to the Chairman of his local group in Twickenham in February 1958, and alternative versions were shown at the inaugural meeting of the London CND. The first mark on paper, according to Mr Holtom, was a white circle within a black square, followed by various versions of the Christian cross within the circle. But the cross, for these people, had too many wrong associations—with the Crusaders, with military medals, with the public blessing by an American chaplain of the plane that flew to Hiroshima—and eventually the arms of the cross were allowed to droop, forming the composite basic semaphore signal for the letters N and D, and at the same time a gesture of human despair against the background of the round globe.

After Aldermaston Eric Austen, who adapted the symbol from Holtom's waterproof "lollipops" on sticks to ceramic lapel badges, discovered that the "gesture of despair" motif had long been associated with "the death of man", and the circle with "the unborn child".*

Aldermaston was, said Alex Comfort, "the greatest movement in this island since the days of the Chartists". This claim was often repeated in later years as the March grew to 50,000 or so. It should be treated with reserve. On Women's Day 1908, when seven Suffragette processions converged on Hyde Park, *The Times* reported: "The organisers had counted on an attendance of 250,000. That expectation was certainly fulfilled. Probably it was doubled; and it would be difficult to contradict anyone who asserted confidently that it was trebled." *The Times* may have been more generous to the fair sex than it ever was to the Canon —but then, the available population in South-East England was a great deal smaller in 1908. The CND's crowds were very large by the standards of the time, and more cannot be said. But size of demonstration, in an age when most people prefer to watch this sort of thing on their television sets, is not the point. Aldermaston had started something new, and the sixteens to twenty-threes, the generation whom the advertisers categorise as the teenage market, took to it like the children of Hamelin to the music of the Pied Piper.

The appeal was on several levels. There were the guitars and the singing, the fleeting glimpses of cultural heroes, the general air of not-too-tightly organised jamboree in which a boy and a girl could slip off of an evening to fry sausages on sticks beside the Thames. (The newspapers naturally suspected less reputable amusements, more titillating to their readers, and where they could not find them they set out to manufacture them. On the 1963 March a popular Sunday newspaper even went so far as to dress a girl reporter up as a marcher and send her out among the sleeping-bags at Reading in search of moral danger.) The generation of Aldermaston is an emancipated one, and where its parents have not consented to emancipation it has emancipated itself, using the money its predecessors never had to buy travel, jazz, and long conversations in coffee bars. Aldermaston made a refreshing change from Easter with the family in Southend.

There has been no professional social survey of CND or the Aldermaston Marches, but an amateur attempt was made by *Perspective*, a Leftish magazine edited and produced by young

* The symbol, it was later pointed out, could also be interpreted as a symbol of virility, like the rockets themselves, upended on their launching pads. Mr Holtom had unwittingly discovered what William James would have had to call the psycho-sexual equivalent of war.

people, in 1959. A team of twenty interviewed a "10 p.c. random sample" of the 1959 Aldermaston March. They estimated that 41 p.c. of the marchers were under 21, and drawing on their own experience thought that this was a much higher percentage than the previous year. About 60 p.c. of the marchers considered themselves to be active in politics, and 70 p.c. were participating in the March because they hoped it would have political effects. Nine out of ten young people (and the proportion was even higher among the over-twenty-fives) said that they supported the Campaign for moral reasons, and 34 p.c. professed a religious faith (these were often the ones who were not active in politics). The *Manchester Guardian* was read by 78 p.c. of the marchers, the *Observer* by 80 p.c., and the *New Statesman* by 53 p.c. *Reynolds News*, *Peace News*, and the *News Chronicle* were each read by about 20 p.c., and no popular daily scored more than 5 p.c. This may, of course, have had something to do with the treatment which the popular dailies had meted out to CND during the year, but the survey also suggested that not more than 4 p.c. of the marchers could be described as "working class". Teachers were the largest single occupational group, after students, and there were also many librarians, clerks, civil servants, journalists [*sic*], and social workers. Only 6 p.c. supported the "voters' veto" campaign then being run by the Direct Action Committee, but 31 p.c. supported the DAC demonstrations at Swaffham. (This last figure should be set against what happened on the 1963 March, when about a fifth of the marchers turned off, against their leaders' advice, to invade the "Regional Seat of Government" at Warren Row.)

Thus, at a deeper level than the annual picnic, there is no doubt that the vast majority of marchers in all years felt committed to the words they were singing and the actions they were taking. (It should not be forgotten that the participants were by no means the same people every year. Inquiry on the 1963 March revealed very few who had been on all the marches, and very many who were taking part in their first or second March.) There seems little reason to quarrel with the assessment of E. P. Thompson, published in his *New Reasoner* in the summer of 1959:

"The young people who marched from Aldermaston do not mean to give their enthusiasm cheaply away to any routine machine. They expect the politicians to do their best to trick and betray them. At meetings they listen attentively, watching for insincerities, more ready with ironic applause than with cheers of acclaim. They prefer the amateur organisation and the amateurish platforms of the CND to the method and manner of the Left-wing professional . . .

"The Labour Executive has appointed a Commission to sit on questions of youth. But youth has been making its own inquiries and the Labour Party Executive does not come out of them too well . . .

"It is a difficult generation for the Old Left to understand. It is, to begin with, the first in the history of mankind to experience adolescence within a culture where the possibility of human annihilation has become an after-dinner platitude."

This analysis is nowhere better confirmed than by the folk-songs of the anti-nuclear revival. The official songsheet at the first Aldermaston March was, according to an article in *Peace News* later,* "the only real fiasco".

"The Englishman, unlike the American, doesn't sing edifying songs, and unlike the Irishman hasn't any songs of recent currency known to middle-class marchers which symbolise 'damn the Government', like the Peeler and the Goat, or the Sean Bhean Bhocht, even when only whistled."

Going by soldiers' preferences the songs which a solemn protest against atomic war would produce would be "ribald, flippant, and effective", like the one which London medical students sang after Aldermaston to the tune of "John Brown's Body":

"To hell with all the humbug and to hell with all the lies,
To hell with all the strontium continuing to rise,
To hell with all the Charlies with a gift for compromise,
If they won't ban the H-bomb now.

(Ban, ban, ban the bloody H-bomb
Ban, ban, ban the bloody H-bomb
Ban, ban, ban the bloody H-bomb
If you want to stay alive next year.)

"Macmillan and the Tories are out to wait and see,
They think the great deterrent will secure the victory—
I don't know if they scare the Reds: by God, they frighten me,
If they won't ban the H-bomb now.

"Gaitskell and Nye Bevan are preparing for a sell,
They want to get the votes and keep the atom bomb as well,
But NATO's going to send us all to shovel coal in hell,
If we don't ban the H-bomb now.

"Now half of them are barmy, and half of them are blind,
They've all been talking long enough, it's time they all resigned;
And the way to shift a donkey is to wallop its behind,
If he won't ban the H-bomb now.

* May 16, 1958.

61

"We're going to stop the loonies and preserve the human race,
We're going to save our country for we like the dear old place,
We're going to stuff a rocket up Mr Dulles' base,
    If they don't ban the H-bomb now.

"Oh they sent the papers down to say that marching was a farce:
Hailsham rang his handbell and declared 'They shall not pass'.
But 20,000 boots went marching straight across his—grass
    Since he won't ban the H-bomb now.

"The feet have started marching and they've only just begun,
They're going to put the fear of hell in every mother's son:
Aldermaston, Downing Street and Chequers here we come
    If you don't ban the H-bomb now."

CHAPTER THREE

"SEEK YE FIRST THE POLITICAL KINGDOM"

The Campaign proposes . . .

"I say for the Transport and General Workers' Union, and I say as a father, that I cannot and will not see a situation where I could be a party to using this weapon against anyone."

Frank Cousins at Blackpool, September 9, 1959
(TUC Conference Report), p. 402

IN 1955 the "romantic singularity" of Sir Richard Acland, Bt., could embarrass but not destroy the Labour Party. Five years later the romantic collectivism of a popular mass movement swept up and bound in with Sir Richard teenagers, Trotskyites, television personalities and—most dangerous of all—thousands of ordinary, apolitical, vaguely progressive men and women. Together, they all had the Labour Party by the throat at a moment which even without their intervention would have been critically dangerous: the moment of self-doubt after the loss of a third successive General Election. Beaten off with difficulty, the dogs of peace can still be heard growling in the background, awaiting another opportunity.

A few weeks after the first Aldermaston March, the political correspondent of *Peace News* wrote:

"The most salutary and remarkable effect of the early stages of CND was the panic it produced in the party headquarters.

"It was the type of movement which career politicians most fear—a largely spontaneous and self-organised wave of protest on a single issue, which could neither be side-tracked nor readily exploited within existing party programmes, and which had a large element of moral indignation behind it.

"The battle is, of course, far from being won. Those who organise a campaign without a rigid and professional machine are tackling a tough undertaking—one which proved too tough for the Chartists and almost too tough for the Suffragettes . . ."*

Some people on both sides have inevitably been tempted to interpret the battle in terms of its outcome. This interpretation appealed to the unilateralists, who could see themselves as Davids, chosen by the Lord to challenge and conquer the Goliath of the trade union block vote in the Labour Party. The multi-lateralists, equally, were able to regard themselves as successful counter-revolutionaries who had, by intelligence and self-discipline, converted millions of honest but bewildered toilers back to the status quo. But, in fact, it was not like that at all. By October 1960, when the Labour Party met at Scarborough, the Campaign for Nuclear Disarmament was already well past its peak. Over the whole period of the debate it is doubtful whether more than a small minority of the active participants changed their minds in one direction or the other, and even when they did, the minds were sometimes changing in one direction while the votes were changing in the other. Yet the story of

* May 16, 1958.

64

CND's personal and intellectual involvement with the Labour Party, together with the reasons for its partial success and ultimate failure, provide a classic example of what is liable to happen when progressive public opinion in Britain gets temporarily out of step with its natural political outlet. There is space here for no more than an essay on this theme, but the following are elements in the situation which have to be weighed:

(*a*) The political structure and attitudes of CND and associated organisations.

(*b*) The types of argument presented by the Campaign to the Labour Party and the public at large.

(*c*) The structure and condition of the Labour Party, both in Parliament and at its annual Conference.

(*d*) The evolution of the parties' defence policy, in response to internal pressure and external events.

(*e*) The movement of public opinion, expressed through polls and by-elections.

If the Campaign had a membership it might be possible to say or guess what proportion of it was, at the peak period, Labour by membership or voting habit. But the Campaign never has had a membership. At its second meeting the Executive agreed that "the Campaign would not have individual members or affiliated branches but should continue along the same lines as the NCANWT". This system involved enrolling supporters' names and addresses, and recording donations if any, but not exacting subscriptions. The Executive and Co-ordinating Committee considered that their view on this matter was shared by local groups as a whole, and it was, in fact, upheld by the first National Conference in March 1959. At this Conference the Executive announced: "CND is not a political party and has no political ambitions other than to see its aims adopted by Parliament. It is not intended to be a permanent organisation."

This wording, recalling Canon Collins' original summons to "a sharp, virile, and successful campaign", was no doubt intended as a stimulant to morale, and the Executive was also anxious to avoid the administrative work involved in a formal membership. Nor had formal membership been enough to preserve other comparable organisations from infiltration by Communist and other "wrecking" bodies: indeed, formal membership, voting for officers, and the other trappings of democracy often facilitate this type of infiltration, as the recent history of the London Co-operative Society has demonstrated. Nevertheless, the chief arguments against membership were left prudently unstated. For the Campaign to be kept on the rails which the Executive had laid down, the Executive itself had to be as nearly as possible self-perpetuating. (A vote on the chairmanship was not held in the Campaign until the 1963 annual conference.) CND National Conferences were delicate enough affairs to handle already, without the presence of "members" with "rights" to add to the difficulties. The case was clinched by the probability that if CND became a "visible" organisation with rules, policy and a membership it would be instantly proscribed by the Labour Party, with the consequent disappearance of all MPs from its stationery and all Labour Party members from its committees. Just how eagerly the Labour Party would have seized any opportunity presented may be judged from the National Executive's clumsy attempt in 1962 to expel Canon Collins and Lord Russell from the party for sponsoring the Moscow Peace Conference.

There was always a conflict within CND, a conflict which was never resolved and which expressed itself in a variety of ways, between the Labour loyalties or responsibilities of most Executive and Co-ordinating Committee members and the deep suspicion of the Labour Party (and indeed of all established channels of political action), which was a feature of the rank and file. It is true that some of the Labour MPs who supported CND were persistently accused by their colleagues in Parliament and by trade union leaders of disloyalty and irresponsibility. It is also true that the weapon of anti-nuclear campaigning came handy to the hand of some Labour MPs who already had other reasons for opposing the party leadership. But however suspect they might be to their colleagues on the Right, most of these men reacted sharply against the more extreme forms of action proposed by the CND rank and file, not only because their own standing with Transport House and the public at large suffered damage by association with extremism, but because as professional politicians they could not accept that CND could achieve anything outside the context of party politics. When the unions one by one were going unilateralist in the summer of 1960, "Critic" (Kingsley Martin) wrote in the *New Statesman*:

"I know of no way of obtaining a non-nuclear Britain except by converting the Labour Party. Unless they work through the Labour movement, nuclear disarmers are simply marching about to satisfy their own consciences and expressing their sense of the sin and horror of nuclear war."*

Many in the rank and file of CND would have echoed Mr Martin's view. But not all. Mr Denis Knight, in his account of the first Aldermaston March, records that when at a public

* July 2, 1960.

meeting in Reading addressed by Mr Ian Mikardo, MP, the Chairman suggested that the collection should be divided between CND and the Labour Party's own campaign, the audience insisted on the money being all given to CND. Mr A. J. P. Taylor's highly successful speech at the Campaign's opening meeting was successful in part because it contained—as one of his future colleagues on the Executive grumbled—"sneering remarks" about all political parties. A contemporaneously written account of CND's first National Conference in March 1959 (to which the press were not admitted) observes that many of the speeches were characterised by considerable hostility to the Labour Party, and by a feeling that neither in the long nor the short term could the Campaign expect much more support from Labour than from the Conservatives. Since during 1958 the Conservative Minister of Defence, Mr Duncan Sandys, was able to describe official Labour Defence policy as "99·5 p.c. sound", the Campaign's early cynicism was understandable.

The issue came to a head in what came to be called the "voters' veto" controversy, which raged intermittently during 1958 and 1959. The first by-election to be held after the Campaign's inception was at Rochdale, and the prospective ILP candidate there, Mr Haycock, publicly offered to stand down if Mr J. B. Priestley would stand as an Independent anti-nuclear weapons candidate. Mr Priestley declined, though when shortly afterwards Mr Emanuel Shinwell described him in the House of Commons as "about as woolly as any person I have known since the days of Ramsay Macdonald", he may have regretted his decision. Mr Haycock in the end failed to stand, and the Labour candidate elected, Mr Jack McCann, apparently changed from a multilateralist to a unilateralist position during the election, telling *Tribune*: "I don't think we ought to scrap the bombs we've got until we can persuade America and Russia to do the same", and telling a meeting in Rochdale a few days later: "I believe that the position is so critical that this country should be prepared to take the risk of unilateral disarmament as an example to the world." Since the Liberal candidate, Ludovic Kennedy, who came second, was in line with the policy of his Party's Parliamentary Committee, which was already in favour of abandoning the independent British deterrent, CND hardly needed to worry much about Rochdale. The worry was the Prime Minister's, and on television Mr Macmillan said that he was "concerned" that 80 p.c. of the Rochdale electors had voted for candidates who did not want a British H-bomb.

In April the Torrington by-election, with its Liberal victory, passed without CND intervention. But this constituency would have been a difficult one for the Campaign to work, and at the time up and down the country CND supporters were canvassing support for a Mass Lobby of MPs which took place on May 20. Ten thousand people thronged Parliament Square, carrying banners which included, "No votes for MPs who do not support unilateralism." The week before, the Political Correspondent of *Peace News*, in the article already quoted, had outlined two of the next tasks facing CND as:

"Control votes as well as demonstrations, so that the H-bomb issue can jeopardise results across party boundaries.

"Find a lawful but effective form of day to day protest which ordinary people can undertake without stopping work and marching, which will hurt the Government but not annoy the neighbours, and which will carry self-evident signs of its success."*

In April the CND Executive had resolved that wherever possible CND would hold an independent meeting in constituencies where by-elections were taking place, but in June they were pressed to go farther by a group of London University undergraduates, headed by William Crampton, who proposed a campaign to encourage people to withhold their votes from any Parliamentary candidate not in favour of CND policy. The Executive turned the scheme down flat. But it was put forward again by the Direct Action Committee, and hung fire for the rest of the year while CND itself was outlining what it considered the legitimate approaches to the problem. The Executive asked local groups to miss no opportunity of influencing candidates, and to make sure of attending selection conferences if they were entitled to do so. Formidable questionnaires were circulated. (Manchester's ran to 25 detailed questions, covering not only the candidates' views but their reasons for holding them.)

"Voter's veto" was much discussed in local groups at this time, and was a seriously divisive factor in some. But it did not alarm the Labour Party much until January 1959, when the Labour MP for S.W. Norfolk, Mr Sidney Dye, was killed in a car crash. S.W. Norfolk included the rocket bases at Swaffham and North Pickenham, where the first Direct Action civil disobedience demonstrations had taken place the previous month. Over 50 of the participants had been gaoled and Mr Dye had described them as "utter idiots". The Labour Party's candidate in the by-election, Mr A. V. Hilton, was not a unilateralist, nor was the local party sympathetic. The seat was marginal. Direct Action launched a vigorous "No votes for the H-bomb" campaign, circulating Labour and trade union branches, and canvassing electors. In a pamphlet, *Political Implications of a Voters' Veto*, the Direct Action Committee outlined its case. The electorate, the

* *Peace News*, May 16, 1958.

Committee claimed, had been disfranchised on "the supremely important moral issue" of the H-bomb. Even CND supporters in Parliament were not prepared to do more than abstain on nuclear issues in Parliament, and they allowed vital decisions to be made in closed meetings:

"The decision of the Parliamentary Labour Party to support the British manufacture of the H-bomb was made at a meeting of the Parliamentary Labour Party which did not even have prior notice that it was going to be discussed.

"The DAC is not primarily interested in the return of any particular party at the next election ... Is it better to have a slightly more moderate Government with a Right-wing Opposition, or a Conservative Government with dynamic and radical elements in the Opposition who are supported by an active campaign in the country?"

The DAC argued that if a Labour Government were returned after an election in which nuclear disarmament had not figured largely, it would have no incentive to change its policies, nor to fear rebellion, unless at election time CND supporters in the Party had shown themselves prepared to put nuclear disarmament above a Labour electoral victory.

Mr Benn Levy, a sponsor of the DAC, put the official reply in a special supplement to the monthly CND Bulletin.* He argued, first that the Voters' Veto would not work because political blackmail always boomeranged, and because voters were anyway unwilling to disfranchise themselves on other issues by abstaining on one; second, that even the loss of a seat or seats would provide Transport House with a scapegoat rather than bring it to heel; and third, that a "full-scale insurrection" of Labour MPs could not be expected until the General Election had been either won or lost. Mr Levy added:

"If a Conservative Government were returned ... unilateral disarmament would be a dead duck for five long years. In that time a bomb could drop. Where is the sense of urgency? A Conservative Government would be virtually immune from pressure on this issue, even though the Campaign includes, of course, a number of Conservative adherents for whose support it is grateful ..."

Labour held the seat at S.W. Norfolk, though its share of the vote only rose by 0·7 p.c.—an ominous result in an Election year. Dr Edith Summerskill withdrew her support from the 1959 Aldermaston March in protest against the DAC's behaviour, and Voter's Veto was pursued only intermittently thereafter. Later,

* February 1959.

however, in response to critics of the Campaign who complained that if it was serious about its cause it should put up candidates at elections, Michael Craft founded INDEC (Independent Nuclear Disarmament Election Committee), which ran several candidates against Labour opposition at local elections and a Parliamentary candidate in Twickenham at the 1964 General Election. INDEC, though duly proscribed by the Labour Party, was sufficiently separate from CND itself not to become a major embarrassment, and in 1961 a Mr Roy Hewitt, who proposed to stand for Northampton as an Independent Conservative Nuclear Disarmament candidate, asked Mr Michael Foot if he would vote for a Conservative or Liberal unilateralist if the Labour candidate in his constituency supported the Bomb. "Certainly not," Mr Foot replied.

Mr Levy was right about the Conservatives among the Campaign's early supporters. At the first meeting of Manchester CND a woman in the audience complained of the number of times the Labour Party was mentioned when the Conservatives were after all in power. She was put on the committee. And a Gallup Poll published in April 1959 showed that a fifth of Conservative voters would approve if Britain gave up her H-bombs, even if other countries did not do so.

But for the first year of its existence the Campaign's image was not as firmly set as it afterwards became, and the political situation was confused. Mr A. J. P. Taylor, summing up the first six months of the Campaign, complained both of narrowness in its sociological spread and vagueness in its political objectives. Members of audiences were "over 50 or under 25". It was "a movement of eggheads for eggheads, with no industrial workers". Nor were there enough nuclear physicists on the platform. In America and Germany the physicists had led the agitation, and even in Russia Peter Kapitza had with singular courage held out against working on nuclear weapons. But in Britain the physicists did what they were told, and only the biologists were militant. There were still traces in the Campaign of "the attempt to include everyone—the handicap of a non-political movement".

This last point came uncomfortably near the Executive itself. In December 1958 one of its members, Lord Simon of Wythenshawe, put down a motion in the House of Lords which was debated the following month.* (The delay was due to a request from the Government, which did not wish such a debate to take place until the conclusion of the current disarmament talks at Geneva.) Lord Simon's motion advocated a British attempt to form a "non-nuclear club" of all the industrial nations except the USA and the USSR:

* Hansard, February 11, 1959, cols. 74 *et seq.*

"The first thing would be to get the present non-nuclear powers to sign a treaty not to own, manufacture, or use nuclear weapons. The second would be, as part of that treaty *and, of course, contingent upon it*, that Britain would cease to manufacture nuclear weapons, would never use them, and would undertake to destroy her stocks." (My italics.)

Lord Wilmot, who had until recently been Treasurer of CND, said:

"There is no intention of taking unilateral action, and there is no intention whatever of being false to the American alliance, which is absolutely necessary if we are to maintain our position in the present circumstances."

The Campaign thought the debate had been useful, and indeed, the views expressed by Lord Russell, Lord Adrian, and the three bishops who spoke contrasted sharply with the verdict of Lord Strang, a former head of the Foreign Office, who looked forward to the day when as many nations as possible had the H-bomb, for "the extension of the balance of terror might be a very salutary thing for humanity". But it is instructive to compare the modest proposals of the noble Campaigners with the virulent anti-Americanism expressed at times by their colleagues in the columns of *Tribune*, and with the all-or-nothing behaviour of the Direct Action demonstrators, just emerging from their first spell in prison at the time of the House of Lords debate, who regarded all nuclear weapons as equally abhorrent, whether possessed by Britain, Russia, or the United States. Speaking for this last section, Mr Nicolas Walter later criticised the half-hearted pacifism of CND and its sentimental belief that it could get rid of the British Bomb without changing anything else. But he added:

"Nevertheless, CND has served a most useful service—for pacifism, despite itself, because it has built up mass support for protest action against not only the Bomb but all bombs; and for anarchism too, even more despite itself, because it has also built up mass support for protest action against the State that makes the Bomb and the whole social system that maintains the State ... Thus the rank and file of CND have been consistently and increasingly more militant than the leadership; CND began as a pressure-group to make the Labour Party unilateralist, but it became an unwilling vanguard of utopia, the nucleus of Alex Comfort's 'maquis of the peace' ..."*

A movement whose spread was so broad cannot be comprehended within George Orwell's famous catalogue of "fruit-juice drinkers, nudists, sandal-wearers, sex maniacs, Quakers, 'Nature

* *Anarchy*, March 13, 1962, p. 90.

Cure' quacks, pacifists, and feminists", even if one adds in Mr David Marquand's description—accurate as far as it goes—of an important section of the Campaign:

"Among the marchers to Aldermaston you can find much of the slightly faded political driftwood left behind by the storms of the last thirty years; former members of the ILP, former subscribers to the Left Book Club, former ardent supporters of the Spanish Republic, former opponents of the foreign policy of Ernest Bevin and of the rearmament of Western Germany."*

It was the very comprehensive character of CND, and the unfamiliarity of some of its elements, which contributed to the failure of the Communists and their close fellow-travellers to exercise any significant influence within it. Energetic attempts by the Government and the Conservative press to tar the CND with this particular brush had surprisingly little success. The public were quite ready to believe that CND policy, if implemented, would "only help the Communists", but this was not the same as believing that Communists controlled the movement, which they transparently did not. Despite extensive early coverage by the *Daily Worker* the Communist Party as such did not begin to support CND systematically till 1959, and at the 1957 Labour Party Conference Communist-controlled votes were actually cast against the unilateralist motion. By 1960 the position was reversed, and Communist activity in unions on behalf of unilateralism, though probably not decisive in terms of votes, did give plausibility to Mr Gaitskell's outburst at Scarborough against "pacifists, unilateralists, and fellow-travellers". At Scarborough itself, Communists were unusually conspicuous among the CND claque. But the more popular CND's own brand of protest became, the less point there was in the Communist Party crying up what it had failed to control. Indeed, if the King Street commissars were not so invincibly stupid, they would have insisted that the movement be left severely alone from start to finish. As it was, in April 1961, Canon Collins even felt strong enough to give a patronising interview to the *Daily Worker* saying: "We accept with pleasure the support of any individuals or groups who genuinely share our concern and wish our policy to succeed." Coming from a man who had once won a libel action against a Right-wing journal which had called him a Red, this was a bold step.

The Canon's confidence grew, perhaps, from the strange form of inverted nationalism which many observers have attributed to CND. The movement sprang, after all, from soil watered by Suez, and its leaders mostly believed and said that the policy

* *Commentary*, May 1960, p. 381.

which they proposed would leave Britain not only safer and more independent but in a sense greater than before. This messianic emphasis gave the Campaign little taste for the squirmings of a political party which took its instructions from a foreign power. Nor is it hard to see a connection between the assumptions which governed the early British unilateralists and the assumptions which then governed American foreign policy. The Campaign's certainty that some practical effect could be achieved by Britain's giving a "moral lead" cannot be separated from Mr Dulles' belief that rigorous moral attitudes were appropriate for the West's dealings with the East. After Mr Dulles' death, when a more pragmatic attitude entered American diplomacy, CND too began to substitute feasibility for fervour.

A final element in the make-up of the Left during the rise of CND has already been noticed. In 1958 it had only recently appeared on the scene. This was the New Left, originally a circle formed in the universities round the *Universities and Left Review* (later combined with E. P. Thompson's *New Reasoner* to form the *New Left Review*), which was founded in 1956. More than any other element in the politics of unilateralism this group belonged to its time. It had no connection with what were sometimes called the Old Woollies—those survivors of departed Leftist and pacifist movements who clung to CND, as King David did to Abishag the Shunamite, more to warm their old bones than in hope of a successful engagement. The ULR group was Marxist, but in a new-fangled, self-conscious way. They went to "the scriptures" (as they revealingly tended to call the works of Karl Marx) more for a cultural point of reference than for a narrowly political or economic one. They would interpret the adolescent rebellion of their time in terms of the Marxist theory of alienation. They resisted the suggestion, implicit in the work of some sociologists, that a movement like CND was a disease of mass society, an example of demagogic leaders manipulating detached, aimless, but anxious masses to bring direct pressure on the ruling elites.* A New Left sociologist, Dr John Rex, has attacked the proposition that people who are "to some extent alienated from the values of their society" must necessarily be disturbed, mentally sick, or at least misguided. He adds, in a paragraph which does much to explain the diversification of activities later embarked upon by a Campaign which was initially wholly concentrated upon nuclear weapons:

"On one point it would be wrong to resist the arguments of our critics. This is that there are additional reasons for joining and

* Cf. Kornhauser, *The Politics of Mass Society* (Routledge, 1960), pp. 63–4, 234–7.

staying in CND other than support for the cause of nuclear disarmament. Only, whereas they would say that this involves a devastating condemnation of the movement, we should say that with so many unresolved points of tension and political conflict which orthodox political channels have failed to resolve, it is not surprising that many people should see in this movement the hope of creating a better society." (Others, as Mr Rex also points out, started voting Liberal after 1959 in the same hope.) "Indeed, the way a CND sympathiser would put this is to say that the nuclear disarmament movement has become a centre in which all the best social tendencies of our society can gain expression."*

The New Left represented a reaction against the intellectual and aesthetic dowdiness which by 1956 had become the most conspicuous feature of the official Labour Party. Its survival was ensured by Hungary and Suez, which at one stroke turned the most sensitive minds of their generation equally away from Communist leanings and from all forms of political bipartisanship within this country. By an accident of timing as much as by conscious choice, unilateralism became the group's guiding orthodoxy, and one of its moving spirits, Chuck Taylor, a 26-year-old French-Canadian philosopher at All Souls, became the first President of the Oxford University Campaign for Nuclear Disarmament.

The group was not of the type which acquires, or even desires, direct political power in a party. Unilateralism apart, it had a mildly rejuvenating effect upon the Labour Party, as even Mr Gaitskell on occasion ruefully recognised. But it assisted CND to gain a hold over the universities which was later dislodged by junior versions of the Campaign for Democratic Socialism, using methods more ruthless, if anything, than their elders'. Undergraduate politics are always red in tooth and claw. Moreover, through Stuart Hall and others, the New Left later developed the political and military case for CND beyond the naïve oversimplifications of Canon Collins' short-term campaign to rid Britain of nuclear weapons. By doing so, it effectively delayed the return of a whole generation of the student intelligentsia to a conventional Labour obedience. The New Left, as such, did not organise the young people who harried Mr Gaitskell up and down the country at public meetings after his "fight and fight and fight again" speech at Scarborough in 1960. But indirectly the group helped to give the young a sense of corporate unity in dissent which people under thirty-five could not have felt merely by association with the Foots and the Silvermans of the Labour

* *War and Peace*, January 1963, p. 52.

74

Party. Even *Peace News,* formerly an "old pacifist" publication, had its staff refreshed by an injection of New Left disciples. And when at last the folk-hero of the Old Left acceded to the leadership of the Labour Party, Mr Hall wrote of the "wary, tentative response" which CND made to the new Wilson image.*

Since the CND umbrella sheltered such a wide variety of people beneath it, and since nuclear weapons themselves presented a problem which affected people's lives in many different ways, it is not surprising that the lines of argument employed by Campaigners to commend their policy should themselves have been many and various and occasionally mutually incompatible. Moral, political, strategic, and economic arguments were deployed by Campaign spokesmen, and are still, though the balance has shifted sharply over the years away from morals and towards strategy. Most of the important lines of argument were brought out during the first year of the Campaign, and it was what was said then, rather than what was said at the time, which swung the Labour Party Conference in 1960 into the unilateralist fold. The democratic process within the Labour Party is not a fast-moving or flexible instrument, and in 1959 the General Election, by preventing a Conference from being held and by putting Party unity at a premium, further postponed the date at which the ground-swell of opinion in the Party could be formally expressed.

The great debate which reached its peak during 1958 naturally centred on the particular aspects of the nuclear dilemma that were then topical. The chief of these was the decision taken at the December 1957 NATO meeting in Paris to instal Thor IRBMs in the territories of Britain and other member nations. Already, the public—including *The Times*—had been agitated by the revelation that American aeroplanes carrying nuclear weapons were patrolling British skies round the clock. Both these disclosures concentrated attention, first on the extreme vulnerability of Britain in the kind of war for which she appeared to be preparing, and second on the passing of responsibility from elected governments to military commanders: a step apparently inherent in the military logic of the situation. Few of these doubts were allayed by Ministerial and military statements at the time. Thus, Mr R. A. Butler assured the House of Commons that "these weapons are at all times in a safe, that is, unarmed, condition while they are being carried over this country", and was answered by Mr Bevan:

"If these weapons cannot be put into the position of being exploded by the aircrews themselves, why are they carried? If

* *New Statesman,* April 12, 1963.

they can be put into the position of being exploded, then the Prime Minister is deceiving the country."*

The situation was exacerbated by the Prime Minister's subsequent admission that he would have to consult President Eisenhower to discover what precisely the procedure was. As for the chain of command problem, Viscount Montgomery was on record two years earlier with a characteristically frank utterance:

"We at SHAPE . . . with the full political agreement of the NATO Council, are basing our plans upon the fact that if we are attacked we use nuclear weapons in our defence. The proviso is that the politicians have to be asked first. That might be a bit awkward, of course, and personally I would use nuclear weapons first and ask afterwards."†

In January and February 1958 the first cries of the infant CND were further stimulated by news of precautions being taken in the United States (but apparently not in Britain) to protect the civilian population from the consequences of an H-bomb plane crash, and in March by news of such a plane actually crashing in South Carolina, and irradiating a wide area. On February 26 an article in a special hydrogen bomb issue of the Oxford University magazine *Isis* alleged that British Intelligence Services close to the Warsaw Pact countries sometimes deliberately provoked Soviet defences to test their responses. (The authors of the article were later prosecuted and imprisoned under the Official Secrets Act, and though the trial was mainly in camera the publicity was enormous.) In January 9,235 scientists from 44 nations begged the governments of the world to stop nuclear tests and halt the arms race, and in February General Norstad said that it was "absolutely essential" that the West German forces should be armed with tactical atomic weapons. In March the NATO Council agreed, and a debate similar to the British one was set off in West Germany, with the Komittee gegen Atomrustung, supported by the Social Democratic Party and the trade unions, attracting 120,000 people to a rally in Hamburg. And in February, again, the annual British Defence White Paper clinched the message of its 1957 predecessor with the statement: "But it must be well understood that, if Russia were to launch a major attack on them (British forces), even with conventional forces only, they would have to hit back with strategic nuclear weapons." *The Times*, whose newsroom was at this time neglecting CND as an organisation, attacked the

* Hansard, January 23, 1958, col. 1255. † *Royal United Services Journal*, November 1956.

76

White Paper fiercely in its leader columns, to the fury of Conservative MPs:

"If Mr Sandys really means what he says he should make way for someone who realises that the aim of defence is to defend us and not destroy us ... The point to drive home is not that the deterrent is no use, but that it is so absolute that it has severe limitations. It is a valid deterrent only against its like—global nuclear war."*

The CND was thus presented with an extremely strong debating case—and it possessed some useful debaters. Morally, the case put normally amounted to little more than a proclamation—a more or less sophisticated version of the banner which a teenage girl was seen to be carrying on the second Aldermaston March, reading "Caroline Says No". All sections of the Campaign were unanimous that the use of nuclear weapons on civilian populations would be immoral, and it was not for the Campaign's speakers to introduce casuistical refinements. Indeed, they could achieve far more gratifying effects by ridiculing the behaviour of the Churches which, since not all their members were Campaigners, were obliged to argue in finicky detail the moral problems raised by multilateralism and unilateralism alike. For CND, it was a question of choosing which type of moral revulsion one preferred: against the genocidal implications of all-out nuclear war, against the sacrifice of future generations' health in return for the present expediency of nuclear testing, or more generally against the assumption, implicit in the White Paper and the reasoning of some of the new generation of defence experts, that moral considerations of any kind were any way irrelevant to the formation of a nation's "policy for survival". Subsidiary moral points made by CND asserted the impropriety of nuclear bluff as well as of nuclear action, and the desirability—on grounds of obligation as well as of expediency—of diverting some at least of British defence expenditure to under-developed countries. It was noteworthy that points of this latter kind, which raised practical as well as moral questions, exposed CND to counter-attacks which it could not easily rebut without more intellectual cohesion than it possessed.

Bluff and deterrence are after all psychological weapons whose effectiveness depends on their credibility—that is, on the effect they produce in the mind of an enemy. It is possible to argue that bluffing with nuclear weapons is extremely unwise, since if the bluff is called, one's own and the world's predicament is serious; but only the Anarchist or absolutist minority in CND

* February 26, 1958.

77

which held that all forms of international deceit were necessarily wrong could claim that deterrent theory and nuclear bluff were morally on a level with the actual use of nuclear weapons.

The diversion of British defence expenditure was another area in which the CND was highly vulnerable. It was quickly forgotten—at least at local level—in the movement that Mr Sandys' purpose in putting all his eggs in the nuclear basket had been the crude political one of decreasing defence expenditure, not of increasing it. In 1961, when the defence budget represented 7 p.c. of the British gross national product, Mr Harold Watkinson (then Minister of Defence) said:

"The cost of our nuclear strategic deterrent is about 10 p.c. of the defence budget. The cost of our air defences, worldwide, is about 10 p.c. of the total defence budget. Of this second 10 p.c. about one-third is attributable to the requirements of the deterrent."

Mr Watkinson had every incentive to underestimate the proportions, and the cost of—for example—the Rhine Army's tactical nuclear weapons was not included. But the saving on the deterrent, as strategists of all political colours have long insisted, would hardly suffice to buy the conventional forces needed to replace it. The CND, itself a political organisation subject to internal pressures from its pacifist core, generally shrank from emphasising this aspect of the situation.

A further issue of importance which could be dressed up as a moral one by a politician with a mind to do so, was used not by CND but against it, as a kind of anti-missile missile. As has already been seen, the CND did not officially formulate its opposition to "all nuclear weapons and alliances" (i.e. NATO) until it had been challenged with the "immorality" of Britain's abandoning her own deterrent and sheltering under the American one instead. In fact, of course, no country that could completely rely on the protection of a foreign power would on moral grounds alone insist on remaining independent. But putting the issue in these terms brought out into the open at an early stage CND's attitude to NATO, and at the close of the debate on unilateralism in the 1958 Labour Party Conference Mr Gaitskell was able to say:

"The unilateralist argument rests on the belief, I don't doubt it is sincere, that if we do this Russia and America will follow suit. There is not a shred of evidence that if we did take this action Russia or America would do anything of the kind. I say flatly and bluntly, that if we were to do this on our own and remain in the NATO Alliance, all we are doing is to shelter behind the American bombs."

78

In reply to shouts of "Get out of NATO, then" Mr Gaitskell said that he would regard this as "disastrously dangerous to the peace of the world", mentioned the possibility that America might adopt an isolationist policy, and attacked the unilateralists on one of their historic apprehensions—German rearmament:

"Germany then becomes a leading power. What sort of influence should we have over America? If you break up the NATO alliance and try to get into a sort of Switzerland or Sweden position, you may as well give up all hope of influencing American policy."

Politically and strategically, once it was clear that NATO was to be rejected, CND's case settled down quite swiftly into a plea for a positive neutralism. At the outset of the Campaign, in his book *Defence in the Nuclear Age*,* Sir Stephen King-Hall made explicit his own view of the power choices open to a Britain deprived of nuclear weapons and alliances:

"Those who advocate the abandonment of the H-bomb may not appreciate that by a kind of chain reaction in reverse, this decision also means a decision not only to abandon the use of nuclear energy in war but the abandonment of the maintenance of conventional weapons for use in major wars" (p. 142).

Sir Stephen goes on to envisage the possibilities if the Soviet Union were to confront a lightly armed Britain with a demand for bases to use against the United States and were met with a rebuff. The Russians might then:

"(*a*) Threaten to open up a nuclear attack on the West.

(*b*) Declare that they would move into Western Europe with conventional forces.

(*c*) Accept the rebuff.

(*d*) In the case of Britain, threaten or establish a naval blockade."

The answers which Sir Stephen gives to this problem arise out of the main thesis of his book, which is that in the modern age systematic non-violent resistance has become a more practicable means than any other for this nation to stave off the aggression of a nuclear power. He believes that in the circumstances outlined Britain should manoeuvre to compel the Russians to adopt choice (*b*) and undertake an occupation or to adopt choice (*c*) and accept the rebuff. The country should prepare itself to withstand a blockade for long enough to mobilise worldwide political and economic pressure on the USSR, and should discipline itself to challenge the USSR to fulfil any threat it might make to initiate

* Gollancz, 1958.

a nuclear attack on an unarmed country for the sake of bases. Sir Stephen thought that the entire reorientation of the national posture which he was proposing could be completed within ten years.

Less radical approaches were, of course, put forward within CND. Some thought that it would be possible for Britain to renounce nuclear weapons, expel American nuclear bases, but remain in NATO on the strength of increased conventional capacity. Others, like A. J. P. Taylor, thought that in or out of NATO Britain should increase her conventional armament—as the Swiss have done—to the point where it could effectively deter an invader. (The proponents of this view did not usually examine as carefully as Sir Stephen what would then happen if the adversary began a course of city-by-city nuclear blackmail.) But the vast majority of CND activists—that is, excluding those people who supported the movement merely because up to April 1960 it was the only significant political organisation other than the Liberal Party which rejected the British "independent deterrent"—were on both practical and emotional grounds against remaining in NATO. As an organisation, boasting at once the membership of Spain and Portugal and a specially composed hymn about the free world, NATO was in itself infinitely distasteful. But continued membership would also prevent Britain from using her uncommitted status to take the initiatives she ought to take, for example in Germany, and in the Middle and Far East:

"What a narrow view of the world it is which asserts that Britain would be isolating herself if she cut loose from the nuclear strategy! We should, in fact, be taking the same road as nations all round the globe, from Yugoslavia to Ghana and from Ireland to Indonesia. More than that; we should be abreast of an irreversible trend, of the course of future history."

(Mervyn Jones, of *Tribune*, from whose pamphlet *Freed From Fear* this extract is taken, spoke at 20 public meetings during the first year of the Campaign—more than any other member of the Executive except Canon Collins, who was himself certainly no NATO-lover.)

Leaving NATO was not made an explicit plank in CND policy until the Campaign's annual Conference in June 1960, when a resolution to that effect was put forward by London Region CND and carried. As I show in the next section of this chapter, that decision—or rather clarification—came *after* the key union conferences of that year which predetermined the Scarborough decision in October. But even in the fuzzy atmosphere of the Labour Party's debates and embroilments at that time, CND's intentions ought to have been clear to everyone long before June 1960. It is instructive to compare two pamphlets by Stuart Hall, one of the Campaign's leading "practical" thinkers. The first, published late in 1958, asks:

"Should Britain follow her unilateral action (suspending the testing and manufacture of nuclear weapons) by renouncing altogether the NATO Alliance? This is an attractive argument, but it is not necessarily as *radical* as may at first appear . . . Since the mutual dissolution of the two camps can be effected only through negotiation, *Britain's role must be to prepare the West to negotiate.* In order to do this, she must be present during the difficult period in which NATO reconstructs its attitude towards disarmament and disengagement . . . She must be present at these crucial discussions, working actively to reshape the whole basis of the alliance, putting the case time and again, and making sure that the discarded proposals are taken up and acted upon. She cannot do this critical task from a position of neutrality in Europe; and she cannot afford to leave NATO to its own devices."*

The second, published in May 1960, argues that CND should extend its protest to cover the whole nuclear strategy, and "What is NATO without the bomber commands, the missile launching pads, the flotilla of submarines at the ready, the early warning stations, the mobile nuclear units, and the reconnaissance flights?" Mr Hall went on:

"The Labour Party apologists for ten years of bipartisan support for NATO often argue that, so long as she remains within the alliance, Britain can at least exercise a restraining influence on her less temperate allies. This case does not bear examination. On every important issue Britain has capitulated to the strategic and military imperatives of a nuclear alliance. Britain acted as midwife to the West German army: she reconciled herself to the position of an advanced and exposed aircraft carrier for American nuclear missiles and bombers: she was unable to restrain France from entering the nuclear race: she is going to have to accept, with ill grace, nuclear weapons in West Germany: indeed, at the time of Suez, it was a NATO ally, recognising the possible danger of a general war, *which restrained Britain,* rather than the other way round. The logic of the Cold War is inexorable: once Britain accepted the basic premises of the NATO alliance, she was obliged to follow every other dangerous twist in the weapons race."†

* *Breakthrough* (Combined Universities CND, 1958), p. 16.   † *NATO and the Alliances* (London Regional Council of CND, 1960) p. 4.

It is evident from Mr Hall's volte-face that Campaigners who considered the arguments at all realised that they were finely balanced. Strategically, it was possible to argue that without a national nuclear force and American rocket bases Britain would run less risk of being drawn into a nuclear war which had already started if she opted for neutralism instead of NATO. But this was, of course, a question secondary to the problem of how to prevent such a war occurring at all. CND never evolved a satisfactory answer to the objection that by upsetting the balance of power in the world so radically Britain would induce a jitteriness in the major nuclear powers which would make war more likely. Partly as an answer to this difficulty, and partly in response to events, more recent CND pamphlets have tended to take the line that NATO is breaking up anyway, and should be given an extra crack on the shell to help it on its way.*

However, the core of the populist CND case never rested on such nice calculations of military probability, and Campaign annual conferences tended to be impatient when they were asked to listen to them. The strategists and the military arithmeticians —such as Herman Kahn—were chiefly used in debate to prove that the acknowledged dangers of existing national policy were quite as terrifying as the CND alternative. The constructive emotional force behind unilateralism, when the negative elements of fear and abhorrence were set aside, rested fairly and squarely on English liberal humanism, dashed with Socialism. They expressed sensitivity to the human and economic needs of developing countries, needs symbolised by India as a great—but neutral—developing power. This symbol, set against the continued absorption of some £200 million per annum and over half the country's trained scientific manpower in the maintenance of an "independent" deterrent, gave the unilateralists a staying-power which sheer apprehension of nuclear war could not have provided by itself.

* See *NATO's Final Decade*, by John Gittings and Richard Gott (London Region CND 1964), and *Balance of Risks: Communism or Nuclear War?* by Terence Heelas (North-West CND, 1964). Mr Gittings and Mr Gott belong to Chatham House; Mr Heelas is a member of the Institute for Strategic Studies. The Gittings–Gott pamphlet argues that the myth of Soviet superiority in conventional forces has now been dissipated. The "Soviet threat" no longer exists. Both European and NATO deterrents, and the proposed multilateral force, proliferate nuclear weapons unnecessarily. Both NATO and the Warsaw Pact could now begin to dissolve. Britain should leave NATO in 1969 if the alliance is then given a new lease of life, and meanwhile oppose all spread of ownership or control of nuclear weapons within NATO, seek disengagement in central Europe, and try to secure balanced reductions of conventional and nuclear systems on both sides, "at least down to 'minimum deterrent' level".

CHAPTER FOUR

"SEEK YE FIRST THE POLITICAL KINGDOM"

... The Party Disposes

"If Conservatives have a fault, it is perhaps that we have not thought enough about the bomb ... Labour, on the other hand, has thought too much."

Julian Critchley, MP,
Spectator, February 21, 1964

THE decision for unilateral nuclear disarmament taken at the Labour Party's Scarborough Conference in 1960 was in part the result of popular pressure at the grass roots of politics: local Labour Parties, trade union branches, Women's Co-operative Guilds, and all the sparsely attended but (by the few) enthusiastically cultivated bodies which comprise the Labour movement. But the decision was also the culminating point of resentments which had been building up in the party for at least a decade. Finally it reversed two myths about the workings of Party democracy which had been widely believed by the Labour rank and file: that the Party Conference was sovereign, and that the union block vote at it was impregnably reactionary.

In the early fifties, the days of the Bevanite revolts over such issues as German rearmament and health service prescription charges, it was an article of faith with the Left that full-blooded Socialist doctrine, expressed in the resolutions and votes of the constituency Labour Parties, was prevented from becoming the official policy of the Party by the actions of a few Right-wing trade union leaders, whose block votes at Conference outnumbered the constituency votes by about 5 to 1. It was argued by the Left that the block votes did not represent their nominal owners. "The Labour Movement," said Mrs Barbara Castle, MP, at Brighton in 1953, "is in danger of dying a death of three million cuts—the block votes of four men. Their vote was not representative of the working trade unionist." At the same time, during the years when a Right-of-Centre Parliamentary Party was consistently supported—especially on defence and foreign policy—by Right-of-Centre trade union leaders, it was assumed that Conference was, in fact, the final authority of the Labour movement, and that if only the "four men" in the smoke-filled room could be replaced or done down, the Party would automatically become Socialist again.

This persecution complex, readily discernible in the political career of Aneurin Bevan, further encouraged the growth, anyway inevitable in a party of the Left, of Parliamentary and extra-Parliamentary ginger groups, dedicated to remaking the Party in a more Socialist image. Victory for Socialism, revived in 1957, after a period of inanition, to sponsor a Labour campaign against the H-bomb, is an obvious example. Its Chairman in 1957 was Hugh Jenkins, Secretary of Actors' Equity and a London county councillor, who had fought his Parliamentary election campaign in Mitcham and Wallington in 1955 mainly on the H-bomb issue. Victory for Socialism's Parliamentary membership oscillated around 40 MPs. This compares with the figure of about 70 MPs, including 25 actual pacifists, in the 1959–64 Parliament who were prepared to support unilateralism in the House of Commons, usually by abstaining on official Labour defence motions or amendments; and to these should be added another 30 or so who on some issues, like the British H-bomb tests in 1958, sided with the unilateralists.

The first clear sign that there might be something wrong with the old assumptions came in 1956. First, Frank Cousins became General Secretary of the Transport and General Workers Union. The TGWU is the largest union in the country, casting a million votes at the Labour Party Conference, and between 1945 and 1955 it was led by Mr Arthur Deakin, a militant anti-Communist who had very little difficulty in persuading his biennial Conferences to vote against any Left-wing policy. When the union under Mr Cousins began to take definite darts to the Left, both industrially and politically, it was even easier than before for its critics to believe that its policy was made by the General Secretary rather than by the membership, or even the other officers.

At the same time, the main political event of 1956, Suez and the public reactions to it, had given the Left an awkward reminder that working-class Labour voters are, on defence and foreign policy issues, much more conservative and chauvinistic than the Labour Party at Westminster. It thus seemed that in this area of policy-making the Right-wing trade union leader might in fact be a more faithful representative of his membership than a Left-wing one. It was this fact about the British Labour movement, temporarily obscured during the rush of public feeling about nuclear weapons in 1959, that helped to produce the crushingly successful roll-back of forces between Scarborough 1960 and Blackpool 1961. As Mr Martin Harrison has written:

"In general, drawing from their industrial experience, the unions have been sceptical that abandoning British nuclear weapons was likely to persuade other nations to follow the example. They have always been less sentimental about using power than many members of the local parties.

"Consequently the unions' support for unilateral disarmament was exceptionally low in 1957 and 1958—a mere 200,000 to 300,000 according to the terms of the motion."*

It is true that the constituency parties at this time were also only beginning to show the influence of the Campaign, and were about equally divided on this issue. Two years later the myth of

* *Trade Unions and the Labour Party since 1945* (Allen & Unwin, 1960), pp. 237–8.

the invulnerability of the unions to sudden change, breached from above by Mr Cousins' impact upon the Transport and General Workers, was shattered from below by the unilateralist upheaval set in motion, for the most part, at local level. Union after union toppled—"almost casually", as Mr Roy Jenkins has put it*—and indeed, the process took place without CND itself putting in an organisational effort in any way comparable to that which was mobilised after Scarborough by the Campaign for Democratic Socialism, with the aim of reversing the decision taken there.

"This swing of opinion," said the CND after Scarborough,† "was not achieved by lobbying and infiltration, but by a public campaign which affected trade unionists along with the rest of the population. It was at Aldermaston that the victory of Scarborough was won." Nevertheless, the possession by the Campaign of leaders who knew the internal structure of the Labour Party inside out was undoubtedly a help. Peggy Duff, for example, had been on the drafting committee of the 1958 Labour Conference. Kingsley Martin was editor of the *New Statesman*, Michael Foot editor of *Tribune*. The Campaign did not lack informed tactical advice.

But even though CND managed to surmount the politico-sociological obstacle set up by the attitudes of the Labour movement's industrial rank and file, it was almost inevitably baulked in the end, partly by the nature of its cause and partly by the Labour Party's widely misunderstood constitutional processes. As Mr Harrison writes:

"It is all but impossible to formulate an atomic policy in the hundred words or so of a Conference resolution. Moreover, unilateral disarmament was not a policy in itself, it was a mere fraction of a policy. It could not be separated from the complete recasting of defence and international policy which would inevitably follow. Yet the nuclear disarmers were not only trying to persuade Conference to adopt this morsel of a policy, but to mandate a future Labour Government to it regardless of events at the time, in utter ignorance of what the circumstances would be ... They were unable to present Conference with a coherent formulation of the international policy for Britain after nuclear disarmament because their unity scarcely extended beyond their single demand."‡

In July 1959, when it looked for a time as though the unions would turn as massively unilateralist as they eventually did the following year, Mr Gaitskell went out of his way to insist in his Workington speech that annual Conference did not "mandate"

* *Encounter*, February 1964. † *Bulletin*, October 1960. ‡ *Ibid.*, p. 236.

a Government, and that the Parliamentary Party must be free to decide its own line. This principle, despite Mr Wilson's personal concern for the sanctity of Conference decisions, is now more clearly established than it has ever been.

Between 1958 and 1961 newspaper readers and television viewers were treated to the spectacle of Britain's alternative Government methodically tearing itself apart over an issue which affected, one way or another, the continuance of Britain as a major world power. The argument was variously described at the time as a dignified example of democratic decision-making, and as a squalid personal vendetta in which the handiest weapons happened to be the Bomb and public concern about it. There was a similar division of opinion, when the combatants had fallen back exhausted, over what the struggle had achieved. True, there was a winner, but he did not live very long to enjoy the fruits of his victory, and when he died, he was succeeded by some-one who had been holding a coat for the opposite side. Labour's defence policy was preserved from pacifism, neutralism, and fellow-travelling, but on the other hand, it was no longer being described by Conservative Ministers as "99.5 p.c. sound". It is still open to argument whether this result was achieved by popular pressure, or by the logic of external events, and whether the bloodiest part of the duel could have been averted if the policy had been modified earlier than it was.

The Campaign for Nuclear Disarmament, in its early days, puzzled the Labour leadership. Any professional politician on the Left could remember many apparently comparable protest movements, and the failure of Labour's own H-bomb National Campaign three years previously did not suggest that the issue was one on which the public would be easy to arouse. The tests, admittedly, were arousing widespread concern, but this aspect of the matter was not politically disturbing. Labour could afford to go a long way with the opposition to testing, and could show willing on minor issues like the "H-Bomb patrols". But on the central issue of Britain's defences and alliances, there could be no compromise. Two factors strengthened, or were considered to strengthen, the leadership's position. Aneurin Bevan, who in 1955 had used the hydrogen bomb issue against Mr Attlee in the House of Commons, had at Brighton in September 1957 abandon-ed his former fellow-rebels and spoken of the need not to send a British Foreign Secretary "naked into the conference chamber". And time favoured the leadership: in a few months, it would be possible to appeal for Party unity in face of an imminent General Election.

Less than three weeks after CND's Central Hall inaugural meeting, a joint Labour and TUC Committee issued a statement designed to let the Party ride the crest of public feeling rather than drown in it. The committee contained two known doubters about nuclear weapons: Frank Cousins, Secretary of the Transport and General Workers since 1956, and Tom Driberg, MP, who was in the chair by virtue of his office as Chairman of the Party that year. Otherwise the trade union side consisted of two old reliables, Sir Thomas Williamson of the Municipal Workers and Sir Thomas Yates of the Seamen's Union; while the Parliamentary Party was represented by Mr Gaitskell, Mr Bevan, and Mr James Griffiths. The agreed statement said that Britain should at once suspend thermo-nuclear tests unilaterally for a limited period in the hope that this would hasten permanent international agreement on tests, and lead on to a general disarmament convention. The way to the banning of nuclear weapons was through a negotiated removal of the Soviet preponderance in conventional arms. The Government had "failed to show that it is necessary for British-based aircraft to carry nuclear weapons on either patrols or training flights", and no physical steps should be taken to set up the East Anglian missile bases until a further attempt had been made to negotiate with the Russians. The bases, if they were set up, should remain "effectively under British control".

The effect of this statement was slightly spoilt by events both before and after its publication. On February 25 the usually reliable *Daily Herald* came out with its own line, calling for unilateral cessation of hydrogen bomb manufacture and refusal to accept missile bases. The Secretary of the Labour Party, Morgan Phillips, described this approach as "seriously in conflict with the policy of the Labour Party" and "an ill-considered attempt, supported by misleading information, to interfere in current private discussion between the Labour Party and the TUC". Then on April 4 John Strachey, MP, issued a conservative pamphlet roguishly entitled *Scrap All the H-Bombs*, with a foreword by Mr Gaitskell. To the vast irritation of some of his colleagues, Mr Gaitskell said that though Mr Strachey's pamphlet was "not an official statement" it had been thought by the Executive to be "a most useful background document", which was being issued in connection with the Labour–TUC campaign. Mr Strachey argued that Britain must have the H-bomb to be able to diverge from America if need arose, but added: "We cannot help bitterly resenting it when those people who attack the Labour Party pretend that the Labour Party is 'for the H-Bomb'."

Outwardly at least, the Conservative Party did not mind being attacked on this account nearly as much as Mr Strachey did. "If we believe we should defend our way of life, then we should be prepared to defend it whatever the cost," said the Prime Minister in February, and Sir David Eccles, speaking about tests, said that it was a wicked thing for "third-rate people, doctors, people who have no experience like the people who advise us in the Government" to play on people's fears and serve the cause of the enemy.* Most Conservative speakers, in the House of Lords especially, were not well informed enough about CND to be puzzled by it, though Lord Home, in philosophical mood, did tell their Lordships: "Today, under the impact of the hydrogen bomb, people are bewildered. The young put up a brave façade but they cannot conceal that their faith in the future and purpose of life is wavering."†

Mr Macmillan, moreover, took an early opportunity of analysing in Parliament the views that were being put forward in the country:

"We could, of course, throw in our hand altogether. In other words, we could accept, either from high principle or from less respectable motives, the pacifist solution. There have always been some people in this country, by tradition, who support the pacifist view, but I do not think it would commend itself to any government likely to be formed in Britain.

"There is a variation of this which is equally dangerous. It is that we could unilaterally abandon nuclear weapons. I think there are Hon. Members who favour this view, and I have certainly drawn this conclusion from the number of letters and resolutions which are sent to me from time to time. But this unilateral nuclear disarmament is not a tenable position, either. For if the British were to abandon this weapon only to shelter under the American nuclear power, this seems to me to have little moral value, and it is, indeed, somewhat disingenuous. If on the other hand it means that the whole of the West is unilaterally to abandon nuclear defence, then I think we must see that this would put us completely at the mercy of the Soviets."‡

Mr Macmillan's political antennae were far more sensitive than most of his colleagues', and he was not the man to remain indifferent to a movement whose spontaneity and force were attested by his postbag. "Either from high principle or from less respectable motives", he put the public pursuit of peace high on his agenda. He won the 1959 Election partly on the strength of the impending (though in the event, disastrous) Summit, and at the end of his career, after the signing of the 1963 Test Ban Treaty, he received a warm letter of congratulation from President Kennedy. Even his famous nerve was vulnerable to nuclear

* The *Observer*, March 16, 1958.   † Hansard, March 6, 1958, col. 1275.
‡ Hansard, February 19, 1958, col. 1217–18.

anxiety, and it was remarked at the time of the 1962 Cuban crisis that the strength and firmness of the messages emanating from Lord Home at the Foreign Office were in marked contrast to the more hesitant signals from Admiralty House.

A later indication of Mr Macmillan's flexibility was his reception, in March 1962, of a deputation from the Women's Committee of the CND to protest against the renewed use of Christmas Island for nuclear bomb testing. The deputation, which was led by Dame Alix Meynell, consisted of Dr Janet Aitken, Mrs Diana Collins, Miss Jacquetta Hawkes, Professor Dorothy Hodgkin, Miss Marghanita Laski, Dr Dorothy Needham, Dr Antoinette Pirie, and Mrs Mary Stocks. Dame Alix urged Mr Macmillan to take a strong and if necessary separate line in the Test Ban negotiations, and to use his great influence with the Americans to persuade them to modify their demands for inspection. Miss Laski thought that the nuclear arms race soured the idealism of many young people. It might account for the rise in juvenile delinquency: it certainly made students distrust the State and its instruments and direct their energies into negative political pressure groups instead of study and constructive activities. Miss Hawkes thought that a "moral mutation" in human history, comparable with the abandonment of human sacrifice, cannibalism, or slavery, was imminent, but that the mutation—the abandonment of warfare—would take a generation or two to arrive. Britain should renounce her nuclear weapons as a contribution to the world's survival in the interim period. Mrs Collins quoted the World Council of Churches judgement that governments should never get themselves into the position where they contemplated the first use of nuclear weapons, and protested against the United Kingdom's abstention in the United Nations on a proposal to establish a nuclear-free zone in Africa.

Mr Macmillan is said to have replied that he considered juvenile delinquency to be primarily the result of the lack of religion among the young; that the only circumstances in which this country might use nuclear weapons first were if Europe were seized and the enemy were at the Channel ports; that he had persuaded President Eisenhower on several occasions not to test and that President Kennedy wanted a test agreement "passionately", but that there must be some form of verification; that the Pentagon would welcome British abandonment of her deterrent but that we should lose our influence on the Americans if we dissociated ourselves from the American tests.

The tests remained in the forefront of public anxiety during the summer of 1958, while the British and Americans were testing and the Russians were offering a suspension, but receded from view when the Geneva Conference began in the autumn. At the Labour Party Conference in September CND had to be content with a small increase in the unilateralist vote (it just topped the million mark on a motion against missile bases) and with a hint from Mr Gaitskell that he was coming round to the idea of the "non-nuclear club", which the *Manchester Guardian* had been pressing upon him since the month of CND's inaugural meeting, but which itself lacked the unilateral ingredient necessary to satisfy the Campaign. The idea also left open the question of what was to be done if the non-nuclear club failed to persuade France and China to join. Properly speaking, it represented an initiative rather than a fully watertight policy.

CND arranged a Nuclear Week in September, and the Labour Party a simultaneous and parallel campaign, by comparison very poorly supported, which according to A. J. P. Taylor was designed "to kill us, not the Bomb". There was more comfort for the Campaign in the Liberal Party Assembly, which voted by a huge majority for an end to British hydrogen bomb tests and renunciation of the "independent deterrent".

During the winter, with the first Direct Action demonstrations and arrests in Norfolk, the CND proper fell somewhat out of the limelight. But on March 25 Mr Anthony Greenwood, MP—"whose young daughter's views on the bomb" (wrote John Cole in the *Manchester Guardian*) "have hitherto been better known to the public than his own"—raised anew in Labour's National Executive Committee the question of the Party's attitude to nuclear weapons. Mr Gaitskell said that the question of a non-nuclear club had been discussed at the last Conference and need not be reopened before the Labour Government came in. But five days later Trafalgar Square was thronged with 20,000 people at the end of the second Aldermaston March. Although the marchers were deprived of Dr Edith Summerskill's support,* Bob Willis, the year's Chairman of the TUC, chaired the final meeting and Mr Frank Cousins was espied with his children on the edge of the crowd. On June 23 the non-nuclear club, which China had already described as "hypothetical, hypocritical and humbug", was formally proposed by the Labour Executive to the TUC. The old wrangle over whether Labour meant to stop or only to suspend tests was covered by the proposal that if tests started again, Labour would call discussions to obtain further suspensions, and the possibility of opening Britain and even her NATO bases to UN inspection was mentioned. But on the independent deterrent the statement guardedly said: "It is impossible to assess in Opposition whether any technical and military merits such a policy may possess are sufficient to outweigh its obvious political

* See p. 69.

91

drawbacks." Mr Cousins and Mr Willis declined to sign this statement, though the meeting had been specially advanced from late July in the hopes that they would be able to do so in time for the big union conferences.

Already—with the Election, as it turned out, only three months away—the leadership was in grave trouble. On June 4 the National Union of General and Municipal Workers, normally one of the most docile in the TUC, went unilateralist by 150 to 126 with 75 abstaining. "What do lavatory attendants know about nuclear weapons?" said one Labour MP when he heard the news, and it was openly rumoured that the missing multi-lateralists had all been having tea when the vote was taken. But the damage was done, and within a week 78 Labour MPs, ignoring the request of the leadership, had signed a motion opposing the transfer of American nuclear warheads and aircraft from France to Britain after France had refused to accept them.

In the event, Mr Gaitskell was granted a year's grace. Of the big unions, only the Transport and General, whose 760 delegates were all sent a full copy of the 3,000-word Labour–TUC statement on *The Next Step*, went unilateralist, voting for a seven-point motion which, according to Mr Cousins, contained nothing which had not at one time or another been part of official Labour Party policy. The whole, however, was more than the sum of its parts. On July 12 Mr Gaitskell, speaking at Workington, moved some way towards satisfying Mr Cousins by saying: "I think we could safely say that we would never use the H-bomb first. I think the policy of being prepared to use even tactical atomic weapons first is, to say the least, questionable." On August 21 the Municipal Workers, recalled by their leaders to hold another conference on the excuse that Labour's new defence policy statement could not have been considered at the last one, reversed its vote by 194 to 139, though one speaker translated the Chinese view of the non-nuclear club into trade-union English, saying: "I have never heard such a lot of tripe as this club lark." And for the platform Mr Fred Hayday praised the "moral and Christian grounds" of the unilateralists, adding: "They are most disturbing, but you cannot formulate political programmes and policies on these principles. Disarmament is a question of hard negotiations."

At Blackpool in September, the TUC agreed. (No Labour Party Conference was held in 1959, because of the General Election. Mr Gaitskell addressed the TUC by invitation instead.) The seven-point Transport and General motion was lost by 5,133,000 to 2,795,000. A motion protesting against the installation of missile bases was narrowly carried. In October the Labour Party lost its third successive General Election, and while recriminations were still proceeding, an article in the *New States-man** by Professor P. M. S. Blackett, the leading military scien-tist of the Left and not a member of CND, further revealed how far some of the Campaign's conclusions had in the past two years become part of the received progressive wisdom. "I can see no plausible way in which the European defence community can survive either with its own jointly owned nuclear forces or with individual national nuclear forces," Professor Blackett said, anticipating Mr McNamara's Ann Arbor speech by over three years. "The criticism of the 1957 and 1958 White Papers is over-whelming . . . When official policy is to do impossible things, then, if put to the test, nothing is done." The whole policy of massive retaliation, Professor Blackett pointed out, would have been possible in the days when one side had the monopoly of nuclear weapons, but had become impossible by the time it was formulated in 1954.

"Once a nation pledges its safety to an absolute weapon, it becomes emotionally essential to believe in an absolute enemy . . . It is ironical that the policy of massive retaliation—that is, atomic attack on civilians—was the chosen slogan of Mr John Foster Dulles, the most passionate political moralist of our times. There is a deeper irony in the fact that it was not the first use of the atomic bomb in 1945 but the loss of its monopoly by the West which sent the moralists back to their morals and the theo-logians back to Grotius' formulation 300 years ago of the *Principles of the Just War*."

Professor Blackett boldly argued that the "non-nuclear club", to which Labour had cautiously come round, was good in itself even if it was not complete—"The risk that Britain might be atom bombed by France or Sweden won't disturb my sleep."

The signs were that official Labour policy was once again going to be left one fatal step behind what the Party and its supporters were ready for. The penalties for inflexibility were set out clearly in the early months of 1960. CND's annual conference reported that the number of local groups had grown over the past year from 272 to 459, and at Easter a four-mile long column snaked its way from Aldermaston to London, ending as a Trafalgar Square crowd whose estimated size varied from 30,000 to 100,000.

The stir in the country was mirrored in Parliament. On March 1 43 Labour MPs abstained from voting in the defence debate. They included Mr R. H. S. Crossman, whose settled opposition to the British independent strategic nuclear deterrent dated back at least to March 1954.† Abstention in the debate

* December 5, 1959. † See p. 25.

compelled Mr Crossman to resign his position as an official party spokesman, and he remarked:

"If only 43 Conservatives had had the courage of their convictions and carried their criticisms to the point of abstention, Parliament might have achieved the total abandonment of a strategy whose weaknesses are becoming clearer year by year."

At this stage the TUC's International Committee was apparently confident that it could continue to withstand unilateralist resolutions at the annual Congress, as it had done so often in the past. But the Committee had reckoned without the effect of the Government's cancellation of Blue Streak, the missile which was to carry Britain's independent deterrent from the mid-sixties on, at a write-off cost of £87 million. This event, coupled with the Communist Party's swing to support unilateralism, brought support for British renunciation of the Bomb to a new height, both in the country and at union conferences, and in April three important conferences—the Co-operative Party, the Shopworkers, and the Engineers—passed unilateralist resolutions.

By this time the Party line was coming round to Mr Crossman's position. In the middle of March Mr Denis Healey had written in the American magazine *New Leader*: "Stopping the spread of nuclear weapons is likely to depend on NATO finding a strategy for the defence of Western Europe which does not require America's allies to possess atomic weapons for themselves." And in the Blue Streak debate in the Commons on April 27, when Mr Harold Watkinson expressed a touching but misplaced faith in the Skybolt missile which the Government had ordered from the United States to replace Blue Streak, Mr George Brown, Labour's Defence spokesman, began to wonder whether Britain could afford a deterrent of her own. A few days later, when Mr Gaitskell returned from a Socialist International meeting in Haifa, he discovered that his Party's line had changed while he was away.

The Campaign was justifiably unimpressed by this conversion. Blue Streak was a vulnerable liquid-fuelled rocket open to many of the objections raised against the Thor missiles in East Anglia, whose installation Labour had already come round to resisting. The weapon's failure was more important politically than technically. For it was the events of the early spring which secured the Scarborough victory. In May, with the U-2 crisis and the bitter collapse of the long-awaited Summit talks in Paris, the public mood swung again. On May 23 Mr Gaitskell delivered an impassioned speech to the General and Municipal Workers, who had played truant in 1959, stating clearly that Britain should stay in NATO and that NATO must remain nuclear.

Next day the union voted against unilateralism by 260 to 80. But the damage had been done. When in late June the Labour Party's National Executive Committee and the TUC finally accepted "the truth that a country of our size cannot remain in any real sense of the word an 'independent nuclear power' " it was too late to convince the Miners, the Railwaymen and the Transport Workers' delegates that Labour's policy met the desires and anxieties of their sons and daughters, embodied on the long hard road from Aldermaston. On September 7, in Douglas, Isle of Man, the Trades Union Congress delighted the newspapers by voting in favour both of the official Labour–TUC statement and of a professedly unilateralist motion proposed by Frank Cousins, which opposed any defence policy based on nuclear weapons or the threat of using nuclear weapons. Mr Cousins' motion got the largest majority.

The Labour Party went to Scarborough knowing that only a miracle could save the platform from defeat. A miracle would almost certainly be ruled out of order at a Labour Party Conference. The CND published a daily bulletin for delegates. In the event, the margin of unilateralist victory was narrower than had been expected. Mr Gaitskell concluded his brave, reasoned but uncompromising speech with a peroration telling delegates that Labour MPs would not quickly become the "pacifists, neutralists, and fellow-travellers that other people are", and offering to "fight and fight and fight again to save the Party we love". Many of the constituency party delegates forgot their mandate, and it has been calculated that about 60 p.c. (no exact figures for constituency Party votes are ever obtainable) voted for the platform. But the union block vote, in its reversed role, carried by 407,000 votes the Engineers' motion demanding "the unilateral renunciation of the testing, manufacture, stockpiling and basing of all nuclear weapons in Great Britain". The Transport and General motion in a similar sense was carried by 43,000, and the TUC–NEC statement rejected by 297,000. CND had surpassed the Chartists in constitutional success even if it could not surpass them in numbers. Or so it seemed until the National Agent (now General Secretary) of the Labour Party, Mr Len Williams, quietly quoted a forgotten clause in the Labour Party's constitution: "No proposal shall be included in the Party programme unless it has been adopted by the Party Conference by a majority of not less than two-thirds of the votes recorded on a card vote."

On October 19 the counter-revolution began. Twenty-six former Labour candidates, councillors and trade unionists launched a campaign initially called "Victory for Sanity", and later "Campaign for Democratic Socialism". The Secretary was

Mr Bill Rodgers, a former Secretary of the Fabian Society, and later MP for Stockton. The group made the reasonable assumption that the Labour Party was still basically sceptical about the wisdom of unilateral nuclear disarmament, and that the case for multilateralism and NATO membership had gone by default during 1960 at hundreds of local party meetings and trade union branches. They recruited 250 local "whips", and distributed from Mr Rodgers' London office model speeches, motions and amendments, as well as (from January 1961) a monthly bulletin, aggressive in tone, called *Campaign*. Far from finding that a posse of determined unilateralists awaited them in every trade union branch, the CDS discovered that a little encouragement went a very long way in quarters where pressure group politics had not hitherto penetrated.

At the same time, at Westminster, the Labour Party's attempts during 1961 to reshape its defence policy in time for the Blackpool Conference were distinguished from those of 1960 by the emergence of a "centre party", represented by Mr Crossman and Mr Walter Padley (General Secretary of the Shopworkers). Mr Padley—like Mr Wilson, who after Scarborough was bullied by the Left into standing against Mr Gaitskell for the leadership of the Party, thus earning for himself the lasting distrust of the Labour Right—stood for the sovereignty of Conference decisions. The Crossman–Padley draft, as it became known, attempted the virtually impossible task of reaching a modus vivendi which would shelter both Mr Gaitskell and Mr Cousins. The draft, though it pressed for "radical reconstruction of NATO to end the need for American nuclear bases in Europe, including Britain", and rejected absolutely "a NATO strategy based on the threat to use nuclear weapons first, and a defence policy which compels armies to rely upon them", was attacked by the *Daily Worker* as well as by Mr Gaitskell, but as a compromise it was enough to withdraw the Shopworkers' Conference in May from the unilateralist camp. The Engineers, the Miners, and the Railwaymen then fell in behind the official Labour–TUC statement, and at the Transport and General conference, which stayed unilateralist by a 3 to 1 majority, a London busman complained: "The manipulations that took place to change some union votes make the ETU ballot-rigging look like a childish prank." The Labour Party Conference met at Blackpool in the middle of the prolonged Berlin crisis and the agitation over the Great Powers' renewal of testing, culminating in the Committee of 100's Trafalgar Square sit-down. But the Transport and General unilateralist resolution was defeated by 2,418,000 votes. Only a mile-long parade by the CND along Blackpool's front, votes against the installation of Polaris and the training of

German troops in Britain, and the refusal of four of his platform colleagues to applaud Mr Gaitskell's speech, betrayed the damage that had been done; though Mr Crossman later correctly claimed—against the jubilation of the CDS—that the opinion of the constituency parties had in fact hardened against the platform since 1960 by about 10 p.c.

The facts of this controversy were later analysed by Keith Hindell and Philip Williams in the *Political Quarterly*.* Against *Tribune*'s optimistic assertion that there was a constituency party majority against the platform of 60 to 40 at Scarborough and 80 to 20 at Blackpool, they were able to show that at both conferences the majority of the constituency parties voted for the official policy (an unheard-of event during the German rearmament controversy a decade previously). In 1960 the constituency parties voted for the platform by 521,000 to 260,000, with about a fifth of the whole abstaining. In 1960 there were fewer abstentions, and the constituency party vote was 548,000 to 320,000 in favour of the platform. In other words, the issue was decided from start to finish by the unions. There was even a moment in 1961 when it looked as though the entire foreign policy of the Opposition hung upon a single branch election in the Yorkshire coal field.

The same article provides some concrete evidence for the success of the Campaign for Democratic Socialism in changing the minds of constituency parties on this issue. From a questionnaire answered by members of 148 local parties in which the CDS was active, Messrs Hindell and Williams conclude that one in three of these parties swung from unilateralism to support of the leadership between Scarborough and Blackpool. "It follows that among parties not in the sample there was probably a slight shift in the other direction." Calculations based on Labour Party Conference votes are necessarily inexact, and and it should not be too readily assumed—as the authors point out—that CDS caused the effect with which it was associated. Moreover, numerical analysis cannot do justice to the qualitative influence of unilateralism. If one had subtracted the CND supporters from constituency parties, there would not have been much left to fight an election with in some places. But for this, the demoralisation of the Labour Party during 1960–1 would not have gone so deep.

As every by-election bears witness, it is possible, if one is so minded, to prove almost anything from the results of a public opinion poll. However, the availability of this reasonably accurate and scientific method of assessing the will of the nation on particular issues antedates the first use of nuclear weapons. (It

* July–September 1962, pp. 306–20.

will be recalled that when the *News Chronicle*'s Gallup Poll correctly forecast the result of the 1945 General Election, the newspaper was too sceptical to print it.)

Unfortunately, the polls have not asked any single question on nuclear weapons in the same form at regular intervals since 1945, so a graph of public concern and judgement on this issue can hardly be drawn. But it is relevant to the placing of CND in its historical context to recall that in August 1945, 72 p.c. of the British people approved of the use of atomic bombs on Japan and 21 p.c. disapproved; and that of the disapprovers, the highest proportion was in the middle socio-economic grade and the lowest proportion in the upper.

By the time CND itself was founded, the public opinion polls were much more firmly established in public esteem, and were taken much more seriously by politicians. The impact of the Campaign is in fact graphically portrayed in a question which the Gallup Poll has asked at intervals between May 1957 and May 1963:

"Does all this talk about H-bombs, rockets, satellites and guided missiles worry you a lot, a little, or not at all?"

%	May 1957	Oct. 1957	Oct. 1958	Jan. 1959	Mar. 1960	Sept. 1961	Oct. 1961	May 1963
A lot	13	24	24	22	24	27	25	12
A little	36	33	41	39	37	35	40	31
Not at all ⎫ Don't know ⎭	51	43	35	39	39	38	35	57

It is difficult from this table to deduce any conclusion about the peak date of CND's influence. The peak of public concern seems to have been September 1961, the month of reaction to the renewal of Russian and American H-bomb tests, and of the Committee of 100's Trafalgar Square sit-down. But this was also the month before the Labour Party Conference returned to multilateralism. Within the five or six years of the NCANWT–CND's popular success it seems to have been external events rather than internal political or propaganda successes that dictated the level of public alarm. (It is a pity the question designed to discover this level was not asked immediately after the Cuban crisis of October 1962.) But equally, it is clear that CND was made possible by a level of public concern which had been rising rapidly during 1957, and which did not lose way seriously until after the West had, over Cuba, confronted and survived, if not its first nuclear crisis, at least the first that was publicly recognised as perilous.

On the other hand, support for CND's policy did not run parallel with alarm about nuclear weapons. With comparatively slight variants the Gallup Poll asked the following question at intervals between April 1958 and April 1962:

"Would you approve or disapprove if Britain gave up her H-bombs even if other countries did not do so?"

%	Apr. 1958	Sept. 1958	Mar. 1959	Sept. 1961	Dec. 1961	Apr. 1962
Approve	25	30	30	21	31	22
Disapprove	61	57	50	62	55	64
Don't know	14	13	20	17	14	14

This can be compared with another set of questions asked by the Gallup Poll during the 18 months of argument within the Labour Party:

"What policy should Britain follow about nuclear weapons?"

%	Mar. 1960	Apr. 1960	June 1960	Late Sept. 1960	Oct. 1960	Mar. 1961	Apr. 1961	June 1961	Aug. 1962
Give up nuclear weapons entirely?	26	33	27	21	21	22	19	20	23
Pool all nuclear weapons with other NATO countries and rely mainly on American production?	19	27	34	31	32	29	26	30	25
Continue to make our own nuclear weapons?	31	24	28	36	37	41	36	35	37
Don't know	24	16	11	12	10	8	19	15	15

Taken together, these polls seem to demonstrate that the Campaign had a definite influence upon public opinion during its first year, winning as converts 5 p.c. of the population between April and September 1958, but that its peak did not come until April 1960, when its groups were sufficiently generalised throughout the country to take advantage of a fortuitous bonus like the failure of Blue Streak. And it was in this month that the Co-operative Party, Engineers, and Shopworkers annual Conferences went unilateralist and started the stampede within the Labour Party. But then came the Summit failure, and by the time of Scarborough much of this support had fallen away. It is noteworthy that as the debate continued the number of "don't knows" fell to a low of 8 p.c. in March 1961, and that almost all of these doubters switched to open support of Britain's manufacture of her own nuclear weapons. The Russian and American resumption of testing in September 1961 also brought with it, not only increased public alarm in Britain, but increased reluctance to depend on American nuclear weapons for national safety.

The Campaign itself was not slow to use the public opinion poll as part of the technique of persuasion, and in the universities in particular, during 1958, the compilation, circulation and analysis of elaborate questionnaires on nuclear weapons to—in some cases—remarkably high proportions of the undergraduate bodies gave the university CNDs considerable impetus. The questions asked were originally designed in Oxford University to stimulate public discussion rather than to elicit clear-cut unilateralist answers. But some indication of both the strength and variety of feeling in the universities in 1958 can be found in comparing the results obtained in Oxford, where almost half the undergraduate body voted; and in Cambridge, where a different set of questions was used and where 37 p.c. of the undergraduate body responded. (Subsequent sample surveys in both places showed that there was no significant discrepancy between the views of those who had and of those who had not voted.) In Oxford, undergraduates rejected by 10–20 p.c. majorities the assertion that Britain's possession of the hydrogen bomb decreased the risk of war, and the argument that retention of the Bomb was justified by the greater influence it gave this country in negotiations. They voted 53 p.c. to 29 p.c., with 10 p.c. doubtful, that Britain should "do everything in her power, including if need be renunciation of her own nuclear arms, to stop any further countries acquiring or developing nuclear weapons". The Campaign in Oxford University for Nuclear Disarmament developed the following year into the largest of all the undergraduate societies, outnumbering Conservative, Labour, and Liberal Clubs, and contemporary undergraduate commentators (David Marquand, Richard Exley) have remarked on the singularly unemotional, pragmatic tone of the university campaign at this time—an atmosphere which the spokesmen of the CND itself, when they addressed a public meeting in Oxford, failed to appreciate.

Cambridge at this period was far less emphatically unilateralist than Oxford. Only 22 p.c. agreed, and 72 p.c. disagreed, with the idea of unilateral nuclear disarmament, and only 33 p.c. thought that Britain should in no circumstances use the hydrogen bomb. Voting undergraduates were rather more tolerant of the presence of American missile bases in the country than was the population at large. (In December 1957 a majority of the population, according to Gallup, was against the setting up of these bases.)

A further student survey, conducted by the Combined Universities Campaign for Nuclear Disarmament, was conducted during November and December 1960. Questionnaires were sent to a random sample of 4,050 students in seven provincial and Scottish universities. There was a 72 p.c. response. The students were asked, among other detailed questions on the moral and practical aspects of nuclear war, which policy they would prefer for Britain in "the present situation". They chose as follows:

Renunciation by Great Britain of her own independent nuclear weapons in favour of their collective ownership under NATO	36 p.c.
Unilateral nuclear disarmament by Great Britain	21 p.c.
The development of an exclusively British nuclear deterrent	11 p.c.
The continuing development of the British nuclear deterrent with US aid	29 p.c.

Over two-thirds of the respondents were in favour of Britain remaining in NATO as it stood, and only a fifth opted for neutralism. Asked whether there were any circumstances in which they would approve of Britain using nuclear weapons, 60 p.c. said yes, 31 p.c. said no, and 8 p.c. were uncertain. On the other hand, only a small majority of students thought that the use of these weapons would be morally justifiable, and they decided (by an equally small majority) that occupation by a foreign power would be preferable to a nuclear war.

Despite the well known anxiety of politicians about their popularity ratings, surprisingly little has been done to correlate the findings of modern, scientifically conducted public opinion polls with the credibility or incredibility of the nation's deterrent posture at the time. In March 1958, for example, over half Gallup's sample (80 p.c. of those who ventured an opinion) did not expect as much as half the population of Britain to survive a nuclear war between Russia and the West. This finding may usefully be compared with a passage in which Herman Kahn discusses what proportion of her 180 million population the United States might be willing to pay to "punish the Soviets for their aggression":

"I have discussed this question with many Americans and after about fifteen minutes of discussion their estimates of an acceptable price generally fall between 10 and 60 million, clustering towards the upper number ... No American that I have spoken to who was at all serious about the matter believed that any United States action, limited or unlimited, would be justified—no matter what our commitments were—if more than half of our population would be killed in retaliation."*

Mr Kahn also found that European estimates of what Ameri-
* On Thermonuclear War (OUP 1960), pp. 29-30

can decision-makers or planners might accept in order to live up to their obligations were rather lower, varying between 2 and 20 million dead. Assuming that Britons are no less fond of life and of the society in which they live than Americans are, it follows that any rational and democratic British Prime Minister would in fact submit to any insult or aggressive act on the part of a foreign power if the certain alternative were a dozen 10-megaton bombs on British cities.

A possible conclusion from all the public opinion surveys and public discussion of the past few years is that the British people as a whole are more acutely aware of their strategic vulnerability than either the Civil Defence authorities or the CND have given them credit for, but that they are extraordinarily phlegmatic about the risks involved. It is agreed on all sides that unless the proliferation of nuclear weapons in the world is stopped, at least one of them will eventually be exploded, accidentally or intentionally, in or over one of the world's capitals. But until that happens, or until some comparable event or series of events changes the face of international politics, it seems unlikely that an anti-nuclear movement in Britain can ever again get to the point of capturing for neutralism a major political party. We have lived long enough on the brink to have become rather blasé about it. In May 1955, according to Gallup, a majority of voters in all parties were of the opinion that Britain should not make the hydrogen bomb, but should devote atomic energy to peaceful uses—"as France is doing", was how the question was then phrased. On this basis, Sir Richard Acland might even have won his by-election, had he been allowed to fight it in March of that year. But by the time CND came into being, the lines of opinion had hardened, and over the ensuing years people became at once better informed on the subject, more sceptical about the value of an all-British deterrent, but (apart from a hard core of 20–30 p.c.) more firmly opposed to neutralism, unilateralism, and grand gestures. After 1960 the Campaign was forced to choose. It could match brains with the strategists and the politicians in a long-term attempt to rid, not Britain only, but the world from the tyranny of nuclear strategies; or it could become a monitory, chiliastic sect, keeping alive a certain vision of a new Jerusalem without bothering overmuch about its architecture and construction. As we shall see, some chose the one course, some chose the other, and the eventual outcome was rapid decline.

It should finally be noted that the British political party most likely to be captured by a movement like CND has learnt a few lessons in the art of repelling boarders. It is true that some of the more obvious defensive measures which the Labour Party could take (constitutional reform and speedier, more flexible devices for reconciling official policy with radical opinion) have as yet failed to commend themselves. The party is, after all, one of the most conservative political institutions in Europe. But the presence in 1960 and 1961 of a tough captain on the bridge established firmly for the future where the chain of command lies in similar situations. Mr Gaitskell did not unite his crew, and a few of those whom he battened down under hatches could safely have been allowed on deck. But he spelt out more clearly than any Labour leader has ever done while in Opposition the qualifications required for a party which the British people are prepared to regard as an alternative Government. By insisting that even in the nuclear age, international idealism is not by itself a guarantee of national self-preservation, Mr Gaitskell virtually completed a process which had already taken almost 50 years: he turned a party of protest into a party of power.

CHAPTER FIVE

SIT WITH RUSSELL: STAND
WITH COLLINS

"It is important, if democracy is to be preserved, both to
avoid the circumstances that produce general excitement,
and to educate in such a way that the population shall be
little prone to moods of this sort. Where a spirit of ferocious
dogmatism prevails, any opinion with which men disagree
is liable to provoke a breach of the peace . . ."

Bertrand Russell,
Power (Allen & Unwin 1938), p. 308

Six days before nuclear disarmament reached its constitutional zenith in the Spa Grand Hall, Scarborough, a letter intended for the Secretary of the Noise Abatement Society, Mr John Connell, reached the Tory journalist of the same name. The two are often confused, but on this occasion the mistake triggered off in the anti-nuclear movement a fission–fusion–fission reaction whose fall-out continued to descend for years. The letter, which Mr Connell passed to the *Evening Standard*, was signed by Lord Russell, President of the CND, and the Revd. Michael Scott, a long-standing member of the Direct Action Committee. It invited the recipient to join a "Committee of 100" to express through non-violent civil disobedience their opposition to "the ever-growing menace of nuclear war". The letter went on:

"A group of people from within the CND is concerned to find ways of carrying these proposals into practical action. They have conceived the idea of forming this committee in the belief that this will spread the responsibility for the proposed action. It is felt that if there are no office holders the danger of the work being paralysed by action against key individuals will be minimised.

"It is proposed that no demonstration or other action will be undertaken without a minimum number of 2,000 volunteers."

The Russell–Scott proposal inevitably brought into the open within the Campaign the old division about methods—a division which could be contained while the group favouring civil disobedience was limited to the small, idealistic Direct Action Committee. But the manner of the announcement made the break a jagged one. On the week before the *Standard* broke the story, those members of the existing CND Executive who had received invitations were busy ringing up their colleagues, many of whom had not been so favoured. Marghanita Laski had had one: the Priestleys not. Canon Collins told inquirers that "speaking as an individual" he considered Lord Russell's action "the greatest possible mistake". A civil disobedience campaign would do nothing but harm to the cause of CND.

Within a few days, the origins of the Committee of 100 were lost under the highly coloured image which the newspapers and its own leading personalities conferred upon it. But it is the origins which explain subsequent events, and they must now be recalled.

Since the first Aldermaston March the Direct Action Committee, whose Chairman, Michael Randle, became the first Secretary of the Committee of 100, had been acting to some purpose. Immediately after the March, 31 people undertook a week's day and night vigil at the gates of Aldermaston Atomic Research Establishment, and for ten weeks in the summer of 1958 150 people picketed the establishment, canvassing, holding meetings in the area and asking workers to leave their jobs. (A few did.) The picketing culminated in an attempt to persuade the Director of the AWRE to grant an interview. He refused, and 27 pickets, including the Revd. Dr Donald Soper, sat down in the forecourt day and night for a week to make him change his mind. He did not, but no one was arrested.

In the autumn the DAC turned its attention to the East Anglian rocket bases, which were then being built at great speed. (Back in February, *Peace News* had offered a copy of *The Hunting of the Snark* to the first readers who reported their location, and in August the Cambridge Labour Party and Trades Council, disregarding official warnings, organised a March to the base at Mepal.) A small DAC group lobbied workers and unions in the North Pickenham area, and on December 6 the group held a public meeting in Swaffham, marched to the base, entered the site, and tried non-violently to obstruct work by squatting in front of a lorry and beside a concrete mixer. Evicted, they returned next morning, slipped over the barbed-wire fence and mounted the cement mixer. The Irish workmen went wild and the demonstrators, who had been carefully briefed beforehand on what to expect and how to behave, had to stand up to being dunked in mud and concrete, pulled out by the hair, and drenched from fire tenders. Fights broke out among the labourers, some of whom agreed and some of whom disagreed with this treatment, and in the House of Commons the Secretary of State for Air, Mr George Ward, alleged that demonstrators had used a great deal of violent resistance to the police. He was later forced to withdraw. No arrests were made, but it was clear that action would have to be taken if the demonstrations continued, and the DAC announced that they would be back on December 20. On that day their coaches to Norfolk were cancelled after the operators had been warned that they might be liable to a conspiracy charge, but about 100 marchers appeared at Swaffham, stopped briefly at the gates of the base for prayer or reflection, and proceeded to obstruct the passage of lorries. The 45 people arrested included Michael Scott.

Most of those arrested refused bail, and with the first pictures of puffing policemen hauling away limp bodies the British public now took in the fact that 37 otherwise respectable citizens were spending Christmas in gaol for being too enthusiastic about peace on earth. Over 3,000 letters, postcards, telegrams, and cables arrived from all over the world, together with so much food, fruit, and sweets that consignments had to be passed on to hospitals. And in Norwich Prison an officer, coming across a silent group in a corridor and asking what it was, learnt from a colleague that there was a religious meeting in progress and exploded: "There's a time and place for everything."

Canon Collins was caught off balance by this public relations coup, and his announcement that the CND was not in favour of civil disobedience or sabotage was not well received by the Campaign. A clarification was issued:

"We have great sympathy and admiration for those who, with deep sincerity and self-sacrifice, went to North Pickenham and subsequently to prison. But if we accepted civil disobedience as a part of Campaign strategy, in a country with full democratic rights, we would inevitably split the Campaign."

Lord Russell, on the other hand, took a different view:

"My own feeling is that the demonstration at North Pickenham was abundantly justified. The Press, with very few exceptions, has boycotted news of peaceful and orderly activities by those who hope to prevent nuclear warfare ... Until the press pursues a wiser policy, it is only by such methods that public opinion can be made aware of the fact that our population is being led blindfold towards mass extinction."

But the Campaign Executive was determined to maintain the distinction between its own and the DAC's activities. The Executive declined to join the DAC in a proposed deputation to the Prime Minister (the DAC did in fact succeed in having 45 minutes "full and frank discussion" with Mr Sandys on March 9), and at the end of a long debate on Direct Action at CND's first national conference in the spring of 1959, the Executive threatened to resign if the conference carried even the following comparatively mild resolution:

"The Campaign Executive, while believing in political action rather than in civil disobedience, welcomes the activities of the Direct Action Committee at North Pickenham rocket base in focusing public attention on our aims."

During 1959 the DAC concentrated on political and industrial activities, through the Voter's Veto campaign and a campaign to get labour withdrawn from the two large missile factories in Stevenage (where the ill-fated Blue Streak was being built). The latter campaign was successful in persuading three local trade union branches to call for token strike action in favour of more peaceful industry being brought to the town. Similar campaigns, without significant acts of civil disobedience, were conducted at rocket bases in Suffolk and the East Midlands. In 1960 the DAC spread its wings farther, and the civil disobedience demonstrations which took place at Harrington in January and at Foulness (not organised by the DAC as such) in April and May were chiefly notable for increasingly severe sentences passed on the participants and distinctly more sympathetic comments in the press. The authorities, faced with the threat of the Harrington demonstration, summoned nine members of the DAC for "inciting the public to commit a breach of the peace" by issuing leaflets about the forthcoming demonstration. Michael Randle and Michael Scott were at the time engaged on an attempt to enter the Sahara, where the French were proposing to explode their first atomic weapon, and so could not be apprehended, but six of the remaining seven—Hugh Brock, April Carter, Frances Edwards, Allen Skinner, Pat Arrowsmith, and Will Warren—were imprisoned for two months for refusing to be bound over. The *Daily Herald* was "scandalised", and the London *Star* declared: "A society which is strong enough to make allowance for conscientious objection in other matters should be able to accept the pinpricks of anti-nuclear demonstrators without rounding on them and treating them like criminals."

Thirty-eight MPs petitioned the Home Secretary to release the six before Christmas on the grounds that they were of good character, that there were constitutional dangers in this method of preventive arrest, and that the Act under which they were sentenced had been passed in 1361 to deal only with rogues and vagabonds. But the Home Secretary (Mr Butler) refused. The result was 82 arrests at Harrington on January 2, 1960, supported by a non-disobedient march of 250 led by Canon Collins, and over a hundred reporters and photographers. The accused included the grand-daughter of a judge and the daughter of two magistrates, and the police superintendent said he had never had such co-operative defendants. Almost all refused bail, but the magistrates had a new trick to play: the accused were conditionally discharged, and though a few of the most fervid demonstrators afterwards expressed disappointment that they had not been led straight back to the base on discharge, the DAC's substitute leaders argued that the great majority of the demonstrators were "psychologically unprepared to undertake another action" after being suddenly released from prison. Four months later at Foulness, where the organising body was—significantly—not the DAC but the Southend local CND group, a precisely opposite tactic was used by the magistrates, and 13 people who refused either to be bound over or to pay fines were imprisoned for six months.

During the summer of 1960, in Manchester, Weybridge,

Bristol, and Slough, the DAC and its indefatigable Field Organiser Pat Arrowsmith continued their attempt to lay bare the ramifications of nuclear weapons manufacture in British industry and to stimulate industrial action by workers who supported the Campaign. The overt successes were minor: 15 out of 50 trade union meetings addressed passed resolutions in support of the Campaign, and in Bristol at Siddeley Engines 100 workers out of 500 who listened to Donald Soper at the factory gate deliberately prolonged their lunch hour by 20 minutes to extend the meeting. The DAC also drew up a declaration of intention not to work on nuclear weapon development for circulation in the universities, and launched a revenue refusal campaign. This last idea had been previously tried in America, but under the British PAYE system it is almost impossible to withhold proportions of taxes attributable to particular objects. Members of the DAC itself, what with prison sentences and subsistence salaries, were in some cases more often taking out money from the State than putting it in, and a Committee minute of November 24, 1959, apropos of the DAC Relief Fund, observes:

"This Fund is *not* intended to be a substitute for State benefits (i.e. unemployment benefit or National Assistance). It may, however, be used to supplement State benefits if this seems necessary particularly to help the dependents of those in prison."

(There was £226 in the fund at that time. It was also used to cover legal costs and help workers who left rocket site jobs as a result of the DAC campaign.)

However, artists, writers, and clergymen, assessed under Schedule D, were in a better position to confront the tax authorities, and in November 1960 Arnold Wesker, George Melly, John Berger, and others formed a sub-committee "Against Tax for Nuclear Arms". One member of the group of tax-refusers, Mr Eric Walker, a public address engineer, fought his case through the Inland Revenue, tax tribunals and the courts between 1961 and 1963, seeking to prove that it would be illegal for him to finance the production of nuclear weapons because they emitted "a noxious by-product", and were therefore outlawed in international law under a Hague convention. When the judgement went against him, he paid up.

Even before the Foulness sentences, the Chairman of the Campaign showed that he was not proof against the developing militancy of his followers, nor against a recurrent surge of anti-Americanism on the Left as the get-out-of-NATO theme became more explicit. On March 5, addressing 1,000 people who had marched from Wethersfield to the nearby base to present petitions, Canon Collins said:

"Today we are an American satellite ... a forward base for rocket-firing on Russia ... Everyone at the Top knows there is no defence to nuclear warfare. We are being fobbed off with a goddam lie ... because we are a satellite of a nation of which the people are charming, but with a government riddled with the folly of thinking in the past and with hysteria against Communism, which puts them in the hands of their military gentlemen at the Pentagon ..."*

But not for the last time, and despite this strong language, the Canon had to watch his followers streaming on ahead of him.

On the Aldermaston road that year the Canon's regiment stretched out over four miles, consuming 80,000 cups of tea and 30 tons of food on the way from the AWRE to Trafalgar Square. Estimates of the final crowd varied from 30,000 to 100,000, and the *Daily Mirror*, under a banner headline "Well done, Marchers!" said: "Right or wrong in their ideas" (the *Mirror* thought they were wrong) "the Ban-the-Bomb marchers have given grand and irresistible proof that ordinary people CAN AND DO CARE about the way the world is run." At the Easter Monday rally Mr A. J. P. Taylor alleged that an unnamed member of the Labour Shadow Cabinet had been forbidden by Mr Gaitskell to join the March. Amid these public manifestations of enthusiasm no reporter noticed a bearded, fast-talking American political scientist who was canvassing support on the March for a new anti-Bomb body that would commit civil disobedience not in symbolic tens and twenties but in thousands and tens of thousands.

Ralph Schoenman, who at this time was 24, had come to England from Princeton in 1958 to do a postgraduate course at the London School of Economics. While the Campaign was flexing its muscles, Schoenman was studying the Young Conservatives, as an example, he thought, of American-style political organisation being introduced into Britain. He never finished his thesis. Instead, he began reflecting upon the inadequacy of the Direct Action Committee to achieve the objects which it had in mind. He compares its members, in their purity of motive, to the early Christians. "They commanded a kind of nervous respect, but not emulation. And in fact they felt uncomfortable if they were involved with large numbers of people with conflicting impulses and the usual hostages to fortune in the shape of families and jobs."†

The same point had been made by Bayard Rustin shortly after the first Aldermaston March, out of his own transatlantic experience:

* *Reynolds News*, March 6, 1960.   † In a conversation with the author.

"We're not going to get people who believe in non-violence in principle ever to be socially organised; for one thing, once they believe it in principle, two-thirds of them are unorganisable. There's something that happens which gives you the strength, on the one side, to stand out so vigorously against society, and the other side of that coin is absolute individualism. Most of the people who were engaged in the campaign in Montgomery were the same old people with the same old prejudices, who came into it for very vulgar reasons of their own, but in the process got whipped into something new. At this moment they do not believe in non-violence in principle."*

During the spring of 1960 Schoenman, who was on the Youth CND Executive, was meeting a number of acquaintances in the basement of the Partisan, a club frequented by the New Left. The group included Alan Lovell, Stuart Hall, and Ralph Miliband from the New Left, with Hugh Brock and April Carter from the Direct Action Committee. There was also a painter called Gustav Metzger. Both Schoenman and Metzger at the time were reading in the Italian Renaissance period, and they decided afterwards that the title "Committee of 100" had been a subconscious reminiscence of the Guelphs and their "Council of 100". But the idea had not got as far as this yet. They began by going from group to group within the Campaign, and sending round chain letters. "But by the time the letter had got to Newcastle and back," Schoenman says, "people hadn't the faintest idea who the people were who were sponsoring this thing."

At this stage Schoenman wrote to Russell, whose private secretary he afterwards became (and remains), outlining his ideas. He got a favourable response, and the plan for mass civil disobedience, launched by a committee of "big names", and guaranteeing that no sit-down would take place without at least 2,000 previously obtained pledges to join in, began to take shape. Various ideas were canvassed. Schoenman's own favourite was an interruption of the State Opening of Parliament, but he bowed to advice that this would tend to bring in the essentially irrelevant issue of Royalty. Piccadilly Circus, Chequers, and Parliament Square were other venues suggested for the opening demonstration.

Nowadays, a faint chill tends to come over the conversation of nuclear disarmers when Schoenman's name is mentioned. Unpredictable, sympathetic to Anarchism, and intellectually extravagant, he was at this period regarded by Canon Collins with patronising amusement rather than active distrust. During August 1960 Schoenman went to see Collins to tell him that a

* *Peace News*, May 30, 1964.

civil disobedience demonstration was planned for mid-September, at the end of the Edinburgh–London March organised by the DAC. By this time a split between the President and the Chairman of the Campaign was imminent. For the time being, however, the courtesies were observed. On September 4 Canon Collins received a letter from Lord Russell which said:

"When I speak in Trafalgar Square on September 24, I plan to say something in support of those who practise direct action. I believe that they are an essential part in the progress of our campaign. I hope you will not mind my doing this."

The Canon replied asking Lord Russell not to make a statement of this kind a week before the Labour Party Conference, and later suggested a meeting, which took place on September 16 in Lord Russell's house. According to Canon Collins' report to the CND Executive, Lord Russell undertook to resign the Presidency of the Campaign if the Executive considered that his support of Direct Action would harm it, but said nothing of the new civil disobedience campaign being planned nor of the letters which were shortly afterwards sent out over his own and Mr Scott's name. It was agreed at this meeting that Mr Frank Cousins should be asked to tell Lord Russell what effect a statement by Lord Russell in support of direct action might have at Scarborough, and Mr Cousins wrote saying that it would be most unhelpful. Schoenman also contacted Cousins and was told, he says, that Lord Russell must make his own decision. Lord Russell agreed to postpone his statement. On September 23 Victor Gollancz telephoned his old friend Canon Collins to say he had been asked to join a Committee of 100, and what was happening? Lord Russell was telephoned, and explained that nothing would be made public until after the Party conferences. On the 28th, when the news broke in the *Evening Standard*, Canon Collins issued an official statement:

"The CND is bound by conference decision to use legal and democratic methods of argument, persuasion and demonstration to achieve its aims, though, of course, we have sympathy and respect for individuals who feel bound by conscience to use illegal means and undergo imprisonment."

He added the characteristic personal rider:

"This is not to say that if we felt that a minority was holding down a majority, I would be opposed to the organising of civil disobedience."

Next day an emergency meeting of the CND Executive was called. Four of the 27 members were present (though some others were consulted by telephone). The meeting reaffirmed the policy "voted by large majorities at two annual Conferences" that the Campaign should urge its policy only by legal and democratic methods. "Individuals who advocate methods of civil disobedience, whatever their standing, do so without having consulted either the Executive Committee or the rank and file of the Campaign." Next morning, Canon Collins went away to address a pre-Scarborough meeting at Newcastle, and the *Daily Mail* reported that the CND Executive had decided to ask Lord Russell to resign. According to the Canon, this was not only untrue, but he had himself dissuaded the Executive from taking this step. However, Lord Russell and Mr Scott issued a statement the same night saying that Lord Russell had always understood that members of the CND were free as individuals to support civil disobedience, and that he would like evidence that a majority of the Campaign did not agree with his proposals. His resignation offer still stood. The same day Mr Austin Underwood, one of the more militant of CND's regional chairmen and a member of the Executive, complained that Lord Russell's general views were known to Canon Collins and could have been communicated to the Executive earlier, and that statements involving the CND were being "issued by an unrepresentative group, acting in a completely undemocratic manner".

Thereafter, Lord Russell agreed to meet Canon Collins again. Four meetings took place in the week beginning October 3 (while Mr Gaitskell was fighting for his political life at Scarborough), with Michael Mitchell Howard seconding Lord Russell and Arthur Goss seconding Canon Collins, and with a tape-recorder running as a kind of umpire. A further disaster was narrowly averted, since Canon Collins inadvertently left the tape-recorder running when Lord Russell's party had left the room and while those left behind were mulling over the meeting. However, the outcome of the meetings was a Statement of Amity, circulated to the press and all local groups on October 7, which explained that CND policy gave full freedom to individuals who wished to support direct action, and which blamed the misunderstanding between the President and the Chairman on hostile and inaccurate newspaper reports. It was agreed that there should be no more public statements until after the Executive meeting on November 5.

But on October 19 Mr Scott circulated to all groups, regions, and Executive members a document which suggested, among other things, that the Canon's conduct of his press relations had throughout done less than justice to Lord Russell's case. On October 22 the Committee of 100, at its inaugural meeting in Friends House, elected Lord Russell as President, and next day

Canon Collins returned from holiday to find Lord Russell's resignation awaiting him. It declared:

"I cannot countenance the chairman of an organisation of which I am president permitting the policy of that organisation to be misstated in public statements which are said to come from him and have not been publicly repudiated by him."

Lord Russell then prepared an article to be published in the *Observer* on November 6, giving his version of the controversy. But the *Observer* was wary of publishing it, and Lord Russell anyway agreed to withdraw it after a full meeting of the CND Executive, meeting on Guy Fawkes Day, had expressed unreserved confidence in Canon Collins but regretted "that false statements, purporting to come from the Chairman, about the CND's policy and concerning the President's actions, have been made in the press". The Chairman and the ex-President did not meet again until the 1961 Aldermaston March, when Lord Russell spoke in Trafalgar Square. They did not shake hands.

It would be hard to envisage a more ill-matched pair than this for the leadership of a movement which contained inescapable structural and philosophical tensions of its own. Statements, decisions, and policies which the Canon's instinct was to blur offended Lord Russell's logical either–or approach. Nor did the passionate sceptic's own regal inconsistencies of behaviour and attitude over the years commend him to the Canon, whose individual quirks were securely anchored to the solid Broad Church conventions. Nor did the first meeting of the Committee of 100 suggest that the new organisation would be any more successful than its half-brother in achieving permanent, or even initial, unanimity. In the first place, the participation of conscientious Anarchists in the new Committee ensured the failure of the attempts made by the more bourgeois elements to keep the Committee's deliberations secret. The *Guardian* had a full story of the meeting, whose attendance included Lindsay Anderson, Reg Butler, Alex Comfort, Doris Lessing, Christopher Logue, John Osborne, and Arnold Wesker. John Arden, Robert Bolt, John Berger, John Braine, Augustus John, Bernard Kops, Sir Compton Mackenzie, and Sir Herbert Read had their names read out as supporters, but despite this Reg Butler thought the list was short of important people, Alex Comfort regretted the shortage of scientists, and Michael Scott wanted more clergymen.

With so many writers present, it was inevitable that the meeting should reject the draft statement of aims as being "too long, too imprecise, and too badly written"; and that the ideas for civil disobedience projects put forward should be more notable for imagination than practicality. It was suggested that there should be direct action against military installations and centres of authority. Official functions like the Opening of Parliament or Trooping the Colour might be disrupted. They might kidnap the Chancellor of the Exchequer on Budget Day, jam the BBC, or set up a pirate radio station. The press, whose reaction to the first news of the Committee's existence had been extremely hostile, began to smile. The *Guardian*, while citing historical instances of justified civil disobedience against slavery in the United States and British rule in Ireland, opined that the militant Suffragettes had done nothing but harm to the cause of votes for women and concluded:

"If Lord Russell wants to help his cause by a form of direct action which is legal, why does he not initiate a one-man filibuster in the House of Lords? No one could object—and it would take their lordships aback."*

The Direct Action Committee survived by 10 months the founding of the Committee of 100, despite the fact that all but two of the DAC's members were also on the new body. Apart from sentimental loyalty to the DAC, there were several reasons for this. The DAC had a final project on hand: the Polaris Protest, planned after the Prime Minister's announcement on November 1, 1960, that an Anglo-American agreement had been made to station a submarine tender (the *Proteus*) in the Holy Loch at the mouth of the Clyde, to support the US Navy's growing fleet of Polaris-firing submarines. Back in 1957 strong local protests had been made in Aberdeen about the proposed siting of rocket bases near by, and the bases had gone to East Anglia instead. The DAC were determined that Glasgow should inflict a similar humiliation on the Government. Immediately after the 1961 Aldermaston March (whose numbers were up for the fourth year in succession) 35 DAC supporters set off on a 465-mile trek to the Holy Loch, picking up local supporters for odd days on the way, and talking endlessly in pubs, coffee bars, and at factory gates. In Cambuslang, near Glasgow, the management of an engineering works locked out 200 men who deliberately overstayed their lunch hour at a DAC meeting. This was the last of the DAC's long marches, and it ended seven weeks after it began with a march of 2,000 from Dunoon to the Holy Loch and an attempt by 70 pacifistic pirates to board the *Proteus*, while 200 other supporters immobilised the pier at Ardnadam. From American sailors and Scottish police the demonstrators had the roughest treatment they had had since Swaffham in 1958, and this project was chiefly responsible for the £650 debt which had to be cleared before the Committee could officially wind up.

* The *Guardian*, October 10, 1960.

Another reason for the continuance of the Direct Action Committee was that not everyone on it was happy about the way the civil disobedience movement was now going. Canon Collins, perhaps, did not realise sufficiently at the time how fortunate he was in the DAC. Like many British Colonial Secretaries, he diddled the moderates only to find himself met with extremism. As Nicolas Walter has written:

"A non-violent blockage by a few devoted cranks of a single entrance to a remote military base, which is tolerated by the authorities for a few hours and then cleared and punished by small fines and prison sentences, cannot even begin to constitute a real threat to the Warfare State—though no doubt it counts as conduct prejudicial to good order and discipline . . . The so-called 'direct action' demonstrations have really been what April Carter calls 'symbolic action' and have functioned as a form of propaganda by deed. But they aren't very effective deeds, nor are they very effective propaganda . . . The new pacifism is still after all an overwhelmingly middle-class movement (and the middle-class has no tradition of direct action). It belongs to the tradition of minority dissent rather than to the tradition of majority revolution."*

The Committee of 100 was the child both of the rocket-base demonstrations and of the Aldermaston Marches: it was Schoenman's contribution—if it is to be described as a contribution—in the spring of 1960 to see that the two could be combined to forge a new weapon. What he and others did with it must now be examined.

The announcement of the Committee of 100's first demonstration—again anticipated by a leak to the *Guardian*—was made by Lord Russell at a press conference on December 14, 1960. The demonstration, he said, would consist of a four-hour sit-down outside the Ministry of Defence in Whitehall on February 18, to coincide with the expected arrival of the *Proteus* in the Clyde. Lord Russell told a somewhat sceptical group of reporters that the demonstration would not take place unless at least 2,000 people were pledged to take part, and that he was confident that there were more people than that who would rather be alive than dead. If he himself was arrested and fined, he would opt for prison. Casting back 45 years, he said that he had refused to pay a fine before, and that the authorities had sold his Bible to get the money.

Lord Russell's optimism was not shared by all members of the Committee. There had been several resignations, and when the Committee—or half of it—met in the Kingsway Hall on January

* *Anarchy 14* (April 1962), pp. 108-9.

21 to discuss progress it was reported that although Michael Randle had distributed 34,000 leaflets, only 500 pledges had been received. Donations to date amounted to £1,262. There was a long discussion on whether to proceed with the demonstration at all if fewer than 1,200 pledges came in. Arnold Wesker asked how demonstrators at the back of the march would know what was happening at the front, and Dr W. Weinberg suggested that the Committee should *en masse* adopt the pseudonym "Jack Muir" if arrested. He explained that Jacques Muir was a young Frenchman who had refused service in the Algerian War, whose name was being picked up and used by others in France as a symbol. The idea was adopted, but later dropped.

At 3 p.m. on Saturday, February 18 "the quietest, most orderly, most impressive mass demonstration senior police officers could recall" marched in silence down Whitehall and sat for 2½ hours outside the Ministry of Defence. Estimates of its size varied from 1,000 to 6,000. Lord Russell and Michael Scott taped to the door of the Ministry a declaration demanding the "immediate scrapping of the agreement to base Polaris-carrying submarines in Britain" and "the complete rejection by our country of nuclear weapons and all policies and alliances that depend upon them". The declaration concluded:

"We call upon the scientists to refuse to work on nuclear weapons. We call upon workers to black all work connected with them and to use their industrial strength in the struggle for life ... We hereby serve notice on our Government that we can no longer stand aside while they prepare to destroy mankind."

Reporters had to squat down beside Lord Russell and his companions to gather their stories, and the press was sympathetic. The police, though they had warned the magistrates to be prepared for a late sitting, took no action, and the Committee were disappointed. "We do not want for ever to be tolerated by the police," said Lord Russell, and Ralph Schoenman more explicitly added: "We want to put the Government in the position of either gaoling thousands of people or abdicating."

Later, the Committee ceased to regard its stock of well known names as an asset, but in the initial stages the fact that such a high proportion of the country's most admired dramatists (John Osborne, Arnold Wesker, John Arden, Shelagh Delaney, Robert Bolt) were prepared to risk prison for their beliefs undoubtedly created the necessary confidence in hundreds, even thousands, of others. Not that the Committee was bounded by the Royal Court, Sloane Square, and the Theatre Royal, Stratford E. During the year it included an ex-Suffragette (Lady Clare Annesley), several

118

Anarchists (Sir Herbert Read and Dr Alex Comfort), a poet (Hugh MacDiarmid), a Bedford vehicle company owner (Major C. V. Clarke), one of the singers on *Tonight* (Robin Hall), a Scottish Nationalist who could give even Lord Russell a year or two (R. E. Muirhead), a London University ancient historian (Dr John Morris), and Miss Vanessa Redgrave. Of politicians there were not unnaturally few, and it was noticeable that the handful of Labour MPs who sponsored the DAC did not join the Committee of 100, which had to make do with an ex-candidate or two, a Left-wing LCC councillor, and Stephen Swingler's son, Robin.

In 1961 the wearing of a CND badge, which might connote either respectability or lawlessness, took on a fresh significance. Many were the grammar school boys and bank clerks who found it prudent to wear their badges under their lapels, where storybook spies keep their MI6 accreditation; and Robin Hall, who wore his in front of 5 million television viewers on *Tonight*, must have confirmed numerous Conservative Party workers in their long-cherished belief that the BBC is really a Communist front organisation.

Other less well known supporters have undoubtedly been victimised in quiet ways for supporting the Campaign. Peter Moule, a level-headed ex-bank clerk who has worked for War on Want and fasted in Italy with Danilo Dolci, joined the Committee in 1962, later becoming its Secretary. He told me that in one large London catering firm putting on a CND badge was a recognised method of getting one's cards. And in his Birmingham bank, before the Committee of 100 was launched, Moule's employers became worried about the number of CND badges which were being worn in his vicinity, and summoned him to a two-hour interview, in which they explained the difference in his prospects that his attitude would make. The Board held out the alternative of a managership at 35 or stagnation in a country branch. One member remarked: "Look, it's all right for you to have these ideals but you should keep them to yourself. Now, would you like us to get you into a golf club?"

Another of the movement's more colourful personalities, Alistair Graham, who edits a Direct Action magazine from an address on the Duke of Beaufort's Badminton estate, worked at one time in Liberal Party headquarters. He left off his CND badge and wore the less notorious broken-rifle symbol of War Resisters International, together with a badge saying "Free Scotland"—a sentiment many Liberals share.

Not surprisingly, the success of the February 18 sit-down was reflected in the CND conference three weeks later, which expressed the view (without the Executive feeling compelled to resign) that the methods of the CND, the DAC, and the Committee of 100 were to be regarded as "three techniques in a united attack on preparations for nuclear war". The resolution went on to congratulate the "100" for the "timeliness" of its demonstration, and to urge full co-operation between the DAC and the Scottish Council for Nuclear Disarmament on anti-Polaris projects. A Liaison Committee to link the Campaign with the DAC and the "100" was set up, and CND acquired, for the first time, a constitution. Canon Collins, though his leadership was severely criticised, told the newspapers afterwards that it had been "a very happy conference".

At the beginning of April Aldermaston received its annual increment, and though the March as a whole seemed smaller because it was divided into two, one company starting from Aldermaston and another from Wethersfield, the top estimates for the Easter Monday crowd in the Square touched 150,000. But Ralph Schoenman was no longer prepared to regard the Aldermaston March as the Canon's private outing, and at the close he unilaterally led about 600 people a further mile to the American Embassy in Grosvenor Square and invited them to sit down. Unprepared for this challenge, many refused, but about 100 sat down either there, at Savile Row Police Station or at the Soviet Embassy, and were arrested. Canon Collins later wrote to Lord Russell, in accordance with a motion passed at the CND annual conference, asking him to resume the presidency. But Lord Russell thought that his position would be untenable in view of the opposition of many members of CND to non-violent civil disobedience.

He added: "As you no doubt remember, we wasted more time and energy than we can well afford in mutual misunderstandings during the days before the Trafalgar Square meeting." The day after receiving the Canon's letter, speaking to a Youth CND Conference at Birmingham, Lord Russell gave the more placid members of CND further pause by saying:

"We used to call Hitler wicked for killing off the Jews, but Kennedy and Macmillan are much more wicked than Hitler . . . We cannot obey the murderers. They are wicked, they are abominable. They are the wickedest people in the story of man and it is our duty to do what we can against them."*

For the next Committee of 100 sit-down, planned for April 29 in Parliament Square, 100,000 leaflets were distributed. The newspapers took little notice of the preparations this time until the police made it clear that they were going to try a different tactic. Notice of intent to apply Section 52 of the Metropolitan

* The *Observer*, April 16, 1961.

Police Act, 1839, was served, and 3,000 police were drafted into Central London. Over 2,000 people marched down Whitehall towards Parliament Square from Trafalgar Square until they were hemmed in by police, sat down, and awaited arrest.

Working in pairs, the police managed to carry 826 demonstrators to the waiting black marias before sundown. The chief Metropolitan magistrate, Sir Robert Blundell, fined the majority £1 and allowed them seven days to pay to prevent himself having to take them into custody. John Neville and Vanessa Redgrave accepted bail in time to appear in the matinee performance of *Lady from the Sea*, and the chief marshal of the demonstration, George Clark, who shared with the police the credit for its orderliness, told the *Sunday Telegraph*:

"We must learn not to congregate like this. We were surprised really to get away with this. We may have to change our tactics by devising another form of demonstration which will provide a lot of trouble for the Government while not inconveniencing the police so much. We really want the Government to bring us before the High Court."*

It was the Government, not the Committee, which changed its tactics. The Committee—already sullen and cynical about the impending reversal of the Labour Party's Scarborough vote for unilateralism—was given enormous stimulus by rumours of war over Berlin, and by the Russian and American resumption of nuclear weapon testing on August 31 and September 6 respectively. The prompt appearance of 116 sit-downers outside the Soviet Embassy in Kensington Palace Gardens, followed by a CND "march of shame" to the same place, impressed such people as could find the news in their papers with the nuclear disarmers' impartiality. But the sit-downs showed the police what to expect for the parallel demonstrations at the Holy Loch and in Central London, which had been fortuitously arranged and planned by the Committee for Battle of Britain Sunday, September 17. During the first week of September, the Government did the one thing needful to ensure a good turn-out. It summoned 36 of the better known members of the Committee, including Lord and Lady Russell, and invited them at Bow Street to bind themselves over under the 1361 Act to keep the peace for one year. When 32 out of the 36 refused, most were sentenced to two months imprisonment, Lord Russell included. There were shouts in court of "fascists" and "poor old man", and when the magistrate, Mr Bertram Reece, was shown medical certificates about the 89-year-old philosopher, he reduced the sentence to one week. Lord Russell read a short speech about the madness

* April 30, 1961.

of nuclear weapons, despite the efforts of the magistrate to silence him and of the crowd in court to silence the magistrate. He was eventually driven away in a black maria with "Ban the bomb" scrawled on the side, and both police and Committee went back to prepare for the confrontation on September 17.

The Trafalgar Square sit-down on Battle of Britain Sunday, just under a year after the barren triumph of constitutional action at Scarborough, marked the high tide of unconstitutionalism in the Campaign. It may also have marked—though this is less certain—the high tide of public feeling about the peril of nuclear war and nuclear weapon testing. Certainly, it was well for the Government that the Cuban crisis took place in October 1962 and not in September 1961. On one level, the demonstration was extremely successful. There were probably about 12,000 people in the Square for much of the evening. Thousands sat down. The 4,000 police on duty—many of them held in reserve in side streets and in Parliament Square—succeeded in arresting 1,314 people between 6 p.m. and 1 a.m. on the 18th, including Canon Collins and Fenner Brockway, MP, who had come to invigilate proceedings. Simultaneously, at the Holy Loch, 351 people were arrested. Of the Trafalgar Square catch, 658 were bailed, which suggested that all the demonstrators were not as determined to swamp the prisons as Mr Schoenman would have liked. For the first time serious allegations of police brutality were made, and indeed, after midnight, the demonstration got somewhat out of hand. News coverage was enormous. No one could complain that typical, quiet British households were not brought up against the issue the Committee existed to ventilate, and the correspondence columns of the papers were evidence that the opportunity was taken.

A visit to the Committee of 100 headquarters at this time vividly emphasised the distance in social geography between the shabby cul-de-sac behind Finsbury Park Station and the head-masterly study in Amen Court where "the prima donnas of the campaigning business" had delivered CND. The little rooms over the Committee's sympathetic printers, the Goodwin Press, were the sort of place in which Richard Hannay would have expected to find one of the Three Hostages. There was a wall-map of the Trafalgar Square area, with tiny CND flags pin-pointing the places where arrests were made. With equal pleasure, no doubt, did some police superintendent move flagged pins about a board in Scotland Yard to denote the distribution of his forces, or an officer on board the *Proteus* plot the course of his Polaris submarines. That morning two young men from Cambridge were sorting the morning's post: £480-worth of cheques and postal orders, mostly the latter, and nice, gauche letters, mostly from well outside London, apologising for not sending more. Altogether £6,726 was received in September, making over £14,000 for the Committee's first year of operation. This was about £2,000 more than the CND received during its first year of operation. CND, as a supporter has observed to me, was trying to change the course of world history with a budget more appropriate to a moderately prosperous constituency Conservative Association. (CND's peak financial year was 1961, when it had a budget of £30,000. By 1963 it was back to £18,000. Arthur Goss, towards the end of the Campaign's first year, had minuted that an annual income of £100,000 should be a first priority, and suggested trying the Foundations.)

It was not long before the Committee of 100 was reduced again to the chronic penury of the Direct Action Committee. Wages that autumn were running at £90 a week, and in December came the disaster of Wethersfield. The Committee felt able to pay for a full-page advertisement in the *Guardian* (£900) and for further advertising; and a subscription to a press cuttings agency cost it well over £100. It was to be expected that the Committee would overreach itself, and it did. On September 12 the leaders had been imprisoned, and a 23-year-old compositor, Pat Pottle, became Secretary. (He later joined Ralph Schoenman and others on Lord Russell's personal staff.) Lord Russell was released in a week, talking gaily about how little Brixton had changed since he was last in, but Michael Randle, Ralph Schoenman, and George Clark were sentenced to two months.

Schoenman, while in prison, had been woken up one November morning by the BBC news blaring out the information that the Home Office was refusing to renew his visa beyond the middle of the month. He immediately wrote to the Home Secretary saying that the authorities would have to carry him on to the boat, and expounding the reasons why he thought it quite proper for an alien to organise civil disobedience in Britain. He was fortunate in his friends. Fenner Brockway wrote to Mr Butler, who replied that Schoenman was serving two months for refusing to be bound over and that aliens who helped to organise breaches of the law could not be allowed to stay in Britain. It seemed a reasonable position to take. But as luck would have it there was an opportunity for a debate in Parliament on the annual Expiring Laws Continuance Act. Emrys Hughes, MP, described the Home Office decision as "a pettifogging piece of intolerance by a puppet of a police State", and Michael Foot, MP, who had always been a determined opponent of civil disobedience, defended Schoenman, pointing out that Tom Paine had been kicked out of Britain but allowed to propagate his unpopular views in America. A last minute bargain was reached: Schoenman could stay provided he organised no more demonstrations. To Lord Russell, at least, his services had become indispensable, and he decided to stay.

Meanwhile, a Committee Working Group was proposing that on December 9 they should invade and block three American Air Force bases: at Wethersfield, Brize Norton, and Ruislip. (Another suggestion, not pursued, was a request to both BBC and ITV for broadcasting time as "the only genuine Opposition in Britain today", with sit-downs outside the headquarters of these organisations if the request was refused.) By November 26 only 126 pledges had been received for these demonstrations. On December 6 the Special Branch raided the headquarters of the Committee and the homes of five of its workers: Ian Dixon, Terry Chandler, Trevor Hatton, Michael Randle, and Pat Pottle. All of these except the last were pacifists of long standing (though all were under 30). The search warrants were ominously made out on the direction of the Director of Public Prosecutions under the Official Secrets Act. The police took away documents connected with the proposed Wethersfield demonstration.

On December 7 news emerged of the extraordinary precautions being taken at Wethersfield, a previously accessible base. A 12-foot wire fence was erected round the perimeter, all leave for the Essex police was stopped, and in all about 3,000 civil and military police were mobilised. A large secondary school at Braintree was taken over as a courthouse. At Wethersfield, 180 specially erected boards read: "Official Secrets Act. Prohibited Entry. Penalty of two years imprisonment." Tents were pitched at 50-yard intervals inside the wire.

On the 8th, the five Committee members whose homes were searched were arrested and remanded on bail under charges alleging conspiracy under the Official Secrets Act. The coaches ordered were cancelled by the operators. The Committee's briefing meeting at the Kingsway Hall was understandably confused, and a subsequent memorandum from Peter Cadogan (a tough-minded Leftist from Cambridge who organised the breakaway movement on the 1963 Aldermaston March) complained:

"Pat Arrowsmith, Ian Dixon, and Terry Chandler showed that despite their other virtues they had no idea how to organise a mass operation, and the poor response of our supporters was, inter alia, a vote of no confidence in them."

All things considered, it was surprising that 5,000 people braved both threats and weather to take part in the demonstrations, and that 850 were arrested. It was, after all, about 50 times the numbers that the DAC was able to mobilise for similar operations in equally inaccessible spots two years previously, and if the organisers had not shouted the odds too enthusiastically before-hand, they might have been credited with a success—at least until the price was paid at the trial of the six arrested under the Official Secrets Act. (The sixth was Mrs Helen Allegranza, the Committee's welfare officer, who was minding the headquarters when the Special Branch called.) But the internal recriminations in the Committee were bitter. Another of the memoranda submitted to the inquest which was held on December 17 said:

"By its present policy the Committee has succeeded, *vis-à-vis* the public, in putting itself in exactly the same position as the Mosley fascists and the Empire Loyalists. We have become a public spectacle, a group isolated from the general body of public opinion and feeling, a rowdy show to be televised and reported in the press for the interest and amusement of a majority who are not with us."

The solutions advocated were as various as the participants in the discussions, and outside the Committee, too, dawning realisation that the Government disposed of immense powers and could not so easily be stampeded into submission set imaginations roving. Few outdid Mrs Taya Zinkin, whose Indian experience enabled her to describe techniques of civil disobedience which the Committee appeared to have missed. A chosen demonstrator, she suggested, should take a purificatory bath and starve to death, hugging a hot-water bottle, by the side of a large portrait of Lord Russell.* Unilateralists should boycott every product and service which brought the Government revenue, and call on their doctor every day with a new disease. There was more in this vein, and indeed, limited experiments were tried. Some Christians fasted on the steps of St Martin-in-the-Fields, and two members of both CND and the Committee of 100 tried a spot of *satyagraha* on their own leaders, squatting in Lord Russell's front hall in an attempt to persuade him to be reconciled to Canon Collins. Lord Russell had to ask the police to remove them. *Voice of Nuclear Disarmament* was heard late at night on the BBC Television wavelength, and the Committee of 100 distributed labels marked "radioactive", which were attached to milk bottles and left outside the Russian and American Embassies.

More seriously, news arrived of the conclusion of the San Francisco to Moscow Peace March, organised by the Committee for Non-Violent Action, in which an international delegation of 30 had been allowed to distribute leaflets in Moscow against all bombs and demonstrate (spontaneously) outside a military barracks. Joan Littlewood put on a CND rally in the Albert Hall with jazz, mobiles, political speeches, and anti-

* The *Guardian*, October 9, 1961.

Polaris folk songs (including "The misguided missile and the misguided miss"). A newly formed CND Stage Club gave a Christmas show in St Pancras Town Hall entitled *Everybody Sit*, and Michael Frayn complained in the *Guardian* that what with this, the CND Christmas cards and the movement's familiar heresies and schisms, campaigners were clearly set to make a ritualistic religion out of their single negative tenet:

"My wife and I joined in the Whitsun [*sic*] pilgrimage one year but like potential Christian converts who somehow stick at about the twenty-seventh of the Thirty-Nine Articles, we could not bring ourselves to join in the bright little cries of 'Ban the Bomb!' which everyone else was moved to utter at frequent intervals."*

In Goodwin Street, with a serious charge hanging over six of its members, the Committee of 100 was taking life more solemnly than this. Pat Pottle was in hiding, evading arrest with Lord Russell's approval, and giving occasional interviews to the newspapers from anonymous pubs in North London. Terence Chandler wrote from Brixton to a friend about the "two major blunders" of Wethersfield and "a major difference of attitude in the working group between the DA types and the Schoenman gang". George Clark, serving a sentence against which he later successfully appealed, wrote from Wormwood Scrubs:

"It is now self-evident that the Committee has achieved the first simple aims it set itself, i.e. to effect a major publicity breakthrough in the national press and in the Campaign itself. It has been shown that large numbers of people are willing to take action for themselves despite consequences which cause personal hardship and discomfort to themselves and their families. I have been enormously impressed by the people I have met in prison—by their spirit and depth of conviction . . .

"Our position is not dissimilar to that of the early Christians. With us, as with them, the last things have arrived. It is one thing for us to be motivated by this kind of drive—quite another to expect millions to be converted unless it is seen as some twentieth-century religion offering a new form of salvation . . . We must make our movement truly radical. It must permit a variety of types of action: immobilising bases—large scale urban projects—intensive work at the factory level and above all a massive door-to-door campaign . . . A priority for 1962 will be to bring about a consolidation of our actions with CND, with Ruislip as an example. One exception will be Aldermaston which must be a joint project without civil disobedience."

* The *Guardian*, November 22, 1961.

It is probably a good thing that this particular document did not fall into the hands of Michael Frayn at the time. Yet it was faithful to an element of public feeling in the autumn of 1961. This element is perhaps best examined through the women's movements which sprang up spontaneously in America, Britain, and Canada during the Berlin crisis, which Sir Alec Douglas-Home, in his first public speech as Prime Minister, admitted had brought us to the brink of nuclear war. In Britain two such movements, Women Against the Bomb and Voice of Women, were thus created. Women Against the Bomb was formed in November, when a few mothers in London decided to protest at the Russian and American Embassies against the resumption of atmospheric nuclear testing. About 600 people, mostly mothers with young children, arrived. Many of them had wanted to take part in sit-downs and other demonstrations but had felt unable to do so because of their families. The children, then and subsequently, made the outing an attractive one for press photographers, and one of the participants tells me that the heads that were shaken over the "dragging along" of toddlers on such expeditions could not have been more wrong: a short march, in company, with banners, was an ideal solution to the problem of how to find something to do with the children on a Sunday afternoon.

Voice of Women, on the other hand, began in November when Judith Cook, a writer and mother of young children living in Cornwall, watched on television American and Russian tanks confronting each other in Berlin, and heard an American colonel telling a commentator that he reckoned they'd be using nuclear weapons by Tuesday. She wrote to the *Guardian* to ask what, if anything, women could do. Her answer was 1,000 letters in four days—almost 1 p.c. of the paper's entire female readership. Mrs Cook conducted an informal survey of the respondents. The basic sociological grouping was naturally determined by the newspaper in which they had read the original letter: no one familiar with the *Guardian*'s "Mainly for Women" page will be surprised to learn from Mrs Cook that "the typical VOW member would be about 30, with perhaps two children at school and a baby, married to a teacher, with a good sense of personal responsibility and a good educational background". Their politics were about half and half Labour and Liberal, with a few odd Communists and a few who adhered to no party. All were initially opposed to civil disobedience, though the Cuban crisis in 1962 made about a quarter of them change their minds. About 60 p.c. had small children, though there were many members in the 55–70 age group, and one or two ex-Suffragettes in their nineties. It was widely observed at CND and Committee of 100 demonstrations that the generations had a gap in the middle. Even among women, the disillusionments of the Second World War bit deep into people who were adults at the start of it, for as Mrs Cook observes:

"Women in the 35–55 age group would seem to have more time; their children would be off their hands and they would probably be better off and able to afford domestic help. But it doesn't seem to work like that."

The reasons for it not working like that were clearly not confined to the subject of VOW's protest, though half the members had never before taken an interest in any protest movement or women's pressure group. Numbers of them were very lonely, feeling that no one shared their hopes and anxieties, or was willing to do anything about it. Mrs Cook notes:

"In one case a mother who was desperate after the death of her daughter from leukaemia has thrown herself successfully into the organising of women's work for peace in N—— and she says it has kept her sane. Two of the women who wrote to me after my original letter to the *Guardian* were contemplating suicide and another abortion."*

It may well have been one of Mrs Cook's members who wrote to the *Guardian* after others had complained that the September 17 demonstration was a failure because some people accepted bail and paid fines:

"Now I, a grandmother, a person of some respectability who has respected the law from her youth up, sat down in Trafalgar Square, for six hours. It was hard on my clothes and on my bottom, perhaps hardest on my bladder (there are no public conveniences in the Square), but no one will pretend that this is total martyrdom. If I had been arrested I would have accepted bail and paid any fine. If I had known I would be killed or tortured I would not have gone. If I had *known* I would be kicked across the Square, thrown in the fountain, or hosed in a police-station yard, as reliable witnesses testify happened to some people after midnight, I might have thought twice about it. All I knew was that I *might* have to face a fine of £50 or three months imprisonment or both.

"The point is not that some people accepted more, and others less, of inconvenience or sacrifice, but that thousands of people demonstrated their total protest against the insanity of nuclear war *in any circumstances*, and did so in such a way that people actually still remember it a week later."†

* In a letter to the author. † The *Guardian*, September 29, 1961.

The great demos of 1961 were muddled both in cause and in effect, like most significant events. On one level they provided a kind of behaviour therapy for worried mothers and alienated adolescents, something which anyone could do in order to prove to themselves that they had done something. On this level the act of civil disobedience was not political at all, for in their political moments most of the demonstrators would themselves have been shrewd enough to realise that an abrupt British diplomatic volte-face over Berlin, which was what their behaviour apparently demanded, would be a highly unsafe manoeuvre, however desirable in the long term.

But on a second level, something of great significance had occurred. Hugh Brock recalls walking behind two students in Charing Cross Road that autumn, on the way to the Square, and overhearing one say to the other: "We must do it Gandhi's way this time." It gave him a great kick, he says, remembering the pathetic little group, self-styled "Operation Gandhi", sitting outside the War Office nine years previously. On this level, an encouragingly large number of people had decided that they did not know enough about what was going on and that they did not like what they knew; that their votes were comparatively powerless to express their choices in ways that could influence events; and that the 20th century had itself provided an instrument for bypassing the normal political process without recourse to the futilities of violence. In the constant losing battle which British minorities fight to change the mind of the Executive, a place had been found for doing as well as for listening, speaking, thinking, and writing. The process had begun with Aldermaston, but *homo perambulans*, Aldermaston Man, had evolved into *homo sedentarius Russellensis*, and in those days of "sit with Russell or stand with Collins" the Canon could be heard patiently explaining that the CND had never ruled out civil disobedience: "We shall have to rethink our whole technique policy."

But of course, as it was conceived in the minds of some of the Committee of 100's leaders, the operation was a failure. There was all the difference between enlisting the aid of a sympathetic population to use the only weapon at its disposal—unarmed mass—to effect the removal of the British Raj from India, and using the same technique to stampede a highly developed country into adopting a policy which not more than a quarter of the population would accept at a referendum. "Not since the General Strike," wrote the authors of a subsequent ILP–Solidarity pamphlet, *The Hundred Versus the State*, "had the Establishment felt compelled to display such force in peace time, against 'its own' people." But this time it was the deputy leader of the Labour Opposition, Mr George Brown, who begged the Government to see that Wethersfield was properly protected, and said to Conservative cheers: "A declared intention to disrupt the forces of law and order cannot be permitted in a modern democratic State."

That such an intention existed is clear enough from a letter written by Pat Pottle, while in hiding, to the Committee of 100 and to newspapers (which did not publish it):

"Who are the real conspirators? Us or them?

"The Government uses secret police to break into offices, to steal papers, to open letters. Its agents search people in their homes in the early mornings. It taps telephones, sends spies to meetings, whitewashes its own brutality and lies in court . . .

"We say to the people: learn from your experience. As you become more effective, the Government will seek to destroy civil liberties. They bring in troops. They talk of conspiracy. It is the Government itself which is an evil and criminal conspiracy."

Pat Pottle presumably spoke for Lord Russell ("I believe in Pat Pottle . . . In his circumstances I should do as he has done", wrote Lord Russell privately to the Committee on December 14), but it seems unlikely that he spoke for more than a small minority of the sitters-down in Trafalgar Square or at Wethersfield. And though the National Council for Civil Liberties more than once expressed concern about the actions of the police, both at demonstrations and in their searches, during the latter half of 1961, the Committee's lasting conviction that its telephones were being tapped and its letters opened was not enough to lead its troops back to the sound of gunfire. On January 28, 1962, meeting with a deficit of £1,900, the Committee rejected by 32 to 12 with 2 abstentions a motion proposed by Pat Arrowsmith: "That there should be a return to Wethersfield in the near future at such a time as to be clearly associated with the Official Secrets Trial, and to be announced at the end of the Trial." As Cuba, the Greek demonstrations and the 1963 Aldermaston March were to show, the Committee and its supporters could still muster in emergency. But the great days were over; and the Committee was left to its memories. Among these was an enviable reputation for graphic art. In 1962 the Council of Industrial Design Committee, considering its poster awards for 1961, was forced to the conclusion that Ken Garland's "Polaris—No" poster for the Committee of 100, displayed in the London Underground, was way ahead of any competitor. Fortunately for the Council, it had not been submitted and was disqualified. Pictures of the CoID.'s Royal patron presenting the award to Lord Russell would have gone down well in *Time* magazine.

Finally, one of the strangest features of the uprush of radical protest which brought serious political issues—of which the Bomb was the chief but not the only one—down to sixth-form level in Britain during the post-Suez period was the role of the public schools. Charles Radcliffe, who was at Wellington from 1955 to 1959 and became, under pressure of the external movement of ideas and the internal horrors of the school cadet force, an anarcho-pacifist, has recalled* that a treasurer of the Committee of 100 and the secretary of the Committee's Schools for Non-violence were at Wellington with him. He suggests that public schools, which have always harboured individual radicals, have now become typically places where "a number of people, all believing themselves to be isolated, come together". Returning to Wellington in 1962 he was "amazed to see the notice board in my dormitory completely covered with notices of CND meetings, school, local, and national; and Committee of 100 statements and such like". Public school revolt, he feels, tends to be "more realistic, more courageous, more bloody-minded, and more long-lasting" than its grammar school counterpart, though the social distinction this implies is becoming more blurred. He adds:

"I think that the new pacifist movement, much of it purely 'nuclear pacifist', will prove more resilient than the old . . . The limits to which one can go are being pushed back, bit by bit. I don't think, despite the rooted objections of staff, governors and any number of pupils, that the current can be stemmed by the authorities, though they would like to. Rather than the ideas themselves it is the means of perpetuating them that worries the schools so much. After all when people complain about adult society it doesn't take them very long to find a lot wrong with school society as well. If they object to being servile to politicians they often object to being servile to prefects, masters and headmasters. At Wellington, about eighteen months or more ago, there was a mock serious march planned to protest about the use of the cane—'a barbarity which no civilised society should condone'. More recently there was talk of a sit-down against fagging . . ."

So much for Mr Peregrine Worsthorne's recent pronouncement, from his perch in the *Sunday Telegraph*: "I should like my son to go to a public school less because it would help him get into Oxford and Cambridge than because it would help him stay out of the Aldermaston March and such like follies." True, Mr Uwe Kitzinger, in the talk cited at the beginning of Chapter Two, regretfully concluded that this wave of adolescent protest is now ebbing away, after six years of life. But the inevitable

* In a letter to the author, September 30, 1963.

ebbs and flows of fashion cannot dispel the demographic, economic, physiological, and sociological factors which in the late fifties combined to make out of the British teenager, at most social levels, a new, cohesive estate of the realm. In CND, and even more in the Committee of 100, the new estate flexed its muscles.

< note>CHAPTER SIX

EPISODES

"If we lived in a State where virtue was profitable, common sense would make us good"

Sir Thomas More in Robert Bolt's
A Man for All Seasons (Penguin New English
Dramatists: 6)

(i) TO RUSSIA WITH LOVE

"Let them go to the Kremlin and wave their banners there."
(Mr Gaitskell in Glasgow, May 6, 1962)

"I would rather go to Russia as a nuclear disarmament supporter than to America as a beauty queen."
(Miss Suzanna Eaton, disclaiming her Miss Britain title, June 1961)

The scope of this book has been narrowed to exclude the "foreign relations" of CND, though by the time that the International Confederation for Disarmament and Peace was formed at Tyringe in Sweden in January 1964 (after a preliminary conference at Oxford in January 1963) the "International CND" comprised member organisations in almost 30 different countries. When the discontinuance of the British Aldermaston Marches was under discussion before (and even more after) the 1963 Aldermaston, it was advanced by Canon Collins, as a reason for carrying on with an English Easter demonstration, that all over the world Easter marchers were looking to Aldermaston as their origin and exemplar.

The Canon's own role as a globe-trotting disarmer did not develop in earnest until 1962, with the World Without the Bomb Congress at Accra in June (whose control was quickly wrested from Canon Collins' hands by the Ghanaians); and the World Council of Peace Congress in Moscow in July. The CND itself sent only 12 of the 145 Britons who were flown to Moscow in two Russian aeroplanes for this Congress. But the whole episode was so extraordinary, and had so many domestic repercussions, that it would be a pity to by-pass it.

In the first place, it was entirely characteristic of the British Labour Party's luck that an event so suspect that CND's sponsorship of it could be seized by Mr George Brown and others as an excuse for expelling Canon Collins and Lord Russell from the Party should end with—in the words of Mr Victor Zorza—"the most direct challenge to official Soviet policies and ideas to have been presented to the Soviet man in the street since freedom of speech died under Stalin."* It was equally characteristic of the CND that when the Committee of 100 asked it to share in delivering the challenge, the CND delegation declined on the grounds that to do so would be impolite to the Russians.

The long-drawn-out battle of 1960–1 had left both CND and

* The *Guardian*, July 12, 1962.

the Labour Party concerned about their images. An early symptom, perhaps, was a CND Executive minute of November 9, 1961, that the stage designer Sean Kenny should be asked to advise on "dressing the Aldermaston March". (This did not prevent the Communist element—fairly strong at this time in the autonomous Youth CND—showing more strongly at Aldermaston than in previous years, often by dint of sandwiching a group of "legitimate" marchers with a vanguard and rearguard of Young Communists, and passing the lot off to the television cameras as their own unaided work.) At its meeting on March 25 the Executive discussed its plans for a national advertising campaign, financed mainly by a sympathetic businessman and by the Sevenoaks group, which had raised money for this purpose. At the same meeting, post-Aldermaston delegations to New York, Geneva, and Moscow were also discussed, and "it was approved that one of the delegates should be a young and photogenic mother".

But the image was shattered before it had properly taken shape. On May Day 1962 the two principal Labour rallies, addressed in Glasgow by Mr Gaitskell and in London by Mr George Brown, were broken up by people waving the emblems of the CND. In London the microphone was smashed and the meeting ended quickly. In Glasgow there was time for the audience, many of whom had gathered for what they regarded as the climax to a year's legitimate Labour campaigning against the Polaris base in the Holy Loch, hear Mr Gaitskell give a tongue-lashing to the mixture of Young Communists, Socialists, Trotskyists, and YCND that confronted him. "We know," he said, "that when it comes to the ballot and to voting in elections these people are not worth a tinker's curse. They are peanuts. They don't count. Most of them really ought to go back to school." Of the CND itself he said:

"The time has come when we have to say this to them: either they choose to go on wrecking our chances, in which case they ought not to be in the Labour Party at all, or they must agree to accept the official policy of the party, even though they may disagree with certain parts of it, and do their best to get a Labour Government into power."

Canon Collins apologised for the rowdiness of "a small minority" of CND supporters, but blamed it on a feeling of frustration in the Campaign about the failure of the Parliamentary Labour Party to force a debate on the American resumption of nuclear testing, which had been officially opposed by the Party until Mr Gaitskell had accepted a private assurance from President Kennedy that it was necessary. This point of view was reinforced by a full page advertisement in the *Guardian*, reproducing from *Tribune* articles by David Boulton (press officer of CND) and Michael Foot on the Glasgow disturbances. The cost—nearly £1,000—was defrayed almost entirely by the "sympathetic businessman" previously mentioned.

Ten days after May Day, the Organisation sub-committee of the Labour NEC, whose chairman was Mr Brown, made its move not only against the May Day agitators themselves, but against the Campaign's leadership. It threatened to expel Canon Collins, Lord Russell, and Lord Chorley from the Labour Party unless they withdrew their sponsorship of the Moscow World Disarmament Congress, scheduled for July and organised by the World Council of Peace, which is on the Labour Party's long list of proscribed organisations. This manoeuvre swiftly degenerated into broad farce. It was broken to Transport House that the sponsors of the Congress also included Baroness Wootton, who had been one of Mr Gaitskell's first nominations for a life-peerage. The sub-committee then tried an alternative means to dispose of Lord Russell, accusing him of not having paid his 6*d.* a month subscription to the Party for some time. It then turned out that he paid annually by cheque. After this, the sub-committee decided to call it a day.

Canon Collins, meanwhile, had trouble to the Left as well as to the Right. The annual CND conference in June dismayed the Executive by passing a resolution in favour of initiating industrial action—which to the rank and file meant strikes—in support of the Campaign. When the Executive interpreted this resolution as obliging them to do no more than organise factory gate meetings Pat Arrowsmith and Michael Scott, who were at this time back on the CND Executive, resigned.

All told, the omens for the Moscow trip were not good. But on arrival in Moscow on July 8, the prominent Labour Party members among the 145 British delegates and observers took a more sanguine view. Mr Kingsley Martin said that although all the other World Council of Peace Congresses since the war had been bogus, this one would be different because the Communists were now falling over backwards to accommodate people who disagreed with them. And Mr Sydney Silverman, the only MP present, said that it would have been a fatal error to neglect an opportunity to speak freely. Next day the hopes of Western delegates were dashed by the announcement that the American high altitude tests, which had been condemned in advance by Sir Bernard Lovell on scientific grounds, had just taken place in the Pacific. The American delegation agreed to a special resolution condemning the tests, and Mrs Judith Cook, who had recently flown to Washington with her baby son to urge the President to stop them, made a similar appeal. But it was noticeably a day on which most of the Congress listened impatiently to the few genuinely neutral voices: a cool and precise tape-recorded message from Lord Russell, who was ill and could not attend; and an address from Professor Dale Pontius, Professor of Political Science at Roosevelt University, who was applauded when he attacked his own Government's policy towards Cuba and Vietnam, and heard in silence when he condemned the USSR's unilateral rupture of the nuclear test moratorium the previous autumn. *Pravda* the next morning reduced Lord Russell to two paragraphs, and in quoting Professor Pontius on the American tests added: "He spoke critically also of the atomic tests which the Soviet Union was forced to carry out last year."

Next day Mr Khruschev addressed the Congress for $2\frac{1}{2}$ hours and Canon Collins for a somewhat shorter period. The two had an hour's private interview in the evening, after which the Canon said he was grateful for the view he had had of the Soviet leader's mind. He had found Mr Khruschev "resilient and amusing", though insistent that since the Americans had tested first, the Russians must test last. Mr Khruschev's reaction to Canon Collins is not recorded.

Overtly, the British unilateralists at the Congress accomplished little, though their attendance prevented the final message from possessing an anti-Western tone, and the "International CND" 's own neutralist statement, signed by Danilo Dolci, Erich Fromm, Claude Bourdet, and others, was written into the record. Considering some of the speeches they had had to sit through, this was only fair: Mr Oginga Odinga of Kenya, for example, padding out a speech on peace with sentences like, "Come what may, the African masses are more than ever determined to overthrow the imperialists into the depths of the oceans." But the most significant activity of the British took place outside the walls of the Kremlin (where the Congress met). Both the CND and the Committee of 100 had taken with them to Moscow parcels of multilingual leaflets. The CND distributed 5,000 without remark. But the 2,000 leaflets duplicated in Russian for the industrial sub-committee of the London Committee of 100 went much farther than the CND's, uniting unconditional opposition to all states' bombs with a Trotskyist political critique of the Soviet Union's social and economic structure.

After describing—rather wishfully, but the Russian reader was not to know this—the increasing involvement of British workers themselves in direct action against nuclear weapons, the leaflet asked: "But the USSR has the same monstrous weapons. Should not this be different if your society is fundamentally different from ours?" Nationalisation of Soviet industry had not changed the "production relations" of Soviet society, and the roots of

Stalinism were to be found in Lenin's insistence that trade unions should not intervene in the management of enterprises:

"What has happened to your revolution that your rulers should threaten the workers of other lands with these weapons? What has happened to the internationalist ideals of October? The Revolution made sweeping changes in the property relations. But it did not solve the central contradiction of class society, that between rulers and ruled in production."

In Russia, as in America, "someone else" decided what the worker should produce, how much, and at what cost to himself. "Has he chosen to have sputniks rather than butter?" Was this a State that was "beginning to wither away from the moment of the Revolution?" Or was it the kernel of the Socialist programme that had withered away?

Despite the vicious kick of the leaflets against Soviet nuclear tests which "threaten workers all over the world with 'Socialist' leukaemia", the Soviet authorities did not prevent the leaflets from being handed round in Gorki Street and in the suburbs of Moscow, and the Committee of 100 delegates remarked that they were more eagerly received than they would have been in the streets of London. But the Chairman of the Soviet Peace Committee, Mr Korneichuk, asked a British CND delegate for an assurance that the leaflets would no longer be broadcast, and on July 12, when the Committee of 100 delegation made it clear that they proposed to form a picket outside the Kremlin the following day and distribute leaflets in Red Square, the Russian authorities conveyed through a British Peace Committee go-between that the consequence of this might be deportation.

The Russians were, however, in some difficulty. Their press and radio had given great publicity to the Committee of 100 demonstrations in England, and the British authorities' "attack on civil rights". Face would have been lost by banning the proposed demonstration. On the other hand, if it was permitted, some Muscovites might have joined in. Their problem was simplified by the CND group, which issued a statement dissociating itself from the project. "We have learned with regret that the Soviet authorities would regard this as an infringement of their hospitality . . . To take part on this particular occasion in a demonstration in the city might regenerate some of the hostility which the freedom of speech in the congress has done something to dispel."

In the event, Friday afternoon's twenty-strong banner parade in Red Square, including Americans, Canadians, and Scandinavians as well as British, lasted just long enough for the Western photographers to be able to prove to Western newspaper readers that the deed had actually been accomplished—that the Bear had been bearded in his own den. What Eric Jacobs of the *Guardian* described as "a group of middle-aged, rather tubby men and women" unpinned two of the banners and made off with them towards the Palace of Congresses, leaving the third banner—once they had rolled it up—with the slightly nonplussed demonstrators. One of the women said that they were not used to banners in Red Square, and shouldn't they be red rather than white? Old Moscow hands did not believe the impression created that the troop were just ordinary passers-by—more probably Druzhinniki (People's Voluntary Police) with a man from a Ministry standing by. But the demonstration, despite the efficiency of the suppressors, was not quite over. A large crowd had gathered, and the arguments started—according to Christopher Farley, Lord Russell's personal representative in Moscow, later—went on for over two hours. Mr Farley thought that the demonstrators' reiteration of their case made some headway against the Russian feeling that it was impolite to demonstrate in someone else's country, and Mr Jacobs recorded two East Germans trying to prove that because it was the custom to march and sit down in England it was not necessarily correct in Moscow. They were taken aback by the reply: "It's also illegal to sit down in England, and that is why it is done."

It was not the first Western peace demonstration in Moscow— the San Francisco–Moscow marchers had been allowed to hold one the previous year—but it was the first illicit one, and Mr Philip Seed, a Quaker member of the Committee of 100, told reporters that as well as the protests of Mr Korneichuk and the British Peace Committee, they had had to put up with "a certain amount of personal abuse from other members of the delegation". Five days later, they also had to put up with a certain amount of public abuse from *Pravda*. The Soviet newspaper attacked a handful of "smart alecks" from Britain and the United States who had started conversations in the streets on subjects offensive to the Soviet people, thrust provocative, slanderous leaflets into the hands of passers-by, and generally done their utmost "to get themselves arrested or at least beaten up so as to be able to write in the press that peace partisans had been maltreated in the Soviet Union". Bourgeois press correspondents, said the article, had followed the group hoping for a sensational story, but in encountering the provocateurs, Soviet citizens realised immediately what was behind it and did not waver even for a minute in their faith in the great and radiant cause of rallying together all the forces that stand for peace.

Analysing *Pravda* in the *Guardian*,* Victor Zorza recalled that a

* July 19, 1962.

fortnight previously the author of the article, Yuri Zhukov, had been heaping praise on the same demonstrators for their actions in this country, and after quoting Lord Russell at considerable length had concluded:

"Yes, it is not just declarations that are necessary now, but actions, real actions, and Russell is profoundly right when he calls for the organisation of a genuine movement of resistance to war."

The month before, Mr Zhukov had travelled all the way to Wales to ask Lord Russell, in an interview to which *Pravda* gave two columns, how he evaluated the Committee of 100's struggle. Lord Russell had said that the struggle must be extended: "This is precisely why we have decided to take part in the Moscow Congress." Mr Zhukov took this remark down, and *Pravda* printed it.

Altogether, it had been a remarkable episode. But back in England, no meritorious service medals were distributed. Indeed, the reward of Mr David Picton, a mathematics teacher who was one of the Committee of 100's spokesmen in Moscow, was a severe reprimand from the governors of Rickmansworth Grammar School for going to Russia with love, but without leave.

(ii) HANDS OFF CUBA!
October 1962

"The sun:
It will never shine again
Over England
Big Ben is here
But our school is gone—
Sir is a 'gonner'
Hanging from the roof.
Some of the people live
But most die.

The world goes up in smoke
Rats are all over the place
There are no fish in my pond.
Something must have frightened them.
Dear Lord!
Let me wake up from my dream."

(Written by a backward 12-year-old boy who was emotionally disturbed during the Cuban crisis. Reproduced in *Pussies and Tigers*, an anthology published for the National Association for School Magazines.)

"Too close for comfort," murmured one woman to her companion on their way out from the Aldwych Theatre, where *Troilus and Cressida* was being performed during Cuba Week. "Now everything consumes itself in power . . ." The historians may eventually discover precisely how near the world was to nuclear war in those October days. They may even decide that the danger was more remote than most people think. But in international relations, as in the behaviour of crowds and mass movements, what people think has happened is often more important than what did happen, and there is no doubt that on certain nights in the autumn of 1962 millions of people with access to modern means of communication went to bed nursing a doubt, however faint or shamefaced, about their prospects of waking up in the morning.

Paradoxically, the world's first serious nuclear crisis marked the beginning of CND's decline from serious influence. A month before, the Committee of 100 could still obtain 4,000 pledges for a Central London sit-down (which did not take place because the Committee had set its sights higher than 4,000). Six months after Cuba (but well before the signing of the Test Ban Treaty), the Gallup Poll asked for the eighth time in six years the question "Does all this talk about H-Bombs, rockets, satellites and guided missiles worry you a lot, a little, or not at all?" The answers indicated that public worry of this type had fallen back, for the first time, below the level of May 1957.

Right-wing apologists offer clear-cut reasons for the swing in public mood from admitted alarm to unwonted placidity. Expressed moderately by John Mander in *Great Britain or Little England?*,* and to the point of caricature by Peregrine Worsthorne (*passim*), the case runs something like this:

"The British lost their head over Cuba. Five years of CND agitation had sunk deeper into the national psyche than most people had realised. When the chips were down, the evil influence betrayed itself not only in the Left-wing press and the street mobs but in 'reliable' newspapers and even in the Prime Minister's office, so that Britain's reputation was only saved by Lord Home's sterling preference for 'horse-sense' rather than intellectual analysis. But President Kennedy, by his cool judgement of the crisis and by visible assertion of civilian authority over the mythical 'reckless generals', finally convinced the British people that their destinies were in safe hands. Feeling ashamed of themselves for having betrayed their own loss of nerve and faith, they shook off the neutralism or worse represented by Lord Russell and his telegrams, and by the 'Hands Off Cuba' demonstrations.

* Penguin, 1963.

141

In the field of nuclear diplomacy, the West is now solid again, even though in other ways Britain is still in the position described by Mr Acheson, of having 'lost an empire and not found a role.' "

The Campaign, or its shrewder members, would admit that their line had been mistaken and their actions ineffective during Cuba Week itself. In general, their reply might run:

"We admit that we read this crisis wrong. We underestimated Khruschev's rashness, and also his subsequent willingness to accept a humiliating reverse. We also underestimated the restraint built into Kennedy's character and into the American war-making machine. But it was a very near thing. Another President might have ordered a strike against Cuba, or an invasion (as Dean Acheson is said to have advocated) and then where would we have been? Would we have supported an American Suez? As for our initial mistrust, this was the Americans' own fault. The CIA had given false information about Cuba to the Administration before, and we could not be sure that it had not happened again. Besides, the English Left felt justifiably protective towards Cuba. Most that has gone wrong with the Castro revolution can be directly attributed to American support of the Batista regime* while it was in existence and to American spite against Castro for ousting Batista. We stand for self-determination in British colonies: we would have been justly reproached by the Right if we had not supported self-determination in what was, economically speaking, an American colony.

"We are grateful for your flattering estimate of our influence in Britain over the past five years. But you should not assume that it is over. Did you notice the Gallup Poll which the *Daily Telegraph* omitted to publish in November 1962? It asked—a fortnight after Cuba—: "In the present world situation, do you personally think that on the whole Britain should side with the United States, with Russia, or with neither?" The replies were:

Side with United States ..	47 p.c.
Side with Russia	1 p.c.
Side with neither	44 p.c.
Don't know	8 p.c.

"Even allowing a generous margin for nationalism and anti-Americanism on the Right, this would seem to show that non-alignment has more supporters in this country than you think."

But to return from the hindsight to the actuality. What did the nuclear disarmers do and say during the crisis?

The role of Lord Russell is well known. Displaying extra-

* Called by Senator John F. Kennedy in October 1960 "one of the most bloody and repressive dictatorships in the history of Latin America".

ordinary energy for a man of 90 who had been too ill to go to the Moscow Conference in July, he appointed himself as honest broker between Kennedy and Khruschev. It was a role which he had played before, in 1958, when his *New Statesman* Open Letters to Eisenhower and Khruschev had elicited replies from Mr John Foster Dulles and the Soviet leader. Since then, by his pronouncements and imprisonment, his prestige had risen in the neutral and Communist worlds, but fallen in his own country and the United States. News editors had begun to wince when his American secretary, Ralph Schoenman—himself a bitter critic of his own country's policies—telephoned from London or Penrhyndeudraeth (the philosopher's North Wales home) to transmit yet another "statement from Lord Russell". Fewer and fewer of the statements were published, and by the time of the Cuban crisis Lord Russell was convinced that the newspapers were conducting a political vendetta against him. His view was confirmed by Fleet Street's imprudent neglect of his early cables to Kennedy and Khruschev during the crisis—a neglect which was very swiftly repaired when Khruschev began (on the Wednesday of Cuba Week) replying to the cables. Lord Russell has described these exchanges, and contributed his own analysis of the Cuba crisis, in *Unarmed Victory*.* Soon after this book was published a much-respected officer of the Committee of 100 told me that a number of Committee supporters had objected to its anti-American tone; and John Mander, in the book I have cited, pointedly contrasts two of Lord Russell's cables sent on different days during Cuba Week. To President Kennedy:

YOUR ACTION DESPERATE. THREAT TO HUMAN SURVIVAL. NO CONCEIVABLE JUSTIFICATION. CIVILIZED MAN CONDEMNS IT. WE WILL NOT HAVE MASS MURDER. ULTIMATUM MEANS WAR. I DO NOT SPEAK FOR POWER BUT PLEAD FOR CIVILIZED MAN. END THIS MADNESS (*Unarmed Victory*, p. 31).

To Prime Minister Khruschev:

MAY I HUMBLY APPEAL FOR YOUR FURTHER HELP IN LOWERING THE TEMPERATURE DESPITE THE WORSENING SITUATION. YOUR CONTINUED FORBEARANCE IS OUR GREAT HOPE. WITH MY HIGH REGARDS AND SINCERE THANKS (p. 46).

Despite his hour-long interview with Khruschev in July, Canon Collins did not imitate Lord Russell's personal diplomacy. But, acting as Campaign chairman, he dispatched the following letter to the UN Secretary-General, U Thant, a few hours after Kennedy's broadcast announcing the blockade:

* Penguin, 1963.

"The state of crisis which has developed in American–Soviet relations over Cuba dramatically illustrates the way in which the world can be brought to the brink of nuclear war by the failure of policies based on deterrence.

"If the Soviet Union has in fact set up missile bases on Cuba, either for direct military purposes or as a bargaining counter to secure the closure of American bases abroad, it has failed to be deterred by American threats of retaliation. And the Kennedy administration, by its blockade of Cuba, has shown itself undeterred by Soviet threats.

"CND wholeheartedly supports the proposal made by Canada's Prime Minister Diefenbaker, that an 8-man committee of neutrals be appointed immediately to investigate and report on the real situation in Cuba.

"CND also supports every action to ease international tension, particularly the dismantling of all nuclear and missile bases wherever they may be—in Great Britain, Turkey, Pakistan, West Germany and Japan, in Cuba, and in East Europe—and would welcome American withdrawal from Guantanamo Bay.

"The Campaign reaffirms that, so long as the Big Powers continue to compete in a nuclear arms race, crises of this kind—and of the kind that has led to a frontier war between China and India—will continue periodically to threaten the world's people with obliteration.

"In all our demonstrations we are urging that the British Government should not commit the British people to support any action which will increase the risk of nuclear war."

Two points about this statement should be noted. The implied doubt about the reliability of the CIA's photographs of the missile bases on Cuba was made explicit in the number of the CND monthly *Sanity*, which went to press late in Cuba Week. The paper also printed a couple of year-old maps from *US News and World Report*. The first map showed the United States bases ringing the Soviet Union; the second, the major Russian cities which could be wiped out from them. These were the bases referred to in the fourth paragraph of the Campaign's letter to U Thant—a paragraph which obviously required more of the Americans than of the Russians, and implicitly demanded the return of the two Great Powers to their own heartlands. This policy was expanded the following month in a fully fledged reaffirmation of the Campaign's aims, "Steps Towards Peace"; a set of proposals identified with Stuart Hall, who argued them at length in the first number of the Campaign's long-awaited intellectual quarterly, *War and Peace*, published at the beginning of 1963. The first step demanded a British initiative towards the withdrawal of all nuclear weapons based outside the US and the USSR. This initiative was to be supplied by the renunciation of British nuclear weapons, British nuclear tests, and nuclear bases in Britain; by opposition to the establishment of a European deterrent (then being much canvassed in the light of Britain's expected entry into the Common Market); and by proposing disengagement in Central Europe, policed by the United Nations, to make acceptable to the West the withdrawal of strategic and tactical nuclear weapons to the US and the USSR.

The second "step towards peace" was designed to tackle the problem of the spread of nuclear weapons, through a British initiative to extend nuclear-free zones (proposed by Brazil for Latin America, the Australian Labour Party for the southern hemisphere, and by the Accra "World Without the Bomb" Assembly for Africa); and to negotiate an immediate test-ban treaty.

The third British initiative proposed concerned the United Nations, whose Charter, CND thought, should take precedence over regional alliances, and whose agencies should be more used for the distribution of foreign *and military* aid. (My italics.) Communist China and Eastern Germany should be admitted to the United Nations, and there should be a UN "presence" in Berlin, guaranteeing West Berlin's freedom.

The cautious, even feasible character of these proposals made them extremely distasteful to the whole-hoggers in the Campaign, who had always insisted that CND stood for nothing short of unilateral nuclear disarmament by all countries, the US and the USSR included. "Steps Towards Peace" helped to emphasise that the unique CND amalgam of 1958 was beginning to break down again into its constituent ingredients. But the Cuba crisis had also emphasised this process in other ways, more readily apparent to the public. It was widely admitted in the peace movement that the street demonstrations during Cuba Week did the Campaign little credit, especially in London where—as Adam Roberts remarked in *Peace News**—by going to particular embassies one apparently apportioned blame, and by going nowhere one achieved only confusion. The only demonstrators who were really sure where they were going were the Communists and fellow-travellers. The "Hands Off Cuba" slogans which sprouted everywhere apportioned blame unambiguously enough, though outside the context of the crisis itself they could have been conscientiously supported not only by the Campaign, but by the bulk of British public opinion. This, of course, was their merit in Communist eyes.

But in Cuba Week London had no monopoly of public disquiet. *Peace News* afterwards recorded that many reports of local

* November 2, 1962.

demonstrations submitted to the paper were prefaced with remarks like, "If you read this, presumably we are both still alive." A number of strikes by schoolchildren were a reminder of the profound, yet often neglected, impact of the Bomb on the minds of adolescents. Even in the sedate atmosphere of a famous public school, where I happened myself to be spending part of the crucial weekend, a housemaster told me that never in his experience had any external event so darkened the mood of his house. An insurance salesman in Sevenoaks later wrote to *Sanity*:

"I have over 700 families on my books and the thing that struck me most about the Cuban affair was the fact that when the crisis was at its height, nobody dared mention it. My policy-holders, normally talkative, looked worried out of their lives, but paid their premiums like automatons, and studiously avoided any mention of the thing that was obviously uppermost in their minds."*

Probably few people carried their anxiety as far towards its logical conclusion as two members of the Committee of 100, Pat Arrowsmith and Wendy Butlin. As tension mounted in London, they were not to be found, and the Committee of 100, or some of its members, indicated to reporters that they were rather anxious about the two women. Had they, perhaps, been abducted? Anxiety was soon allayed by a letter from the pair in *The Guardian*, written from the West of Ireland where, they said, they had taken refuge on the assumption that nuclear war was about to break out and that this location represented the best chance in the British Isles of surviving the catastrophe. In the euphoric mood which came over Britain when the crisis was past, the two girls' behaviour seemed infinitely comic, and caused the Campaign some embarrassment. Any other British people who had taken similar precautions less publicly had no incentive to reveal the fact, and to this day, most people within and without the Campaign probably believe Miss Arrowsmith and Miss Butlin to have been unique. In fact, such evidence as is available points the other way. Mr Irvin Doress, an American marriage and family counsellor, who himself flew to Australia from Washington on impulse 36 hours after President Kennedy's quarantine speech on October 22, has investigated the case-histories of individuals and families who took, or nearly took, similar action. He writes:

"What I had thought might be my projection of personal problems on to the world scene—a psychogenic malaise—turned out to be, on closer examination, in *West Side Story* terms, a 'social disease'. The anxiety bug had bitten people from all walks of life: schoolchildren, college students, nuclear physicists, business

* December 1962.

executives, housewives, soldiers—even psychologists and psychiatrists, who we suppose, and rightly so, are the most likely to be able to control their anxieties."*

The Boston family that fled by night from the city to Vermont, the New Jersey physicist who packed his family and camping gear into his car and set off for Canada, the prominent nuclear physicist who caught a plane to Europe, the influential West Coast psychiatrist who telephoned a peace movement leader to ask if he should go straight to New Zealand, were clearly untypical of their countrymen, but it would be difficult to argue that they were less rational—only, Mr Doress suggests, more aware and imaginative than most of their fellows. It would be surprising if Miss Arrowsmith and Miss Butlin were their only counterparts in Britain.

Outside London during Cuba Week, demonstrations often had the freshness and spontaneity which they had long since lost in the capital itself. Bristol is a good example. In that city, 80 people, of whom only 10 were over 30, were fined after a sit-down—the city's first. On the Tuesday the *Bristol Evening Post* carried a leader which might almost have been written by Canon Collins, equating the Cuban bases with the American bases in Turkey and calling on the Americans to stop playing "nuclear brinkmanship". Five hundred people marched to the Bristol BBC studios—shades of the peaceful march to Budapest radio station!— to demand time on the air, and threatening to return next night if the letter they handed in was not read out on the local news. The crowd then went off to find the Mayor. Discovering him at a Freedom From Hunger function, they held a collection for this cause before being dispersed by the police.

On Wednesday the BBC read the letter on the local news, and in the evening a thousand people, "silent and pensive", according to Miss Hazel Slatter, Secretary of Bristol University CND, who kept a diary of the week, met at the City Centre. Some sat down. On Thursday the University CND printed "as an act of faith" 30,000 leaflets, and the whole Spanish department was deliberately late for lectures. One lecturer, Dr R. V. Sampson of the Department of Economics, talked on the BBC's regional *Round-up* programme about the civil disobedience in which he had taken part the day before, and the duty of all human beings to resist non-violently what was being done in their name by the Governments of the world. On Friday and Saturday the leaflets were distributed and on Saturday sit-downers were arrested in Bristol for the first time. The police, recorded Miss Slatter, "acted with commendable restraint and reasonableness" (though there were

* *New Society*, March 12, 1964.

complaints, familiar in other places from the Campaign's earlier years, about police photographing speakers and demonstrators). But on Saturday, the most dangerous day in Washington, the sense of crisis had disappeared, and Miss Slatter wrote: "Only those who had read, or had pointed out to them, the front page of the *Guardian* that morning felt that the situation was still urgent . . . One realised, looking at the audience, that it was only the intelligentsia and especially the students—who were probably at least 50 p.c. of the crowd—who were still moved. The general public had again gratefully pushed it to the back of their minds."

Which is where, by and large, Cuba Week has remained. And no doubt it will be harder, if there is a next time, for CND or any organisation that replaces it to get people out on to the streets in a nuclear crisis. Yet it would be dangerous to assume that because people stay at home they are necessarily endorsing the actions of the Government in power. It is of the essence of a nuclear crisis that people prefer to stay at home. In the time-scale of modern war—as Lord Russell himself points out*—it is too late to protest against something that may occur in a matter of minutes; and if a man expects himself and his family shortly to become a digit in a megadeath, he tends to prefer the intimacy of his family circle to the effect—itself dehumanising—of being caught up in an aimless, chanting crowd. CND, up until Cuba, had lived on demonstration: the mass assembly was the fibre of its being. After Cuba, demonstrations began to be left to people who happened to enjoy them. In this strange secular Church, the revival meeting was giving way to the study group and the devotional retreat. No wonder that in 1963, at its annual conference, the Campaign made its first serious (though unsuccessful) attempt to fire its Canon.

(iii) ALDERMASTON '63

"I've got a secret
A nice Official Secret
But it isna for the likes of you and me . . ."

Impromptu song, Easter 1963

The 1963 Aldermaston March was generally expected to be the last, partly because the public were getting bored and partly because the Aldermaston AWRE was scheduled for closure. In the event, boredom was averted, and more newspaper space was devoted to the 1963 March than to any of the previous five. But Canon Collins, the Home Secretary, and the *Daily Worker* were united in their disapproval.

* *Unarmed Victory*, p. 28.

Apart from a few plain-clothes policemen, there was nothing in Falcon Field on Good Friday morning to indicate that anything was amiss. The annual picnic looked smaller and younger than the previous year's, but on the other hand, the Campaign was still clearly being refreshed with new blood: about a third of the marchers were, so to speak, making their first Aldermaston. One of them explained how he had been converted to unilateralism while on a three-year engagement with the RAF: "We used to sit around bitching and moaning and talking about Lord Russell and his ideas. In the RAF you have lots of time on your hands, and they seem to choose slightly more intelligent types than the Army do." At the other end of the age spectrum, a woman chattered to her neighbour:

"I feel insulted. When I tell someone I'm going on the March, they say: 'What, all of it? At your age?' And then they say: 'Well, see you on the telly.' 'No,' I say, 'you have to have a gimmick for that. Lend me a baby and I'll be on.' 'Lend you a *baby*?' they say—and then that starts another argument."

But as the March filed through the Berkshire woods towards Reading, members of the Committee of 100 began distributing, in distinctly conspiratorial fashion, six sheets of duplicated foolscap entitled "Danger! Official Secret: RSG-6". The authors, who described themselves as "Spies for Peace", introduced their pamphlet by saying that it was "about a small group of people who have accepted thermo-nuclear war as a probability, and are consciously and carefully planning for it. They are above the Army, the Police, the Ministries or Civil Defence. They are based in fourteen secret headquarters, each ruled by a Regional Commissioner with absolute power over millions of people. In the whole of Britain only about 5,000 men and women are involved . . . Their headquarters are called Regional Seats of Government."

The remainder of the document, after giving the whereabouts and telephone numbers of twelve of the RSGs, offered a detailed description, with plan, of RSG-6. It also named the departments which would be represented in the bunker, and 42 of their senior staff. It went on to describe what had happened on two recent occasions when the RSG system had been activated—during the exercises Parapluie and Fallex, in the spring and autumn of 1962. Both exercises, according to the pamphlet, had assumed nuclear attacks on Britain. The first had ended in a complete communications breakdown. The second—as *Der Spiegel* had already disclosed in Germany—had revealed widespread devastation and chaos in Britain, including 15 "megadeaths", despite six days of strategic warning for dispersion and mobilisation. The pamphlet added:

"The medical services broke down completely. Every hospital in the Southern Region was destroyed or put out of action by fallout, the death of doctors or lack of supplies. The communications system broke down, and the roads were choked. Gloucester, Oxford and Plymouth were eliminated by small bombs. London was paralysed: to go above ground was death. A lethal belt of radiation extended as far out as Windsor. (We trust the heir to the throne was not mutated.) Three-quarters of the Police in the Southern Region were killed, injured or irradiated. Losses among the civilian population were proportionately even higher. Whoever won the war, *we lost it.*"

The exercise, added the authors, "convinced at least one occupant of at least one RSG that the deterrent is quite futile". This was the only direct clue offered to the source of the security leak, whom the Home Secretary (Mr Henry Brooke) immediately dubbed a traitor. But internal evidence—including a peppering of schoolboyish scatology—suggested that the actual compilers of the pamphlet might be found among the readers of the Trotskyist magazine *Solidarity* ("For Workers' Power"). This, at any rate, was where the police looked. But no arrests were made.

On Friday evening the newspapers, which had also received copies of the pamphlet, were unable to publish the contents. D-notices (official advice to editors, normally obeyed, not to publish the material covered by the notice) were out, and police were confiscating all the copies they could find, as well as questioning marchers in camp at Reading. But the secret had escaped. Late on Saturday morning the March reached the turn-off to a village on the Reading–London road. The junction provided the most unambiguous division between sheep and goats that the Campaign had yet seen. By it there stood a Committee of 100 supporter holding up a placard which pointed the way to the RSG, while Mrs Peggy Duff, using the microphone of a CND van, told marchers to carry on to their lunch break— "No food down there, marchers." However, about a tenth of the 6,000 marchers preferred the bunker to the trough, and went down the lane to have a look, many of them singing "I've got a secret, a nice official secret" to the tune of "I love a lassie". The bunker was not fenced off, and the 20-odd police present were unable to prevent the marchers squatting on the site to view a descending ramp, green doors, a boiler-house, and an oil tank. Later, police reinforcements commanded by the Chief Constable of Berkshire arrived, and after another hour or two the site was clear. There were already some 5,000 copies of the pamphlet in existence, though the first edition comprised only a few hundred, and on Sunday and Monday 20,000–30,000 leaflets summarising the "essential" parts of the document were distributed on the March. The police still collected copies where they found them, and arrested one or two people for distributing them, or for carrying placards naming the RSG. "One man," reported the *Daily Mail*, "was arrested for singing the secret. An inspector and a constable took a note of his words and then led him away as the march neared Hyde Park." But still the D-notices were kept on, more as a deterrent against further revelations and a hint that the breach was being taken seriously than as an attempt at concealment. Curiously enough, it was the *Daily Telegraph*'s patriotism which cracked first. By quoting the summary broadcast over Prague Radio the paper was able to enlighten those of its readers who had not by then had access to the original document. But from Easter Monday on, access was wide. Miss Vanessa Redgrave described the location and purpose of RSG-6 to the March's closing rally in Hyde Park, attended by at least 50,000 people. Photographic copies were sold in Cambridge coffee bars, duplicated ones in Doncaster pubs. The name of the village appeared in letters 4 feet high on a station wall at Harlow, and was scrawled in dust on a black maria. And Canon Collins, whose executive a month later said that it had welcomed the revelations of the Spies for Peace, announced that the demonstrations at RSG-6 would not help the cause.

The disturbances in Central London on Easter Monday helped to ensure that the reaction in Parliament and press should be almost uniformly hostile. Peter Cadogan, a Cambridge teacher who had led the 1958 March to Mepal rocket base and described the episode to the Labour Party Conference in the same year, became the self-appointed leader of a "March Must Decide" Committee; the phrase implying that the Aldermaston March itself was the sovereign body of CND and should be allowed to decide whether or not it wanted to make an act of civil disobedience part of the March. After a stop for rest and debate in Hyde Park, Cadogan's followers and the London Federation of Anarchists, assisted by the anonymous and scarcely non-violent accretions which any metropolitan crowd draws to itself, linked arms and spilled across the road. Half-contained by mounted police the contingent—small in proportion to the whole of the March—eddied along Victoria Street, up Whitehall, and back via Regent Street and Oxford Street to Hyde Park. There were 72 arrests, and a bag of flour was emptied over Canon Collins.

If the Campaign was concerned about its image during 1962, it had fresh cause to be concerned after Aldermaston '63. Fleet Street's leader-writers enjoyed a splenetic Easter.

The Times:

"A much larger group in CND are quite simply very young, or very immature, people for whom the attraction of a cause is irresistible, especially if it involves badges, television cameras, and a dispensation from the normal codes of hygiene and public behaviour. For these carefully dishevelled exhibitionists the annual shuffle from Aldermaston to London . . . has long since ceased to have much direct connexion with nuclear weapons. It has become a slightly tedious annual parade in which the earnest bonhomie of a tube station in the blitz and the opportunity for some remarkably uninhibited carousal have been welded to a formless sense of protest against authority . . .

"One of the disturbing developments in the unilateralist movement has been the gradual eclipse of moderation and the takeover by anarchistic elements."*

The *Daily Telegraph:*

"In its emphasis on the non-elected character of the emergency staffs, its sarcasm about 'our rulers', its wild insinuations about a plot for a military dictatorship, its sneer at the Church of England as a 'Government department', and its cheap minor obscenities, the pamphlet seems to reflect an amalgam of the worst elements of CND: Communist subversion and pure rebellious irresponsibility . . .

"It is really quite ludicrous for Canon Collins and all the other 'respectable' leaders of CND to 'dissociate' themselves from such malignant irresponsibility. They helped to create the fevered atmosphere in which such outrages are possible."†

Tribune:

"We have little interest in the content of the notorious 'Spies for Peace' pamphlet which has done the nuclear disarmament movement a great deal of harm . . . The organisation it describes becomes inevitable once this country accepts a nuclear strategy."‡

For months afterwards the Committee of 100 and associated organisations—by this time largely bereft of the "big names" which had decorated them two years previously—devoted themselves to "exposing" RSGs in different parts of the country. Readers of *Solidarity*, equipped with an article published in the magazine telling them how to jam telephone exchanges, went round London with bicycles and matchsticks trying the secret Security Service numbers which had fallen into their possession (a technique which had already been successfully tried on the American and Russian embassies when the two countries resumed testing). But in Parliament the Prime Minister, who had

* April 16, 1963. † April 16, 1963. ‡ April 19, 1963.

and was to have as much embarrassment over security questions as he could well afford, played down the significance of the Spies for Peace: "The disclosure of the particular information involved is not seriously damaging to the national interest . . . There is little resemblance between this affair and cases of espionage." Mr Macmillan also denied that there was anything mysterious or sinister about the existence of the RSGs. "It is widely known that our defence plans for any future war, whether nuclear or conventional, include provision for essentially civilian organisation . . . To prepare the RSGs and to link them with the headquarters of the local authorities is an obviously essential precaution."* As for the telephoning of Security Services, Mr Macmillan said, all that had happened was that an establishment had been abusively telephoned eight times in 1½ hours. The Anarchists claim that they did a great deal better than this.

In fact, not only had the regional government system for emergency purposes been in existence for 44 years (it was originally devised as a means of keeping essential services going during the strikes and civil disturbances of the twenties, and was reactivated during the 1939–45 War in case communications in the country broke down);† but in outline the system and its application to the nuclear age was publicised in 1961. On February 28 that year the *Daily Mail*'s defence correspondent, Stevenson Pugh, described the "twelve little Governments which . . . have already been set up and staffed to ensure the survival of twelve states of Britain after an H-bomb war", and added that such a war "has been rehearsed in exercises many times". He also visited the London headquarters of the system (presumably in the old Rotunda), which has since been moved to the West Country in deference to the penetrative power of large H-bombs, and an RSG in the Midlands. He called the Regional Commissioners "the Big Leaders". During 1962 the Campaign Caravan—a separate itinerant organisation set up under the leadership of George Clark to initiate and foster local CND groups and activities—heard further rumours. The astonishment of the Campaign's rank and file was an indication of their youth and ignorance. Yet there is no reason to suppose that most MPs were any better informed, and certainly, as had happened with the atomic bomb 15 years earlier, Parliament had voted the money for the construction of the underground fortresses without knowing what it was doing.

The whole episode clearly demonstrated the dangers inherent in the bureaucratic instinct for secrecy. The outline and purpose of the RSG system could not long have been kept secret from any-

* Hansard, April 23, 1963. † Cf. Nicolas Walter, *The RSGs* 1919–1963 (*Solidarity*, pamphlet, 1963).

one who seriously wanted to find out about it, and the vast majority of the population, had they been aware of the system's existence, would have accepted that it was beneficent in intent. As *The Times* pointed out, "If Britain were to reject its military insurance against nuclear attack, the need for efficient passive measures would presumably increase." Few Direct Action groups, given full public knowledge of the whereabouts of RSGs as well as of rocket bases, would perversely have chosen to demonstrate at the former. Nor is it easy to see how any body apart from the Government itself could be entrusted with the task of selecting the people who would earn their preservation in an RSG by being useful in the post-attack world. It is even possible that had the Government been prudent enough to announce its intention of stockpiling a few anti-nuclear poets and dramatists along with the fuel supplies and the emergency rations, the CND's fears for the future of civilisation might have been allayed.

CHAPTER SEVEN

SIDE EFFECTS

"Human history began with an act of disobedience, and it is not unlikely that it will be terminated by an act of obedience."

Erich Fromm in *A Matter of Life* (ed. Urquhart, Cape 1963), p. 97

(i) POLICE

"May all to Athens back again repair
And think no more of this night's accidents
But as the fierce vexation of a dream."

Midsummer Night's Dream, Act IV, Scene I

ON the night of July 10, 1963, when the British Royal Family accompanied the King and Queen of Greece to a performance of *A Midsummer Night's Dream* at the Aldwych Theatre, a man in the crowd outside waved a Union Jack. A London policeman turned on him. "Put that thing away," he said. "Do you want to start a riot?"

The policeman kept his head that night better than some of his colleagues, and better perhaps than the Home Secretary, Mr Henry Brooke, who later told reporters: "The Queen of England has been booed tonight and I am furious." The Greek demonstrations, as they were called, damaged the Campaign more than any other incident in its history. They identified the movement more closely than ever before with the Communists, who had been running a long-standing and for once not altogether unfounded campaign against the prolonged imprisonment of some members of the losing side in the Greek civil war. CND's grouse against the Greeks was different. Some members of the Committee of 100 had been expelled from Greece at Easter when they attempted to participate in a Marathon to Athens anti-nuclear march, which the Greek Government prohibited. And the whole CND had been stirred by the murder in Salonika of a Greek MP, Gregory Lambrakis. Mr Lambrakis had himself at Easter-time been in Britain, taking part in the Aldermaston March, and in January had also attended the Oxford Conference which set up the European Confederation against Nuclear Arms. The murder had apparently been political, and the CND suspected that but for the efforts of Lambrakis' friends, the Greek police would not have tried very hard to find the culprit.

But by the time that the Greek Royal Family arrived in England and began making conciliatory noises about the Greek political prisoners, the leaders of both CND and the Committee of 100 were having serious doubts about what they had got themselves involved in. The doubts were not even allayed by the report that the son of the head of security at the Foreign Office proposed to join the Committee of 100 sit-down. After King Paul had consented to see Mrs Betty Ambatielos, the wife of one of the prisoners, Peter Moule, the Secretary of the Committee of 100, argued strongly that the demonstration should be cancelled, but he was overruled. Loyally, he led it and was eventually imprisoned for four months for incitement to obstruction. Canon Collins, who wrote to the King and Queen of Greece as Chairman of CND warning them that the movement would stage incidents, gave interviews to newspapers explaining that it had all been an error of judgement. He told the *Sunday Times*:

"We decided to take this chance of protesting because the Greek issue blew up at the same time as we were trying to spread CND internationally. Unfortunately, in our position, we can't always stop to consider all the consequences of our actions."*

The *Daily Telegraph* called him a turbulent priest, and the Campaign carried the can for everything that happened, including the booing of the Queen's party. (Nothing could happen inside the theatre because the Foreign Office had taken every seat and filled it with the assorted bric-à-brac of the Establishment. It added up, said one newspaperman present, to the worst audience the Royal Shakespeare Company had ever had.)

And yet, after all this, the chief long-term sufferers were not the Campaign but the Metropolitan Police, four of whose members stood trial in 1964 on a charge which is often made against the police but very rarely substantiated.

They were charged with "planting" evidence. The case arose during the Greek demonstrations out of the arrest of Donald Rooum, a cartoonist for magazines which included the *Spectator* and *Peace News*, and three juveniles on charges which alleged that they were in possession of offensive weapons, to wit pieces of brick. Mr Rooum's version of the whole episode was published in *Anarchy* 36.† He had the presence of mind, and could afford, to get the contents of his pockets analysed and to hire a good lawyer. He was acquitted of the charge and both he and the other youths, who had been convicted, later accepted substantial sums from Scotland Yard in compensation. The policeman in charge, Detective-Sergeant Harold Challenor, was found insane and unfit to plead. Three of his subordinates were sent to prison in June 1964, and several other prisoners who had been convicted on Challenor's evidence were released. *Peace News*, which originally broke the story, celebrated.

This was the second demonstration which had left the image of the police more tarnished than the image of CND. The first occasion was the Committee of 100's Trafalgar Square sit-down on September 17, 1961. It would be too much to say that this occasion was both the beginning and the end of police violence

* February 1964. † July 7, 1963.

in the streets of London, but the Force undoubtedly received a salutary lesson in the unwisdom of applying to articulate middle-class demonstrators, in a widely publicised setting, methods which might have passed muster in a dockside rough-house. Seventy-four complaints were received by the Commissioner—an unprecedented number—and an elaborate inquiry had to be held. Under the highly unsatisfactory procedure then in force, the Metropolitan Police were compelled to be the judges in their own cause, and though the evidence to the inquiry amounts to a 4-inch thick pile of foolscap, the public was mildly sceptical about the findings. It was officially admitted that several people had been dropped in the fountains, that a woman constable had used bad language, and that a sergeant had been too free with a fire hose. The Royal Commission on the Police, which was sitting at the time, studied the inquiry, and found it satisfactory. Suspicion and allegation is not the same as proof, whether the subjects are policemen or criminals. Nevertheless, it is necessary to recall what was alleged, and how the allegations were initially treated.

It took some time for the happenings in the early hours of September 18 to leak out, through letters to the *Guardian*, an article by Adam Roberts in the *New Statesman*, and a dossier compiled by the National Council for Civil Liberties (which was also concerned about the decision to ban the use of the Square to demonstrators). No one person could possibly see everything that took place, but a summary, by a commentator very hostile to CND, is given by Mr Herb Greer in his book on the Campaign:

"Late in the evening Canon Collins, protesting angrily that he was not a demonstrator, was collared and led away. Just before midnight Fenner Brockway, the only prominent figure remaining on the scene, was forcibly dragged out of the Square and put under arrest. Furiously he argued that he was there with permission of the Home Secretary, but the police were bland and quite deaf to what he had to say.

"After midnight the reason for the summary removal of prominent people became suddenly and shockingly obvious. Ranked policemen, surly and foul-tempered at the long hours of struggling and at having weekend leaves cancelled, launched a deliberate and vicious attack against the scattered remnants of the crowd. Cameramen were told abruptly that if they filmed another foot they would be arrested. Demonstrators, onlookers, passers-by— it made no difference—were punched, knocked down, kicked. Squads of constables threw struggling civilians into the icy water of the fountain basins. Middle-aged women were slammed down and dragged by one leg through puddles, face down against the concrete pavement. Several people, alarmed by the thug-like brutality erupting in the Square, tried to flee. They were hauled down from behind and kicked and beaten where they lay.

"Prisoners taken in vans to a courtyard at the police station were not much luckier. Some were battered with high-pressure streams from a fire-hose. One hapless man was lifted by four policemen as high as they could raise him and smashed to the pavement. A girl was thrown bodily from a police van on to the concrete floor of the courtyard. Another demonstrator was kicked in the stomach."*

It took several days for Scotland Yard to admit that an extraordinary number of complaints had been received, and by the time that the result of the inquiry was announced to Parliament six months later, MPs were sufficiently distant from the events concerned to receive Mr Butler's statement with merry laughs.† Scotland Yard, however, had not forgotten. The basic mistake, it was realised at the Yard, had been to keep the same set of policemen on duty all day. Contrary to popular belief, police resources in London were by no means strained to the utmost on September 17. Of the 4,000 on duty, 2,000 were held in reserve in case the demonstrators managed to get through to Parliament Square. If the two battalions had changed places halfway through, fewer constables would have lost their tempers, and there might even have been fewer complaints in the *Police Review* afterwards about poor canteen facilities and arrangements for getting home. At subsequent demonstrations, too, a senior police officer was deputed to sit in a nearby police station to receive public complaints, if any.

The most difficult decisions which the authorities had to take in relation to the September 17 demonstration preceded the day itself. The decisions taken aroused strong criticism, partly because they reminded libertarians just how limited the right of public demonstration is in Britain, and partly because they predictably had the effect of provoking what they purported to prevent: mass defiance of law and order.

To book Trafalgar Square for a meeting, one simply writes to the Ministry of Works. The simplicity of the procedure was amusingly demonstrated in 1962, when a young clerk from Cheam had the idea of booking the Square for Easter Monday the next year on behalf of the barely existent "Keep Britain Great" movement, in order to do down Canon Collins. (The Ministry accepted the booking, and when the Canon applied, told him with a straight face that he was too late. Making a virtue of necessity, the Canon explained to the *Guardian*, when it broke the

* *Mud Pie*, Max Parrish, 1964, p. 59.   † Hansard, March 1, 1962.

story, that the Aldermaston March was now too big for the Square and would have anyway had to wind up in Hyde Park.) The *Guardian* subsequently made some experiments of its own, booking the Square on behalf of an entirely fictitious organisation to see if any inquiries were made. None were. But according to the police the procedure is for the Ministry of Works to consult the police, through the Home Office, about their knowledge of the organisers of a Trafalgar Square meeting.

In 1961 no one needed to inquire about the intentions of the Committee of 100. As the Yard points out, the Committee obligingly publishes a briefing leaflet for its supporters in advance of demonstrations, including, as often as not, tolerably accurate forecasts of how the police are likely to deal with them. The September 17 demonstration was the third during the year at which large-scale civil disobedience had been committed. On the first occasion, outside the Ministry of Defence in February, the demonstrators had confined themselves to the pavement and no arrests were made. At the second, in Parliament Square in April, the Committee got bolder, and Scotland Yard had to decide what it should do about the third.

In the event, the Commissioner of the Metropolitan Police, Sir Joseph Simpson, asked the Home Secretary to exercise his power under the Public Order Act, 1936, to ban processions in the Trafalgar Square area, and when the ban expired on September 17 itself he used a power, available only in London under the Metropolitan Police Act, 1839: he issued regulations, which did not require the Home Secretary's permission, for preventing obstruction for a further 24 hours in the same area. (Since the demonstration went on beyond midnight on the 17th, the regulations had to be further extended.) The decision to summon Lord Russell and other well-known people beforehand for inciting members of the public to commit breaches of the peace was taken by the Director of Public Prosecutions. But Sir Joseph, a scrupulous, almost donnish policeman, probably had even fewer doubts about this course than many Conservative MPs. Politicians take short views. A police chief in a big city looks ahead to the next demonstration, and the next and the next. Sir Joseph told me:

"I normally consult the D.P.P. before acting against someone who has openly said that he will break the law. The decision should not be made purely on the basis of 'Is this going to cause more trouble on this occasion or isn't it?' I have to look farther ahead—I am influenced by the effect that it might have on subsequent events."

The police do not necessarily accept that the imprisonment of Lord Russell and his associates made the September 17 demonstration bigger and more intractable than it would otherwise have been (though, in fact, it would have been surprising if Lord Russell's much-publicised appearance in court, and imprisonment for refusing to be bound over to keep the peace, had had any other effect). But undoubtedly, the loss of its original leaders hamstrung the Committee after September 17, even if not before.

Of course, if a couple of hundred thousand people decided to sit down in Central London, the police could do nothing but cordon off the area and hope that no rival group provoked violence. But apart from the trivial interventions of Empire Loyalists, the Campaign's demonstrations set no problems comparable to the pre-war battles in the East End between Communists and Fascists, and were even more orderly than the Hunger Marches (which tended to attract supernumerary roughnecks when they got to London). The only recent parallel to the Committee of 100's openly expressed intention of breaking the law was the Militant Suffragettes. The Committee of 100, of course, did not hurl bricks through Cabinet Ministers' windows, and professed non-violence, though the police view is that "there are people within the Committee of 100 who do react violently. They don't all go limp, though they very rarely resist arrest. There are some who will charge a cordon and call others on."

The Royal Commission on the Police, using the apparatus of the Government Social Survey as well as other evidence submitted to it, found that there was no evidence of deteriorating relations between police and public, though it had been strongly represented to them—particularly by lawyers—that there was. It depends, of course, upon what one means by deteriorating relations. A growth of scepticism, among magistrates and others, about police methods and veracity would not necessarily strike at the roots of British society, or prevent us from continuing to think, even though less romantically and whole-heartedly than before, that our policemen are better than anyone else's. On the face of it, it would be surprising if the comparatively small-scale CND demonstrations had done a quarter as much as the swelling volume of motoring cases, or the occasional scandal like the Sheffield "rhino whip" inquiry of 1963, to convince the middle classes that policemen have their share of human faults as well as of superhuman virtues. But in one particular age-group, the eighteens to twenty-fives, where the Commission itself found that there was cause for concern, CND and the Committee of 100 formed a natural focus for the general crisis of authority. Within the Campaign itself, despite its overall middle-class character, young people of widely varying backgrounds met on equal terms. Interpreting the police simply as the incarnation of authority and also as the extension of the Government, to be used for any purpose the Home Secretary thought fit, Campaigners lent a ready ear to stories of police violence or duplicity. It was a firm conviction with the Committee of 100 that their telephones were tapped and their correspondence interrupted, and some members even staged various experiments to prove their contention. (The proofs, however, usually left out the possibility that the Committee itself included a police informer.)

Demonstrations, especially in Central London, also tended to attract from outside the Campaign itself the amorphous crowd of new-rich, new-leisured teenagers whom policemen themselves regard as a difficult problem—"Before the war you could tell them to move on and they'd go, but nowadays the answer is more often 'Why pick on me?' " Whether as a direct consequence or not, the attitudes towards the police once current in a particular social class would appear to have been transferred to an age-group instead. What effect it all had upon the policemen themselves is past telling, though it was obvious from casual exchanges with policemen on demonstrations that not many of them either saw the point of what was being done or valued the overtime pay above the hours of lost leisure and stopped leave.

There were, of course, exceptions, and cross-fertilisation, so to speak, between policemen and demonstrators did sometimes occur. At least one young lady, on going limp in the Square, was carried away metaphorically as well as literally by the constable who arrested her, and a marriage was arranged between law and sweet disorder. After the wedding, a mutually satisfactory compromise was arranged: the lady stopped sitting down, and the constable left the Force.

(ii) THE LAW

"Men can exaggerate the extent of their interests and so can the Crown. The servants of the Crown, like other men animated by the highest motives, are capable of formulating a policy *ad hoc* so as to prevent the citizen from doing something that the Crown does not want him to do. It is the duty of the Courts to be as alert now as they have always been to prevent abuse of the prerogative."

Lord Devlin,
Chandler & Others v. *Director of Public Prosecutions*,
July 12, 1962

"Mankind is moving towards death as a sandhill moves, not by any sinister mechanism it contains but by the shifting of its myriad tiny grains in one direction. The campaign of civil disobedience is no device to force it backwards. It simply asks any individual who may be listening to move, himself only, in the opposite direction."

Robert Bolt,
A Matter of Life, ed. Urquhart (Cape 1963), p. 46

In the course of acquiring a martyrology of their own, the nuclear disarmers in Britain became entangled with, and left enduring marks upon, the country's law. One of their number, Mr George Clark, was twice convicted of inciting people to commit a public nuisance by obstructing the highway, and sentenced to prison terms of nine and eighteen months respectively. But twice, after serving a substantial proportion of these sentences, Mr Clark had his conviction quashed on appeal. The second appeal, heard before the Lord Chief Justice in November 1963, followed widely expressed public concern about an extraordinary sentence, passed on Mr Clark by the Deputy Chairman of London Sessions for allegedly directing one of the demonstrations against the King and Queen of Greece in July. But the conviction was quashed on a point of law, and the decision established, according to legal correspondents, that it would no longer be enough for the prosecution in cases against people engaged in political processions to show that they caused an obstruction, even though they might have brought traffic to a standstill. The obstruction must also be "unreasonable". However, the police, though originally somewhat perturbed by this decision, were later reassured by the confirming of sentences on two leaders of the Committee of 100, Peter Moule and Terence Chandler, for similar offences.

CND obstruction cases were not rare—Miss Pat Arrowsmith fought another notable one after an incident in Bootle. Other obscure legal byways were explored. After the Swaffham demonstrations of December 1958 the authorities were much criticised by some newspapers for employing against the demonstrators a statute of 1381, aimed against the marauding vagabonds who survived the Peasant's Revolt, whose translation and meaning were in doubt and whose applicability to a 20th-century clergyman like Michael Scott was not obvious. An even more recherché issue was raised by Terence Chandler, conducting his own defence against the charge arising out of the Greek demonstrations. It concerned the right of an accused to object to jurymen by asking them to "stand by" until the list was exhausted. Chandler was released on bail from Wandsworth Prison to pursue his researches after the Court of Criminal Appeal had rejected his plea that the right to challenge jurors should be enjoyed by the defence equally with the prosecution, and that it did not lie within the discretion of the trial judge. He was eventually refused leave to appeal to the House of Lords.

All these cases were beguiling to lawyers, and important to the defence of British civil liberties. Several of them also showed how much can be achieved under the British system by an ingenious barrack-room lawyer. Terence Chandler is headstrong, indubitably sincere, partly self-educated, and obsessed, like many "absolute" pacifists, with the preservation of his own identity in an impersonal world. George Clark is less intransigent, and university-educated, but dogged and argumentative, possessed of a remarkable talent for organisation and leadership. Neither are people whom it is safe to overlook.

However, cases of this sort were of comparatively minor significance and public interest compared with the Official Secrets Trial, which began at the Old Bailey on February 12, 1962, and was concluded in the House of Lords on July 12 of the same year. In this trial, Michael Randle, Trevor Hatton, Ian Dixon, Terence Chandler, Pat Pottle, and Helen Allegranza, were charged with conspiring together "to incite divers persons to commit a breach of Section I of the Official Secrets Act 1911, namely for a purpose prejudicial to the safety or interests of the State to enter a Royal Air Force station belonging to Her Majesty at Wethersfield". All were found guilty. Helen Allegranza, who committed suicide not long after her release from prison, was sentenced to 12 months, and all the other defendants to 18 months imprisonment.

The Government had made clear before the Wethersfield demonstration took place that the Official Secrets Act would be applied if the aerodrome was trespassed upon. Michael Randle said at a press conference in the Feathers, off Fleet Street, on December 8, 1961, that the Committee thought that the Government was bluffing in threatening to use against them an Act clearly designed to prevent spying, and that if it were used it would constitute a threat to civil liberties. They would not be deterred by it. There was throughout the trial virtually no dispute about the intentions of the defendants, nor about their actions. The case, which began with the Attorney-General (a Minister of the Crown) assuring the jury that this was not a political prosecution, hung upon the decision, made on the third day by Mr Justice Havers, to exclude all evidence relating to the ultimate purpose of the accused in doing what it was admitted they had done. They were therefore unable to call any expert evidence, or cross-examine the Crown's experts, on the possession or use of nuclear weapons by this country. The same ruling made a verdict of guilty inevitable, for it left the Crown as the arbiter of whether the purpose for which people entered a prohibited place was "prejudicial to the safety and interests of the State". The five Law Lords upheld the judge's ruling, though Lord Devlin entered a notable qualification:

"The fact to be proved is the existence of a purpose prejudicial to the State—not a purpose which 'appears to the Crown' to be prejudicial to the State. Words of that sort could have been written into the statute. In emergency legislation they frequently are . . . But there is no suggestion that they are to be implied into this statute. Their place cannot be filled by the common law. There is no rule of common law that whenever questions of national security are being considered by any Court for any purpose, it is what the Crown thinks to be necessary or expedient that counts and not what is necessary or expedient in fact . . . Consequently, the Crown's opinion as to what is or is not prejudicial in this case is just as inadmissible as the Appellants'."

Though the case was decided on law rather than upon evidence, this did not prevent the cross-examination taking a dramatic turn at times. The Committee of 100 ever afterwards claimed as a great victory the cross-examination by Pat Pottle (who conducted his own case) of Air Commodore Graham Magill, Director of Operations at the Air Ministry. The exchange ran:

Pottle: Air Commodore, is there any official order you cannot accept?

Judge: Is there what?

Pottle: Is there any official order from the Government that the Air Commodore would say to himself, "I accept orders, I am a servant of the government, but on this particular occasion I cannot accept this order."

Judge: He is an officer in the forces of Her Majesty.

Pottle: So actually there is no order you would not accept?

Magill: It is my duty to carry out any order that is given to me.

Pottle: Would you press the button that you know is going to annihilate millions of people?

Magill: If the circumstances so demanded it, I would.

Pottle: Would you slit the throats of all the two-year-old children in this country, Air Commodore?

Judge: I think you must stop all that.

Pottle: I feel it was comparable with the effects of nuclear weapons. It was the same as saying he would press the button to explode the nuclear bomb. Have you read the summing-up of the judge at the Eichmann trial?

Judge: Where are we getting to?*

Later, Pottle managed to quote in court the lines from the Eichmann judge's summing-up which Mr Justice Havers had ruled out of order: "The very contention of applying the defence

* Transcript, p. 132.

165

of the act of State to the extermination of helpless people is an insult to justice." However, virtually all the questions which Pottle sought to put to expert witnesses, including Sir Robert Watson Watt and Professor Linus Pauling, who had flown over from the United States to attend the trial, were ruled as inadmissible because they raised "irrelevant" questions about the dangers of nuclear explosions and defence systems. There were other high spots in Pottle's examination of witnesses—for example, Lord Russell's and Miss Vanessa Redgrave's open and intentional self-incrimination in the witness-box—but the most thorough exploration of the defendants' actions and opinions took place during the examination of Michael Randle, who was in the witness-box for the greater part of a day. Randle, who was Secretary of the Committee at the time of Wethersfield, was then 28. He had got married a few days before the trial opened. A thoughtful, if anything over-serious man, a pacifist since long before the Committee had been thought of, Randle had in common with the other defendants a preoccupation almost amounting to an obsession with nuclear weapons, together with great reserves of moral staying power. He was the most articulate of the prisoners. By putting to him extracts from the leaflet *Act or Perish, a call to non-violent action by Earl Russell and Rev. Michael Scott*, Mr Jeremy Hutchinson, QC, who defended all the prisoners other than Pottle, afforded Randle the opportunity to state parts of the Committee's "further purpose" in going to Wethersfield (as opposed, that is, to their immediate purpose of immobilising the base):

"If nuclear weapons were ever used by this country and there was a retaliatory attack, most, if not all, of the people in this country would be destroyed, and therefore I cannot hold that these bases are essential to the defence of this country, or for the defence of any country."*

The Russell–Scott leaflet also contained the words:

"We are told that in a democracy only lawful methods of persuasion should be used. Unfortunately, the opposition to sanity and mercy on the part of those who have power is such as to make persuasion by ordinary methods difficult and slow, with the result that, if such methods alone are employed, we shall probably all be dead before our purpose can be achieved. Respect for law is important and only a very profound conviction can justify actions which flout the law."

Answering questions on this from Mr Hutchinson, Randle said:

* Transcript, p. 147.

166

"I believe it is important to abide by majority decisions. Except in very exceptional circumstances . . . Every individual must finally decide whether millions of lives are threatened by a particular act, and in that situation I think they have the right to make that decision . . .

"There were people in Germany during the Nazi regime who were ordered to commit what have since been defined as crimes against humanity. They would have been going against the law of their country by disobeying their order. I feel they had a moral duty to disobey that order in that situation."*

The judge thereupon intervened:

"As far as I can see it means this, doesn't it, if you disagree with the law, you break it?"

Mr Hutchinson protested, and Randle went on:

"Not in general, only in particular situations. It does not mean that every time I disagree with the law I break it. It only means in particular situations where I disagree with it, and where I think it is flouting basic human rights I will certainly disobey it, and I feel it would be a moral obligation to disobey . . . I feel that the use of nuclear weapons is always contrary to basic human rights. I cannot see any situation in which they would be justified against human beings."

He went on to explain that he would not break just any law to publicise his case: "It must be particular laws that we break which are in some way relevant to the cause that we are advocating."†

Later,‡ in cross-examination by the Attorney-General, Randle repudiated on behalf of the Committee of 100 a statement alleged to have been made by George Clark (who was then a member of the Committee) at a public meeting in July 1961 under Randle's chairmanship, which contained the words: "Police stations will be smothered and the courts overwhelmed, and the result of the demonstration will be that justice will become a farce." The farthest he was prepared to go was to admit that the Committee intended to make it difficult or impossible for the authorities to function effectively without using extraordinary measures. Randle stood up firmly to Sir Reginald Manningham-Buller's attempt to overbear him. (Counsel: "I am not asking you anything about the Eichmann trial." Defendant: "I am just giving it to you gratuitously") and it was the judge who had to explore the phrase "extraordinary measures":

* *Ibid.*, pp. 149–50.   † *Ibid.*, p. 151.   ‡ *Ibid.*, p. 167–8.

"I am not quite sure what that means?"

Randle: "Well, I would say that if the Government were faced with a position where the ordinary courts of law, for example, would have to put aside all other business to deal with us they might set up special administration or special commissions or something to try to deal with us. We would then have placed them in a position where they would have to face up to the logic of being prepared to commit genocide. If they are prepared to do it against people they must be prepared to do it against us. This is the position we want to put them in. That is the real thing I am trying to get to."*

It was hardly to be expected that the Attorney-General would appreciate the nuances of this position, and in his closing speech† to the jury he said:

"You have heard the really astonishing evidence given by Mr Randle. Seldom, I suppose, if ever, in this Court where so many criminal cases have been tried has an accused person had the effrontery to go into the witness box and say—and this is the effect of what Randle said, is it not?—'I have been a member of the Committee from its inception. And right from its inception we intended to embark on a campaign with the deliberate purpose of breaking the law', for the objects which I have just stated. What he said amounted, did it not, to this: 'We have decided what laws we broke, after very careful consideration.' And it appears after having taken legal advice on the penalties involved. 'And where we think fit we break the law.' It is really an admission of rather an astonishing character."

An equal gulf was fixed between Pottle's assertion, in his own closing speech, that the "vast majority" of the social advantages obtained in the last century, from the right of women to vote to the right of a man to join a trade union, had been obtained by civil disobedience, to the Attorney-General's reflections on the rule of law:

"If many other bodies did this, if they succeeded in their efforts, it would be an end, would it not, to the rule of law. It would lead to the end of democracy, to anarchy and possibly to dictatorship ... In this country no one, whether he is a member of the Committee of 100 or not, is above the law. But the Committee of 100, according to Mr Randle, consider they are entitled to break the law whenever they think fit."

Any doubt there may have been about a conviction was removed by the Judge's summing-up, which concluded:

* Transcript, p. 176.   † Ibid., p. 265–7.

"If you can find it in your conscience to come to the conclusion that the purpose was not prejudicial, or if you have any reasonable doubt about the matter, then you should acquit all the accused. If on the other hand you are satisfied so that you can feel sure that the purpose was prejudicial to the safety and the interests of the State, then you should convict, and you will, of course, bear in mind the evidence which Air Commodore Magill has given, and it is for you, and you alone, to say whether you accept that evidence as correct. If you do, you see, it means that that air base was an essential part of the defence of this country, and that those aeroplanes on it had a vital part to play in that defence, and that any interference with the ability of those aeroplanes to take off at any moment would seriously affect their operational effect."*

Since the jury were out for four hours, and when they returned with their findings of "guilty" entered a plea for leniency, it seems probable that at least one of the jurors was unhappy about the way the trial had gone. The prisoners appealed, and the case went to the House of Lords to establish the meaning of the words in the 50-year-old Official Secrets Act about a "purpose prejudicial to the safety or interests of the State", with the accused arguing that evidence on their behalf had been improperly rejected. "State," as Lord Reid remarked, "is not an easy word. It does not mean the Government or the Executive." He added:

"I do not think that it means, as Counsel argued, the individuals who inhabit these islands. The statute cannot be referring to the interests of all those individuals because they may differ and the interests of the majority are not necessarily the same as the interests of the State. Again we have seen only too clearly in some other countries what can happen if you personify and almost deify the State. Perhaps the country or the realm are as good synonyms as one can find, and I would be prepared to accept the organised community as coming as near to a definition as one can get."

Lord Radcliffe dealt with the difficulty about the immediate and ultimate purpose of the defendants in entering the air base by distinguishing between a "purpose" within the meaning of the Act and a motive. If their direct purpose was to cause obstruction, and the obstruction were found of prejudice to the defence dispositions of the State, an offence had been committed. Lord Radcliffe also concluded that evidence about the effects of nuclear weapons inadmissible because the questions it raised were untriable.

"The more one looks at it, the plainer it becomes, I think, that

* Transcript, p. 357.

the question whether it is in the true interests of this country to acquire, retain, or house nuclear armaments depends on an infinity of considerations, military and diplomatic, technical, psychological and moral, and of decisions, tentative or final, which are themselves part assessments of fact and part expectations and hopes. I do not think that there is anything amiss with a legal ruling that does not make this issue a matter for judge and jury."

Lord Devlin's long judgement has already been quoted. The appeal, he said, "embraced big constitutional questions concerning the right to trial by jury and not by judge and the extent to which the Courts can question statements on political matters by the executive. All such questions which concern the liberty of the subject need great care in their consideration. It is to me a special inducement to the exercise of care that these Appellants have not traded their liberty for personal gain but for what they sincerely, and however mistakenly, believe to be the safety of the world."

The clash between the 100 and the State was inevitable, and insoluble. It is arguable that the members of the Committee, holding the beliefs which they did and do, were entirely right to provoke it. The right of conscientious objection to military service was established in Britain after a long, hard, and comparatively recent battle; and in several civilised Western European countries it is not properly established yet. But most thinking people would presumably hold that a man who believed he ought not to fire a rifle in anger, but who failed to carry his convictions into practice by exercising this right where it existed, deserved some form of censure. We might even blame him in a country where the right did not exist, provided that the penalty for this particular form of civil disobedience was so slight that anyone holding these beliefs could reasonably be expected to pay it. The only reason why we do not blame the Germans very much for failing to stop the extermination of the Jews is that the penalties for trying are known to have been terrible. But if an Englishman in 1961 genuinely thought that the only way to preserve the world from nuclear annihilation was to trespass upon Wethersfield base at the cost of a few months in gaol, he was surely as right to do so as the judge was right to impose the specified penalty. It is disturbing that the then Attorney-General, and many others, failed to recognise this.

(iii) PRISONS

"Some reform in prison conditions one noted since former imprisonment. Ordinary prisoners—women who had been there more than once and perhaps often, for the sundry petty offences that victims of bad environment are tempted to commit—were already saying: 'Things are very different here since you ladies began coming.' "

Dame Christabel Pankhurst,
Unshackled (Hutchinson, 1959), p. 112

"I must tell you about a brave stand Marilyn has made on K Wing. The whole wing had been quite artificially spruced up for the visit of some bigwigs, including a previous Governor of Holloway ... Marilyn was standing in the dinner queue when the party came by, and the ex-Governor touched a pretty tablecloth and said how nice it looked. 'Yes, Madam, it's the first time we've seen it,' spoke out Marilyn from the silent queue of waiting prisoners ... Ever since then, K Wing has had tablecloths!'

Jane Buxton and Margaret Turner,
Gate Fever (Cresset Press, 1962), p. 53

The improvement noted by Dame Christabel took place in 1908, 50 years before the participants in the Direct Action Committee's first Swaffham demonstrations launched the 20th century's latest middle-class invasion of the British penal system. Miss Buxton was in Holloway for six months in 1960, for refusing to sign recognisances after the Foulness demonstration. "Instead of just imagining it," she wrote, "I have now myself tasted the experience of belonging to a lower caste."

In men's prisons there had been similar middle-class invasions, but at different periods. When Allen Skinner was in Brixton in 1917 prisoners were not allowed to speak to each other, and were required to turn their faces to the wall if the Governor went by. He emerged half-starved, and broken in health. When he returned to Brixton with a group of Swaffham prisoners in 1958, the Governor asked to see the party, and murmured "That must have been a terrible experience" when Skinner told him that he had been in Brixton 41 years previously. There had certainly been changes. "In the First World War," Skinner later told John Gale of the *Observer*,[*] "a considerable proportion of the warders were really very nasty pieces of work: a strong vein of sadism. I hadn't that feeling at all this time." On the other hand: "Food at Brixton was just horrible. Plentiful in contrast to the First World War but terribly badly cooked ... The whole feeling you have in prison is one of squalor. After two months of that I went the next day into a Lyons teashop and I thought how *gracious* it was."

The ordeal of the No Conscription Fellowship in 1916–18 led to the publication in 1922 of the 700-page report, *English Prisons Today*, edited by Stephen Hobhouse and Fenner Brockway.[†] It

[*] January 14, 1962. [†] London, 1922.

was compiled mainly from questionnaires completed by 290 ex-prisoners and 50 officials (since when the Prison Commissioners have imposed a "silence rule" on their own staff). This "bible for reformers", as Margery Fry called it, put an end to such in-humanities as the silence rule, broad arrows and the convict crop. After the Second World War another questionnaire was completed by 100 ex-prisoners and published in 1948 under the title *Gaol Delivery* (edited by 'Mark Benney').* The Prison Medical Reform Council, which had been constituted during the war by conscientious objectors, saw some of its proposals embodied in the 1948 Criminal Justice Act. But by the 1960s informed public opinion was aware that much was still wrong with the prison system. The effects of the post-war overcrowding had begun to filter through the Home Office security net, and though internal discipline, it seemed, had been relaxed somewhat since the 1940s, there was little evidence that the prisons had kept pace with the advance in the population's own standard of living and conception of human dignity. A well-written memoir by a prisoner—Peter Wildeblood's *Against the Law*,† published in 1955, was an early example—found a receptive public. But just as the experiences of conscientious objectors could expect, at least while the war was actually being fought, only limited attention and sympathy, so the experience of individual middle-class offenders, especially if they belonged to other denigrated and supposedly minority groups like homosexuals, could be officially dismissed as highly coloured and unrepresentative.

It was not so easy to dismiss out of hand the reports brought back by the nuclear disarmers. It is impossible to calculate how many man- or woman-weeks were spent in gaol by demonstrators or plotters of demonstrations between 1958 and 1964, but it certainly runs into thousands. Miss Pat Arrowsmith, one of the most frequently sentenced, received six separate prison sentences. Moreover, although sit-downers were a comparatively small proportion of CND's total support and prisoners (apart from overnight remands) an even smaller proportion of the sit-downers, people who went to prison for Ban the Bomb activities represented something new. Their cause was supported by at least a fifth of the population, and even their method of advocating it was more widely tolerated than many politicians are inclined to suppose. The Gallup Poll in September 1961, after the Committee of 100's Trafalgar Square sit-down, asked: "If another sit-down demonstration is planned, should the authorities take stronger action, such as using force, to get the sitters to move on, or ignore them while it remains peaceful?" The answers were: Should act as last time, 21 p.c.; should take stronger action, 28 p.c.; should

* Longmans, 1948.   † Weidenfeld & Nicolson.

172

ignore them, 37 p.c.; don't know, 14 p.c. This may be compared with a Commonwealth Research Bureau survey which found 27 p.c. of its sample expressing favourable opinions of sit-down protesters, as against 36 p.c. opposed to Britain's possession of her atomic bombs.

The nuclear disarmers who went to prison could thus feel, not merely that they represented a righteous remnant within society, but that a substantial part of society itself sympathised with them. They entered prison, or some of them did, not with the highly charged emotional apparatus of the individual conscientious objector in a country at war, but with the more quizzical, irreverent outlook of an experimental research group. They felt, corporately, that they ought not to be in prison, and felt under no obligation to accept martyrdom when inside. They had no reason to feel guilty about being shut up while friends in the Forces were being shot at. It was peacetime.

Nevertheless, in assessing what nuclear disarmers had to say about their prison experience, it should be remembered that they did as a group have some characteristics which may have affected their account. They belonged, by and large, to the educated middle class or socially mobile working class. Their standards of expectation, alike in personal hygiene and social intercourse, were very different from those of their fellow-prisoners, who were often mentally inadequate as well as socially under-privileged. At the same time they possessed in common the nonconformist streak which had made them demonstrators in the first place. Most of them could have said, as Terence Morris records a "highly intelligent prisoner" telling him in Pentonville:

"The most terrible thing about prison is that no one, at any time, has ever been concerned about me as an individual."*

The nuclear disarmers were not only intensely concerned about themselves as individuals; the subject matter of their campaign entailed a missionary attempt to persuade others to exercise their own individuality. Their time in prison was therefore not only spent on sharp and hypersensitive observation of their own immediate surroundings. They had time to reflect at the Government's expense on the possibilities and limitations inherent in the prison system itself. Laurens Otter, while serving at Eastchurch Open Prison a six-month sentence for his part in one of the 1960 demonstrations at Foulness, was even asked to deliver a paper on prison reform—a difficult task, since he believed that prisons were essentially evil and incapable of being reformed.

"It, however, made me start by asking the jackpot question—

* *Pentonville* (Routledge & Kegan Paul, 1963), p. 167.

what, given the aim of maintaining existing society, is the point of prisons? How far can one make prisons sane, without thereby making people sane enough to wish to overthrow existing society?"*

Not all the nuclear disarmers went as far as this, and indeed, the first that the general newspaper-reading public heard of their experiences was from a report, *Inside Story*,† published in February 1963, which accepted and praised the official policy outlined in *Prisons and Borstals* (4th ed. HMSO 1960), but sought to point out certain discrepancies between the policy and the practice in the 12 English prisons of which the 33 contributors to the report had experience. Their terms of imprisonment varied between one week and eight months, with an average term of 11 weeks, and the wealth of detail in the report, though couched in language less dispassionate than Consumers' Association English, gave it the éclat of a *Which?* on the prison service—and a *Which?* that failed to nominate a best buy. Inevitably, newspapers' attention was concentrated on the more specific or comic of the report's accusations, like the assertion (hotly disputed by the Prison Commissioners) that porridge oats had been dispensed from bags labelled "Grade III Pigmeal", and that one prisoner at Holloway who had lost her toothbrush was advised by an officer to steal someone else's.

Inside Story begins by taking sentences from the Government's declared policy for prisons and borstals and setting them against the reality which the prisoners found. Thus:

". . . responsibility should be strengthened not only in relation to their life in prison but to the life outside to which they must return; they should be encouraged to keep in touch with their families and remember their responsibilities to them and to think constructively about what they are going to make of the future."

(In fact the present system would seem to be designed to destroy family responsibilities and social relations. Little encouragement is given to prepare for release, and such assistance as is given tends to be official and impersonal and consequently ineffectual.)

General judgements of this nature are then supplemented by 115 proposals on 14 particular subjects. I select an example from each section to display both the strengths and the weaknesses of the nuclear disarmers' approach to prison life:

Medical

"We have known a case where a man was imprisoned for four months and had a nervous breakdown halfway through his

* *Anarchy*, November 1961, p. 259. † Prison Reform Council.

sentence but the symptoms were ignored in prison. His general practitioner could have told the MO of the man's history of mental illness but was not contacted until a friendly prisoner did so on his release and ensured that the man was sent to mental hospital. This sort of tragedy could be avoided if the MO always checked with the prisoner's outside doctor (in complete confidence) and asked for medical notes in the case of invalids. This would also ensure that people on a special diet could continue it in prison and avoid a great deal of unnecessary suffering."

Social and Mental Welfare

"In Holloway there is one Welfare Officer to cope with 400 prisoners, which is inevitably quite inadequate. She should have two if not more assistants."

Hygiene

"At present cells are often dirty when the prisoner first goes into them; chamber pots are smelly and rubbish buckets on the landings are filthy. Inspection of cells, bathrooms and recesses and supervision of wing cleaners could ensure that everything was in a healthy state, as there is no shortage of prison labour. There should never be any shortage of cleaning materials—such as exists everywhere at present. Brushes, soap, non-poisonous disinfectants and detergents must be freely available on the wings and in the kitchens. In Stafford prisoners were told to scrub floors with their nailbrushes as no others were provided. In Bedford and Brixton kit inspections required that toothbrushes were laid out on the lids of chamber pots. All of this is in direct contradiction to paragraph 21 of chapter 8 of the Policy Statement which says: 'A high standard of cleanliness is enforced, both in the premises and in the persons of inmates.' "

Clothing

"The embarrassing practice sometimes employed of asking women prisoners to display their knickers before giving them in for laundering should be abolished."

Food

"Some kitchen officers (as in Holloway and Brixton) do not appear to understand the principles of dietetics. The fact that vegetarians are often given jam as a substitute for meat and the value of pulse foods is not appreciated, leads us to have no confidence in their ability to provide a balanced diet for the prisoner in general. When rations are so poor, a proper understanding of food values is essential."

175

Letters, Visits, etc.

"The letter-censoring officer should never be the same person as the landing officer, and anything the officer learns from a letter or during a visit should be confidential and not used as taunts and jibes against a prisoner. This has happened at Holloway, Brixton, and Stafford."

Libraries

"In many prisons there is a prejudice against left-wing newspapers and journals. *Peace News* was sometimes withheld at Stafford and even the *Observer* was frowned upon in Drake Hall. Political pressure of this kind must be removed.

Discipline

"We appreciate that the open prison is a great step forward in the penal system, but the necessary atmosphere of trust which can do so much for the self-respect of the inmate may be entirely destroyed by an over-disciplined administration. This is the case at Eastchurch, which is run on the lines of a military detention centre and seems to be staffed largely by ex-military personnel. Four formal parades a day, four spot-checks in between and the marching of prisoners in military fashion typify the discipline that is imposed, humiliating the prisoners and denying them all sense of responsibility."

Work and Pay

"Pay should be comparable to rates paid outside, with a deduction by the Prison Commission for board. The remaining wage can be divided for (1) an allowance for dependents (rather than the family having to claim National Assistance); (2) recompense to the victim; (3) saving for the prisoner's release (to prevent his being stranded without money and resorting to crime again); and (4) provision for his personal needs in prison.

"We would question the conclusions arrived at in the White Paper 'Penal Practice in a Changing Society' (para 74) that 'it cannot provide a general solution of the prison earnings problem until the general level of productivity and efficiency of prison industry approximates much more closely to that of outside industry.' . . . Prison industries must be brought into line with modern methods, but until they are they will never 'pay their way' or compete with outside industries in productivity or efficiency, and prison workers should not be penalised because of it."

Information to prisoners

"Special provisions must be made for prisoners who do not understand English . . . It has happened that a foreign prisoner who did not understand what was going on went quite berserk with fear, was put in a padded cell and then threatened with Broadmoor."

Miscellaneous

"At most prisons a special show is arranged for the visits of Prison Commissioners. Tablecloths are put out, special meals are served and little extras like condiments and water appear on the meal tables, which are not usually considered important. This window dressing does not give the Commissioners a proper picture and only increases the prisoners' contempt for what he considers to be the dishonesty of the authorities. Surprise visits are the only way of seeing prisons in their normal rout-ine."

Another topic mentioned by the report was the administration of justice within prison. Michael Randle lost several days re-mission for making a noise in support of a cell-mate, suffering from acute diarrhoea, whom a prison officer had refused to allow out to a lavatory. The apparent injustice done to Randle sur-vived both an appeal to the Deputy Governor and an "impartial investigation" by the Home Office. On another occasion, Randle had a letter to his wife stopped without his knowledge. He was told that in it he had been "insulting to the authorities". He had in fact observed, apropos of Mr Macmillan's television appear-ance after the Nassau agreement, that the PM looked as if he was "more than slightly drunk". On this occasion he tried an appeal to the visiting magistrates, also without avail. Nevertheless, his persistence with the Scrubs' conception of justice brought him one short-lived triumph. One day the Principal Officer took it into his head to decorate the bleak central hall of the Scrubs with posters. His choice included a poster of the Aldermaston AWRE. Randle went to the Deputy Governor and asked whether there was any reason, if this were permitted, why the nuclear disarmers in prison should not be allowed to put up a few CND and Com-mittee of 100 posters too. The Deputy Governor could not think up a reason quickly enough, and in his next letter Randle asked for some posters to be sent in. This, however, brought the matter to the attention of the Governor, who sent for Randle and said that he had thought of another solution: all the posters should be taken down.

It is hard to determine the effects of the publication of *Inside Story*, but its impact was very considerable. Within a few hours the Home Office and the Prison Commissioners rejected the report as "unfair and inaccurate", and since the report had been in their possession for six months before publication, their response was presumably considered. Mr Henry Brooke, in Parliament, rejected utterly two specific assertions: that prisoners' porridge was made from Grade III pigmeal and that women in Holloway were compelled to submit to VD tests. Both accusations seem to have been based on justifiable misunderstandings: the first on the assumption by nuclear disarmers working in a prison kitchen that the stencil-mark on the outside of a sack reflected the contents, and the second on a failure to convey to prisoners what their rights were. (Jane Buxton and Margaret Turner had other more serious criticisms of the medical services in Holloway, and it is thought that improvements have been made. The National Health Service does not operate in prisons. As a result, the prison medical service tends to reflect the attitudes and standards of the institution itself.)

In the Commons debate on March 12, 1963 Mr Anthony Greenwood, a well-known supporter of CND, remarked:

"Whatever one may think of civil disobedience—and I am as passionately opposed to it as anyone in this House—it has brought into contact with the prison system men and women of high intelligence, of the utmost probity, and with a profound sense of social responsibility."

By this time the Home Office had provided newspapers with extensive facilities for investigating the nuclear disarmers' complaints, and the *Guardian* alone published five long features on different prisons during March 1963, confirming some of the points made and rejecting others. Curiously enough the writer of two of the articles, Harold Jackson, the paper's assistant news editor, had himself been in Wormwood Scrubs as a conscientious objector 10 years previously, and there developed a sharp dialogue across the years between him and the authors of the report. The notorious slopping-out recess in the Scrubs, Mr Jackson said, had changed "from a vaguely lighted cream and green hole to a reasonably airy half-tiled area that not only looks sanitary but smells it". To this Colin Smart, the Ruskin College criminology student who was Chairman of the *Inside Story* group, replied:

"Was Mr Jackson in Wormwood Scrubs when the bright and airy lavatory recess overflowed with excreta, overspilling on to the ground floor where prisoners were being served with breakfast?"

To this the only possible reply was "No". But the articles brought out clearly enough that little social rehabilitation can be done in prison until a lot more money is spent both on the buildings and the staff (Strangeways, Manchester, a packed-out nick long since condemned, has one welfare officer to every 450 or so prisoners); that the food is about as good as can be expected for 14s. 6d. per prisoner per week, of which 1s. 3d. is the cost at growers' prices of the food supplied from prison farms (1962/3 figures); and that while society itself is still in a muddle about what it expects from its penal system, the prisons and their staff will reflect the muddle. As often, the Prison Commissioners themselves came out of the inquiry rather well. There is the celebrated story of Mr Duncan Fairn (a Commissioner) and Miss April Carter's jeans ... Miss Carter, the first Secretary of the Direct Action Committee, was arrested in December 1958 and dispatched to Holloway wearing the jeans in which she had been demonstrating. On arrival, the jeans were removed on grounds that they were unladylike. Holloway is—or was—a chilly prison, and Miss Carter's need of her jeans was reported to Mr Fairn by a fellow-Quaker. Twenty-four hours later she had them back.

A less-explored side of the nuclear disarmers' incarceration has been their effect on officers and fellow-prisoners. Since officers and prisoners are silent on the subject, there are only the disarmers' estimates to go on. But clearly, the presence in prison of people who could have got out at any time by consenting to be bound over attracted the interest of other inmates. Miss Turner records:

" 'It's like the suffragettes,' they say. They often say we'll never get anywhere with our campaign because it's hopeless trying to fight the established set-up, but generally they think we're right about the bomb and they would be with us if they felt it would do any good" (*op. cit.*, p. 88).

In men's prisons there was not such a ready and suitable comparison to hand as the suffragettes. Colin Smart was listening to a group in Stafford Gaol uttering "the usual abuse about us and the movement in general" when

"the toughest man in the prison turned and told the person to 'belt up', arguing that it was a matter of principle and given our situation he would have done the same. He gave the analogy: 'It's like if one of your mates grasses on yer, it's a matter of principle to do him, ain't it; it's the same thing, like?' "*

As Terence Morris brings out strongly in his book on Pentonville, "both officers and prisoners are heirs to a common culture, that of the urbanised working class". Smart says that the six nuclear disarmers in Stafford were not taken seriously by the officers until they had carried out a hunger strike at the forthcoming execution of a murderer in the prison. "Not only did practically every officer in the place come to the library during the next few days and discuss the motives for the hunger strike, but they wanted to see the action in relation to the Campaign."

* *Isis*, January 23, 1963.

Many nuclear disarmers must have found it difficult to approximate closely enough to the culture of their environment for this much notice to be taken of them in prison. For instance, even those who were not vegetarian to begin with were shrewd enough to realise that they usually got a more palatable diet by registering as such. But by committing self-consistent acts of disobedience within prison they could achieve a collective effect. The weekly fruit ration in Stafford often took the form of an "Outspan" South African orange. The group refused this (it is an offence to refuse food) and were joined by the coloured prisoners. They were naturally labelled "nigger-lovers" thereafter, and both for this and for being pacifists were furiously abused one day by a middle-aged prisoner. They thought no more about it, but a week later the man apologised in front of other prisoners, joined the group in refusing South African oranges, and with unprecedented cheerfulness sat down at table with them, and also with three coloured prisoners.

Implicit in the assumptions of the writers of *Inside Story* are two possibly incompatible beliefs: that prison is bad because it is the negation of human freedom and opportunity to develop in community; and that prisoners are there to be "helped". The point was well made by "C.W." in *Anarchy*:*

"When Colin Smart recommends 'making psychiatric treatment the basis of any sentence', he forgets that he too is a 'criminal'. An American friend of ours was incarcerated in a federal penitentiary during the war for his opposition to it. The war-resisters started a hunger-strike against racial segregation in the mess-hall. They were taken off to the psychiatric ward and harangued by the psychiatrist about their dubious motivation. 'Sure,' our friend replied, 'sure I want to rape my grandmother. Now about this segregation issue . . .'"

The fact that one goes to prison because one has broken the law, and for no other reason, is not only a considerable protection for the individual against excessive "psychological" interference; it is also, in the long run, a protection against bad laws. There is no point in violating the Official Secrets Act as a gesture if the courts and the penal system are going to be more interested in the motivation of the violator than in the public significance of his action. However, merely by concentrating attention on the revolting environment and confused philosophies of British prisons, the nuclear disarmers helped to bring the public up against the fact which is recognised in official policy but widely disregarded in practice and in ordinary people's assumptions: that punishment, deterrence and retribution alike begin and end with the

* November, 1961.

loss of liberty; and that most of the reform that can seriously be expected is best achieved by reproducing inside the walls, or by the hostel system, the mixed, open, welfare society which it is our ambition to achieve outside. Essentially, the nuclear disarmers' ambition, in this as in other matters, was the Conservative Party Conference's nightmare: the creation of prisons so attractive that inadequate people would commit crimes in order to be admitted, and liberty-loving criminals stay law-abiding in order to be excluded.

(iv) CIVIL DEFENCE

"RAF Vulcan and Valiant bombers and four American are taking part in a navigation and nuclear bombing contest over Britain. London, Glasgow, Birmingham, Manchester, and other large cities will be the targets. A cup will be awarded to the winners."

Daily Telegraph, May 19, 1958

One of the conclusions to be drawn from the public opinion surveys on nuclear weapons is that most people in Britain have at some time or other given more than a passing thought to "the next war"—what would happen to them personally if it occurred, and how it should be prevented from occurring. It is not immediately relevant to inquire whether the conclusions they have drawn have been correct, or variable over the years. But it is relevant to the British nuclear debate, latent for 13 years and intensive for six, to inquire whether official actions and announcements have flattered or insulted the common sense of the public. In 1950, Mrs Bessie Braddock's publicly expressed concern about black-out curtains suggested that if the Government had then set out all the ascertainable probabilities about the effects of the Third World War—assuming that it knew what the probabilities were—the country would have had a collective heart-attack. Again, Mr Philip Noel-Baker, MP, has recalled that in 1955 "the Home Office briefed journalists to the effect that London could take eight nuclear bombs and still survive".* Yet by March 1958, 80 p.c. of those who ventured an opinion to the Gallup Poll believed that less than half the population of Britain would survive a nuclear war, and 16 p.c. believed that none of it would.† And although the Home Office, game to the last, launched its 1961 Civil Defence recruiting campaign under the slogan "There will be millions of survivors", the effect was rather spoilt a few days later by the Minister of Defence (Mr Watkinson) telling a Young Conservative audience

* Hansard, March 1, 1963.   † Cf. p. 101.

that in the next war a back-garden air-raid shelter was not going to do much good and that modern weapons could wipe out civilisation. But officially, not only the Conservative Government but the Labour Opposition too still agreed with the Home Office. A recent motion on Civil Defence carried in the House of Commons* commended the work of the 600,000 men and women engaged in Civil Defence in Great Britain, and believed "that they have a vital and effective part to play in the defence forces of these islands even in a nuclear age".

This phrasing indicates one of the main points at issue between the official side and the nuclear disarmers. Long before the CND was formed, pacifists like Professor Kathleen Lonsdale and Dr Alex Comfort argued from the experience of Hiroshima and Nagasaki that there could be no civil defence, as it had been understood in 1939–45, in an atomic war; and claimed that the Government only pretended otherwise in order to silence awkward questions about its preparations to fight a war which the country could not survive. Accordingly the pacifists and later the CND set out to explain to the public in a popular form and in specific detail "what H-bomb war would be like" (to quote the title of the "Black Paper" published by *Peace News* in 1962). Their assessment of the probabilities differed in important details from that of the Government, and still more from semi-official vulgarisations like the WVS One-in-Five talks, but it was not differences about details which generated the steam behind the nuclear disarmers' efforts in this field: it was their conviction that they were doing a job which the Government was deliberately, and for disreputable reasons, neglecting.

Thus, even if Civil Defence had been presented by the Government to the people merely as a conceivably useful rescue service in an admittedly desperate situation, the CND might still have stood out against it on the grounds that its usefulness was being grossly exaggerated. But the Campaign's opposition was clinched by the implicit or explicit allotment to Civil Defence of a supporting role in the defence of the realm "even in a nuclear age". This role carried with it the unspoken suggestion that people who joined the voluntary Civil Defence forces were somehow lending credibility to the British, or the Western, nuclear deterrent. Their willingness to serve could be interpreted, both by the British Government and by any potential enemy, as willingness to stand fast if need arose. On this interpretation, the 600,000 did their bit by enabling Sir Alec Douglas-Home to say (as he was reported over the Berlin crisis on December 14, 1961): "The British people are prepared to be blown to atomic dust if necessary."

* March 1, 1963.

The nuclear disarmers, in short, criticised Civil Defence as a double fraud perpetrated by the Government, the first on the British people, who were to be kept happy by being made to believe that thermo-nuclear war could be tolerated, and the second on Britain's allies and enemies, who were to be impressed by her sang-froid. On the 1963 Aldermaston March a third critique was added. An anonymous group, apparently belonging to the anarchosyndicalist wing of the Committee of 100, obtained and published officially secret details both of the NATO Fallex nuclear exercise in the autumn of 1962, and of the Regional Seats of Government organisation by which Britain was to be administered in the aftermath of a nuclear attack. The first disclosure, the bulk of which had already been made in Germany by *Der Spiegel*, only confirmed CND's accustomed forecasts of the chaos and huge (15–20 million) mortality that would follow even a comparatively modest nuclear attack on Britain. The second disclosure, however, set the Campaign off on a new tack. From the list of names of the designated future occupants of a typical "RSG" it was deduced that power in post-war Britain would be exercised exclusively by a non-elected junta of soldiers and civil servants: "It is colonels and principal officers who will rule after the Bomb drops, not MPs or councillors."

One of the last administrative acts of Mr John Profumo was to reply, through his private secretary, to a constituent of his in Stratford-on-Avon, Mr H. B. Marlow, who had inquired whether there would be a place for him and his family in the RSG nearest his home. Mr Profumo forwarded Mr Marlow's letter to the Home Office on April 29, 1963, and on May 30 Mr Monty Woodhouse, Under-Secretary of State, replied explaining that "these headquarters" were intended to control life-saving operations and co-ordinate essential services after attack, not to ensure the survival of "some specially selected *élite*". On May 31 Mr Profumo's secretary sent the Home Office reply on to Mr Marlow, "as Mr Profumo is at present away and asked me not to delay sending it to you."

Altogether, in the last six years, the sections of the governmental machine entrusted with organising civil defence have had to fight a difficult guerilla war with public opinion. In detail, some of the criticism directed against them has seemed to them unfair, and some—especially that arising out of the RSG disclosures—merely silly. But in general, the Government has had only itself to blame, and the essence of the case against it was put years ago by Professor Blackett in an article criticising the basis of "bluff and politics" which underlay the 1957 and 1958 Defence White Papers.* A deterrent posture relying

* *New Statesman*, December 5, 1959.

wholly on independent air power, Professor Blackett argued, only made sense if one was prepared, by civil defence, to be attacked with the same weapons as one was preparing for the enemy. But of course, in the thermo-nuclear age, Britain of all countries could not afford to be attacked by such weapons. Even Britain's own "independent" thermo-nuclear stockpile, trivial as it is by comparison with the force that the Soviet Union could mobilise against her, would probably be capable of extinguishing all life on this island. (Some 700 megatons might be needed. Russia and America between them certainly possess at least 70,000 megatons.)

Quite early in the fifties, if not in the late forties, the decision was taken not to provide Britain with any Civil *Defence* at all. The sum spent on Civil Defence in 1963/4 was £23 million. This sum, which is 50 p.c. higher than it was three years ago, has been chiefly spent on establishing alternative systems of communication in the hope that some organised life would be possible after a major attack. The sum represents just over 1 p.c. of Britain's total defence expenditure, and at most 10 p.c. of the expenditure attributable to the "independent" nuclear deterrent. At a rough calculation, to provide Britain with her own version of what Dr Herman Kahn describes as "an adequate civil defence programme for America" would cost a sum which equals current British Civil Defence expenditure for 1,000 years. (Dr Kahn budgeted $200 billion over a 15-year period for the shelters, stockpiles, warning, and evacuation mechanisms of a system which "probably cannot be destroyed without the attacker using weapons that either are or come perilously close to being Doomsday machines". But he does not consider the cost of making his system also proof against the cheap biological and chemical weapons which are now available as alternatives to thermo-nuclear warheads.)*

It is difficult for any Government to pretend that it attaches importance to an enterprise on which it spends only derisory sums of money. But before CND, the orders of magnitude involved in nuclear weapons were not widely enough understood for people to be aware just how derisory the sums were. In July 1954—the month after Coventry City Council had refused to discharge its Government-imposed Civil Defence responsibilities —Michael Mitchell Howard, later chief marshal of several Aldermaston Marches and Canon Collins' rival for the chairmanship of CND in 1963, resigned his post with the Crusade for World Government to devote himself to campaigning against Civil Defence in Islington. He was quoted by *Peace News*:†

* *On Thermonuclear War* (Oxford, 1960), pp. 516–18. † July 2, 1954.

"The real danger in Civil Defence lies in the illusion of security which it tries to foster, and in its acceptance of H-bombs as a means of settling disputes . . . It induces people to accept that the only answers to the H-bomb are bigger and better bombs and deeper and larger shelters."

The Government, of course, had no intention of building deeper and larger shelters, and over the ensuing years the main change in its calculations consisted of a gradual upping of the level of casualties to be expected from a nuclear attack on Britain. In January 1957 the Senior Civil Emergency Planning Committee of NATO expected a million dead outright. In September 1962, Fallex '62 yielded 15 million dead in the first few days. But in the intervening period, the other limitations of the Government's approach began to show through. It was not only that very little money was spent on Civil Defence. The calibre of the personnel involved, from the top administration to the volunteer recruits, reflected the sums spent. Even in Parliament Civil Defence was normally only debated when an enthusiastic private Member found time for the subject. Hence, inevitably, the initiative passed to the Government's anti-nuclear critics, who were given plenty of material for both their anxiety and their taste for sick humour to work on. There have been times in the last few years when the *New Statesman* could have filled its "This England" column with little else but Civil Defence. It would have been a duller decade if we had not all been able to comfort ourselves with the reflection that Puddle-town's Civil Defence equipment consisted of seven stretchers, nine blankets, and a billiard table; that Oxford CD Committee had spent £25,000 on a set of artificial ruins to practise on; that "D for Danger" would be tapped out in Morse on dustbin lids during an exercise in Carlisle; and that the designated burial officer of the City of London had been officially advised: "Since the introduction of the hydrogen bomb the whole question of burial of the dead has had to be reconsidered, but up to the present time, nothing satisfactory has been formulated." And when true stories ran out, there was still room for the *ben trovato*. The report published after the Cuba crisis in 1962 that the Government's proposed fall-out shelters in Central London in-cluded the Fleet Street men's lavatory stirred the CND monthly *Sanity* to a series of deadpan comments:

"The Home Office has apparently taken a great deal of trouble to protect the health of those who use the shelter. A colourful poster on the wall gives the address of London hospitals which provide free treatment. There is evidently an intention to provide inmates of the shelter with protective clothing, since a notice warns them not to forget to adjust their dress before leaving . . ."*

Women Campaigners were especially incensed with the Home Office. Already more united and emotionally stirred against nuclear weapons than the male half of the population, women were also the main targets of the Home Office's famous handbook on the hydrogen bomb, with its suggestions for soaking curtains in borax and whitewashing windows during the period (popularly expected to last precisely four minutes) between the warning of an attack and its arrival. The alienation of young professional women from the whole enterprise was further guaranteed by the Government's entrusting of its huge popularisation task to the Women's Voluntary Service, a section of which set out to see that "One in Five" of the nation's womanhood knew how to construct a refuge room and in general to confront the emergency with confident docility. CND, when it was established, quickly became a clearing house for complaints about the unscientific optimism which was displayed by many of the local WVS One-in-Five speakers. Some, it seemed, would have found it difficult to distinguish between a geiger counter and a Jaeger counter, and were certainly not to be trusted with the mathematics involved in explaining how, and why, a properly constructed refuge room in the right sort of house might reduce radiation fortyfold (a scientific estimate which itself had to be radically revised downwards a year or two later).

The gaff was blown on the WVS in 1959 by Mrs Olive Gibbs, an Oxford City Labour councillor, elected Acting Chairman of CND after Canon Collins' resignation in April 1964, who attended one of the lectures with her husband, on being invited to do so by a note brought home from school by their young son. With Dr Antoinette Pirie, an expert on fall-out, Mrs Gibbs compiled a memorandum† comparing what the WVS speaker said with the probable reality. Thus: "The longest you will have to stay in a refuge room is 48 hours . . . Radioactive dust takes two or three days to travel . . . If you get a burn cover it with sticking plaster . . . Radiation sickness is a kind of nasty tummy ache . . . Paint your windows with a mixture of whitewash and curdled milk to prevent blast." The CND women's comments pointed out, for example, that radioactive dust travelled at the same rate as the wind, so that a bomb dropped on Birmingham could affect Oxford in three hours; and quoted the *Bulletin of Atomic Scientists* on the aftermath of a nuclear attack: "At the end of one week external radiation would drop sufficiently for limited outdoor movement, but it would appear wise to live in the

* December 1962.   † Circulated by the Women's Co-operative Guild, August 26, 1959.

186

basement for the first month . . . At the end of one year, a return to ordinary life would be possible."

Dr Pirie had "a local WVS high-up" to tea, and recorded in a letter to Jacquetta Hawkes (January 21, 1960):

"She swings to and fro, saying: (a) they were themselves taught one thing but were not allowed to teach it as it was too alarming. Their instructions come from the Home Office. They are not allowed to say anything about long-term radioactivity. (b) they are talking to simple uneducated people and can save some of them so it's worth while!"

The Atomic Scientists' Committee of the British Association was consulted, and expressed itself "disturbed" about the "grave dangers" inherent in the One-in-Five scheme, namely:

"The inevitable distortion when information is 'relayed' from speaker to speaker without adequate scientific knowledge.

"Over-simplification due to factual selection not based on adequate scientific knowledge."*

The subject, added the Committee, was so complex and the present state of knowledge so imprecise that simplification for explanation to lay audiences was more than usually dangerous. The Committee offered to arrange for a series of lectures to be given to selected WVS speakers.

Armed with this offer, the Women's Committee of the CND proposed a deputation to Lady Reading, Chairman of the WVS. The deputation was to be drawn from Dr Janet Aitken, ex-President of the Medical Women's International Association; Dame Alix Meynell, late Under-Secretary to the Board of Trade; Dr Pirie; Dr Patricia Lindop of the Nuffield Research Unit (to attend as the delegate of the British Association); Mrs Gibbs; Mrs John Collins; Miss Margaret Lane; and Miss Jacquetta Hawkes.

Lady Reading declined to see the deputation, on the grounds that the One-in-Five talks were "based on information obtained from official sources".†

Meanwhile, the authorities themselves were suffering from the lack of open and informed discussion on civil defence in Britain. "The politicians," complained General Sir Sidney Kirkman, Director-General of Civil Defence from 1954 to 1960, in 1961, "have not done enough to educate the public, and

* In a letter to Dr Patricia Lindop, February 15, 1960.   † In a letter to Jacquetta Hawkes, March 11, 1960. It is instructive to recall that two years later the Prime Minister consented to receive a very similar deputation from the Women's Committee. Five of its members were the same people whom Lady Reading had snubbed. See p. 90.

that's the first thing they should have done." Nor had they done much to educate themselves. There has been no British equivalent of the hearings on the biological and environmental effects of nuclear war, conducted in Washington before the Holifield Committee in June 1959. The committee considered the likely effects of a 1,146 megaton attack on the United States in one day (which was then well within the Soviet Union's capabilities). For the whole of the United States, the casualty list was 47 million dead or fatally injured, and 19 million surviving injured, with poor life expectation. In New York, which was allotted two 10-megaton bombs, half the city's 13 million population were dead within two months, with most of the rest surviving injured and irradiated. It was pointed out that by 1965, the scale of the attack in all-out nuclear war would be up to 20,000 megatons, which according to Dr Kahn would kill 160 million Americans if not protected by shelter, evacuation, or both.

In Britain, though the scale of an attack would naturally be smaller, little advantage could be expected from any distinction that might be made between civil and military targets. A 130-megaton attack on targets west of London would kill at least half the city's population from fall-out alone, even if they had provided themselves with the Government's recommended means of protection. But as late as March 1961 the Defence Correspondent of the *Daily Mail*, who was given good facilities for a series of "inside" stories on Civil Defence, was allowed to write:

"In cold statistics applied to the worst case possible in Britain —a big H-bomb dead centre on London—a four-minute warning followed by a universal dive for the simplest form of shelter would result in more than three-quarters of the 8 million population living through the initial holocaust."

As far as can be ascertained, the British authorities have tended throughout to take the optimistic rather than the pessimistic view in their contingency planning.* They have assumed —against the weight of American opinion—that the dropping of H-bombs on built-up areas will not create on an unprecedented scale the kind of firestorm that killed 135,000 people in one night at Dresden in 1945. They have assumed a comparatively small scale of attack. They have assumed several days "strategic warning"—time enough to evacuate 9½ million people (mothers and children, the old and the sick) from cities to "reception areas". They have also not allowed any mere

* Cf. de Kadt, *British Defence Policy and Nuclear War* (Frank Cass, 1964); and Stonier, *Nuclear Disaster* (Penguin, 1964). The latter book includes an excellent bibliography.

nuclear crisis to activate the Civil Defence system. During Cuba week, though Civil Defence was put on the alert in several American cities, the head of Civil Defence for the London region did not even suspend the weekend leave of his key staff, and indeed, on Saturday, October 27, two CND members in Hampstead telephoned nine Civil Defence numbers, central and local, without getting any reply from most or information from any. Nor was the 9d. booklet (Civil Defence Handbook No. 10: *Advising the Householder on Protection Against Nuclear Attack*), which was prepared before the Cuba crisis, put on public sale until January 1963. Naturally, in the middle of a crisis, drastic steps such as evacuation or even mild steps such as the free and wholesale distribution of a booklet might have had the catalytic effect which mobilisation used to have in an earlier genre of war.

Answering Mr Anthony Greenwood in the Commons on December 5, 1962, Mr C. M. Woodhouse, Joint Under-Secretary of State to the Home Office, said that Civil Defence measures could be put into operation, "some in a few hours, some in a few days". But the Cabinet had decided that no measures should be taken in October 1962. He went on:

"I do not deny that there was a crisis. I do not deny—indeed, the Prime Minister himself said that we were very near the edge, but how near the edge is a matter for judgement, and the degree of proximity which would justify the mobilisation of this vast effort is also a matter for judgement."

The "vast effort" presumably referred to the Government's proposed evacuation of 9½ million people.

In view of the line taken, the Home Office has had some difficulty explaining its reluctance to circulate information even at a time when international tension has been relaxed. The reason proffered to Parliament by Mr Woodhouse was that the Home Office did not want to appear to be suggesting to the public that they should actually take immediately the measures suggested in the department's booklet, partly because their daily life would be dislocated, and partly because the advice contained in the booklet was liable to become out of date.

CND has always advised its members to worry away at Civil Defence in their localities. In July 1958 Miss Amabel Williams-Ellis told a Women Against the Bomb meeting: "Go and join the Civil Defence organisation in order to resign. And when you resign, make a bit of a bang about it." INDEC interpreted the advice in their own way, asking residents of Twickenham to vote against the chairman of the local Civil Defence Committee in a 1963 local election. INDEC's leaflet complained that the

Civil Defence Committee had refused to meet a group of anxious Twickenham residents; failed to reply to a letter inquiring where sandbags could be obtained, though official literature suggested that Twickenham would need 5 million in the event of nuclear war; and stated that Government literature on nuclear war was available through booksellers, when it was stocked by no shop or public library in the borough.

This kind of thing undoubtedly had a nuisance value over the years. It can hardly have had any appreciable effect on Civil Defence recruiting—the kind of people who join would be as likely to volunteer to spite CND as to be deterred from volunteering by its propaganda. But if only by publicising material from official (mostly American) sources which the Government has itself not been anxious to communicate to the public, the Campaign has a certain educational achievement to its credit, and several of its physicists and geneticists have done careful studies in particular fields (cf. for example, Dr Antoinette Pirie's book *Fall-out**). Strangely, the Campaign's human scientists seem to have contributed less, and of course the bulk of the national scientific effort has been directed to destruction rather than to survival. It has been Erich Fromm (a leading figure in the United States anti-nuclear movement) who has, with Michael Maccoby, returned a considered answer to the psychological speculation of Dr Kahn about the effect of thermonuclear war on the human psyche. (Fromm effectively quotes the historian Professor William L. Langer's assessment of the Black Death of 1348–49, which in most European towns killed over a third of the population in a few months: "It is perfectly clear that disaster and death threatening an entire community will bring on a mass emotional disturbance, based on a feeling of helpless exposure, disorientation, and common guilt.")†

The greater frankness which has recently been evident in Home Office statements and advertising on Civil Defence may well be a tribute to CND's efforts. The Spies for Peace episode at Easter 1963 at least demonstrated that with the British civilian population in the mood it has been in over the past six years, Civil Defence is not a field in which secrets are easy to keep. Too many people with too many non-military loyalties are involved, and a description of the RSG system duly figured in the Civil Defence advertisements of autumn 1963. But Mr Henry Brooke, who replaced Mr Butler at the Home Office in 1962, was himself as a Conservative backbencher quite a vocal

---

* Macgibbon & Kee, 1958. † Fromm & Maccoby, "The Question of Civil Defence", in *Breakthrough to Peace* (New Directions, New York, 1962). The findings of American "disaster studies" are fully reported in de Kadt (*op. cit.*) and Stonier (*op. cit.*).

critic on the subject of Civil Defence, and his well-known abhorrence of CND and all forms of social rebellion may not have prevented him from meeting the Campaign's grumbles in this one particular. In January 1964 Mr Brooke even asked for a report on the role the clergy could take in a nuclear emergency, after an enthusiastic Warwickshire vicar had produced a document in which he advocated an ecclesiastical chain of command, to take over immediate control of the clergy in the event of a nuclear attack. Regional Seats of Prayer, in fact.

"All lost! To prayers, to prayers. All lost!" During the fifties nuclear war finally developed into something which Britain could risk, or was prepared to risk, but not endure. Official reticence about the development at least preserved this country from the squalors of the 1961 fall-out shelter craze in the United States, with its solemn discussions of whether or not the occupants of a shelter would be morally entitled to shoot the neighbours if they tried to get in. Yet the Government's attitude also bore an unpleasant resemblance to the refusal of old-fashioned doctors to tell cancer patients the nature of their disease: not a fraud, so much as an insult to human dignity.

CHAPTER EIGHT

THE THEOLOGY OF THE UNTHINKABLE

"The day of the Lord will come as a thief in the night: in which the heavens will pass away with a great noise and the elements shall melt with fervent heat; the earth also and the works that are therein shall be burned up."

II Peter, Ch. 2, v. 10

"For all I know it is within the providence of God that the human race should destroy itself in this manner."

Archbishop Fisher,
The Fearful Choice (ed. Toynbee,
Gollancz, 1958), p. 43

Two or three years ago Mr Malcolm Muggeridge, never at a loss for a timely word of advice, is said to have suggested that if the Campaign for Nuclear Disarmament was wondering how to stage its next demonstration, it should gather its cohorts and march *en masse* to the churches on Christmas Day. The move, Mr Muggeridge went on, might give some of the backwoodsmen and backwoodswomen in the pews a nasty turn, but it would be bound to do more good than harm. Recording this opinion at the time, the *New Statesman*'s diarist said that he had put the suggestion to a member of the Committee of 100, who thought that it was cynical, insincere, and propagandist, and should on no account be adopted.

The reaction is as interesting as the suggestion. There is a persistent feeling in this country that protests against the use or possession of weapons of mass destruction ought to be a function, perhaps the chief function, of the Christian Church, and that the Church's failure to speak with one voice on this matter is a major cause of the mass absenteeism which has emptied so many pews in this century. At the same time there is, or has been until recently, a latent respect for the Churches, and a wistful hope that they might yet, against all precedent, start living up to their profession. This respect made it seem entirely natural for the Chairman of CND, from its inception until this year, to be a Canon of St Paul's; and correspondingly unnatural and indecent for a demonstration to be arranged within the context of an act of worship. (Though since the banners of Boy Scouts and Guards Regiments are generally acceptable in Christian sanctuaries, there is no very obvious reason why the symbols of an organisation that does at least seek peace and pursue it should not be accorded the same facilities.)

As CND became younger and more iconoclastic, this deferent attitude towards organised religion began to change. Canon Collins, his leadership widely questioned and his pronouncements giggled at by his own followers, found that CND was emulating the Church chiefly in one unwelcome respect: it was "by schisms rent asunder, by heresies distressed". In 1960 the growing secularity of the Campaign was recognised by the formation of a sub-group called "Christian CND" (swiftly followed by the "Christian Committee of 100"). These groups were charged with carrying nuggets of wisdom called "moral arguments" to people who thought on this level, while the Campaign as a whole got on with the serious business of strategy and politics. It seems doubtful whether the organisers of these groups realised the significance of what they were doing. By making their faith a department, a special interest, within CND itself they were reproducing in minuscule the same false doctrine of church and society which was—to their own distress—stultifying the prophetic function of Christians generally.

It is this function, thrown into relief by nuclear weapons, which I examine in this chapter. The scope of the inquiry must be narrowed to exclude the long and intractable argument among Christians about their participation in war, and concentrate instead on their efforts, in this country, to arrive as a Church at an adequate collective judgement on a particular war problem; albeit a problem which contains enough novel features to render partly obsolete the accumulated wisdom of centuries. All the same, some of these features were taking shape long before August 1945. In this context, it is useful to recall the life of George Bell.

Dr Bell was Bishop of Chichester from 1929 to his death in 1958. From 1933 on, he was an active and public opponent of Hitler and his persecution of the Jews. During the 1939–45 War, he also became an active and public opponent of the British policy of obliteration bombing, which reached its peak in the incineration of 135,000 people, mostly refugees, in Dresden in April 1945. Neither of these activities was much to the pleasure of the Governments in power at the time, and for his speeches in the House of Lords on British bombing policy Dr Bell was bitterly attacked. Since then the British and U.S. strategic bombing surveys, German eye-witnesses, and captured German documents, have revealed that even at the lowest level of self-interest, Dr Bell was justified in what he said: mass bombing of residential suburbs, and the great fire-raids on Hamburg and other German cities, not only failed to impede but in some respects actually stimulated the German war effort.

As the Archbishop of Canterbury's chaplain during the First World War, Dr Bell saw the Church in each nation, not least his own nation, becoming the Church of that particular nation and failing to strike any universal note. In November 1939 he quoted, as a warning against "Christian nationalism" the statements issued by German Protestant theologians and by British church leaders in September 1914. The Germans:

"With the deepest conviction we must attribute the responsibility for the terrible crime of this war to those who have long and secretly been spinning a web of conspiracy against Germany, which now they have flung over us in order to strangle us therein."

The British:

"It has not been a light thing for us to give our assent to the action of the Government of our country in this matter. But the facts of the case as we know them have made it impossible for us to do otherwise . . . We have taken our stand for international good faith, for the safeguarding of smaller nationalities, and for the upholding of the essential conditions of brotherhood among the nations of the world."

These essential conditions of brotherhood were not upheld when the Treaty of Versailles was negotiated in 1919, and for that misfortune "national Christianity" must take its share of the blame. It is doubtful whether the "supra-national" character of the Church even now carries much weight with public opinion in the West. There was no outcry when Nagasaki, one of the historic centres of Christianity in Japan, was selected as the target for the second atomic bomb, and it is hard to believe that the image which Southern Baptists in the United States have of the Soviet Union is seriously coloured by the millions of Christians—Baptists included—who live there.

On February 9, 1944, Dr Bell challenged the Government in the House of Lords on "Bomber" Harris' declared policy of "pulling out every town in Germany like teeth". He cited the 1922 Commission of Jurists' code of rules for aerial warfare: "Aerial bombardment for the purpose of terrorising the civilian population, of destroying or damaging private property not of military character, or of injuring non-combatants, is prohibited." He quoted Swedish papers in support of his thesis that the policy was not even achieving the desired result:

"On November 5 the Secretary of State for Air said that bombing in this way would continue until we had paralysed German war industries, disrupted their transport system and broken their will to war—again leaving the ethical issue aside. It is pure speculation. Up to now the evidence received from neutral countries is to the opposite effect."

He concluded:

"What we do in war—which after all lasts a comparatively short time—affects the whole character of peace, which covers a much longer period. The sufferings of Europe . . . hardly imaginable to those in this country who for the last five years have not been out of this island or had intimate association with Hitler's victims, are not to be healed by the use of power only, power exclusive and unlimited . . . We should so use power that it is always under the control of law."

British bombing policy was derived almost wholly from a

paper written in 1942 by Lord Cherwell, the Prime Minister's chief scientific adviser. According to Sir Charles Snow, it:

"described in quantitative terms the effect of a British bombing offensive on Germany in the next 18 months. The paper laid down a strategic policy. The bombing must be directed essentially against German working-class houses. Middle-class houses have too much space round them, and so are bound to waste bombs; factories and 'military objectives' had long since been forgotten, except in official bulletins, since they were much too difficult to find and hit. The paper claimed that—given a total concentration of effort on the production and use of bombing aircraft—it would be possible, in all the larger towns of Germany (that is, those with more than 50,000 inhabitants), to destroy 50 p.c. of all the houses."

Lord Cherwell's calculations exaggerated fivefold the destructive effect of his policy, since he did not yet have atomic weapons to play with. Sir Charles continues:

"It is possible that some time in the future people living in a more benevolent age than ours may turn over the official records and notice that men like us, men well-educated by the standards of the day, men fairly kindly by the standards of the day and often possessed of strong human feelings, made this kind of calculation. Such calculations, on a much larger scale, are going on at this moment in the most advanced societies we know. Will they say, as Roger Williams said of some of the Massachusetts Indians, that we were wolves with the minds of men? Will they say that we resigned our humanity? They will have the right."*

It goes without saying that Dr Bell's arguments against the fire-raids and area bombing of 1944–5 apply with equal or greater force to the dropping of atomic weapons on Hiroshima and Nagasaki. Once the war was over, however, the debate on this issue was muffled until it was revived by the manufacture of the British H-bomb and the founding of CND (which claimed Dr Bell as an early member). But now that a debate on nuclear weapons is proceeding within the Church at a fairly high level of technical and theological sophistication, it is salutary to recall what Dr Bell, who was not a pacifist, said about the predecessors of these weapons, and what support or lack of support he had at the time from his fellow-Christians.

The immediate post-war years saw the publication of one or two British Christian documents about nuclear weapons† but

* *Science and Government* (OUP, 1961), pp. 48–9. † Notably *The Era of Atomic Power* (British Council of Churches, 1946) and *The Church and the Atom* (Church of England, 1948).

it was not until 1954, when the country became aware that the decision had been taken to make a British H-bomb, that the pronouncements of bishops became frequent—albeit confusing. Dr Bell said in April 1954 that "the duty of man to his Creator, respect for nature and respect for fundamental human rights alike cry out for the complete prohibition of atomic weapons." The Bishop of Exeter, one of the Church of England's most respected moral theologians, told the Convocation of Canterbury (May 11, 1954):

"It would be immoral and unchristian if Britain were to use the hydrogen bomb, either offensively or even in retaliation after attack. The bomb is a weapon of indiscriminate destruction, and those who used it would put themselves on a level with those who, in the days of Old Testament history, massacred their enemies and exterminated men, women and children, regarding themselves as doing the will of God. The hydrogen bomb is destructive of God's natural creation. It can have no conceivable moral warrant, and it would be directed against the helpless."

The bishop added that he would not be able to support such action, and would have to advise Christian people that they could take no part in it.

However, the same session of Convocation also heard different advice. "It might be better to perish," said the Bishop of Winchester, "than submit to the parody of civilisation which seems to be the alternative presented from the other side of the Iron Curtain." The Bishop of Southwell said that the bomb raised no new question, and the Bishop of Derby compared it to a hand-grenade. Moreover, any cutting edge which such statements, had they been unanimous, might have possessed was rather blunted by the Dean of Chichester, who said that it was not the task of Convocation to call on the Government to do anything, and by the Archbishop of Canterbury, who said that the Church "could not become a negotiating party in the politics of the matter, nor could it identify itself (except in extreme cases) with any particular solution to the problem". It should seek simply to represent "the Christian point of view". The idea that the Christian point of view might only find expression through particular judgements was apparently strange to the Archbishop, though he did go so far as to tell the Royal United Services Institution on December 9, 1955, that over the past 10 years the Church had approved of most of the steps which the Government had taken.

It can thus be seen that when CND was formed in 1958, it did not create a new situation for the Church, but only intensified and polarised reactions which had already found expression. (At a different level, the character of CND as a young people's movement, helping to generate a rebellious attitude towards the religious as well as the political establishment, did set the Church a fresh problem, but that is another story.) In 1958 and 1959, however, bishops did in response to public anxiety and argument say a great deal on the subject of nuclear weapons, and for some of it, even at this short distance in time, the authors must occasionally blush. The present Bishop of London (then of Peterborough) was reported (*Church Times*, November 11, 1958) to have said that it was worth doing anything, even destroying humanity, rather than run the risk of enslavement to Communism. The late Bishop of Willesden (*Prism*, September 1958) expressed a downright historical judgement:

"It is, of course, a matter of history that appeasement, coupled with such movements as the Peace Pledge League [*sic*] and the misreading of British opinion which such movements led to, was at least partly responsible for Hitler's war. And it is significant that history is repeating itself today with the various abolitionist Campaigns."

Later in the same article, the Bishop aligned himself with his brother of Peterborough:

"Of course, nuclear war might lead to the destruction of humanity and destroy us all, and therefore it is virtual suicide. That is the risk, a terrible risk, and we have to face it. We also have to face what I believe is equally suicide and that is exposing the world to the most diabolical thing the world has ever seen. As far as I know, there is no biblical authority for assuming that we must save life at *all costs* . . . Life here is not the end, whether there is physical death or the living death of a body bereft of personality and responsible life, a body alive and breathing though its mind is possessed by another. But to me the latter is far more terrible; it is the ultimate sin against a child of God; it is blasphemy, it is the devil. And it has happened, is happening and will happen."

Of these "better-dead-than-Red" arguments the present Archbishop of Canterbury wrote (*York Quarterly*, December 1959): "It is appalling that such a thesis should have come from any Christian lips." The Bishop of Sheffield, in his Diocesan Review (December, 1958) said that it did not make moral sense or any other kind of sense. And Fr. Trevor Huddleston, replying to the Bishop of Willesden in the same issue of *Prism*, commented:

"The prophets of the Old Testament saw the Philistine and the Assyrian as the instruments of God's avenging justice upon his own people's sinfulness and blacksliding. And they called Israel to repentance. The Bishop of Willesden, apparently, sees the Communists as the instruments of Satan, and calls the Christian West to arms. Which is right?"

As CND took shape, there appeared to be about a dozen declared unilateralist bishops and suffragans in England and Wales, out of a total of over 100. They included: Manchester, Birmingham, Chichester, Southwark, Woolwich, Plymouth, Hulme, Llandaff, Bangor. There may well have been others who held these views without publicly expressing them. But the proportion of unilateralists probably represented fairly faithfully the proportion in the Christian community at large, and also among the population.

Other denominations in Britain, though their legislative assemblies are often both more relevant and more representative than Convocation and Church Assembly, are handicapped officially by their lack of universally acknowledged and widely reported spokesmen in between the annual meetings. The British fascination for gaiters, though unfortunate for the Church in many ways, does enable a cross-section of Anglican opinion on various subjects to be readily cropped from the newspapers. But the Methodist Church and the General Assembly of the Church of Scotland, for example, debated nuclear weapons on several occasions between 1946 and 1962. These communions did happen to possess, in the Revd Dr Donald Soper and the Revd Dr George MacLeod respectively, two of the best platform orators in Britain. Both are pacifists. But neither man has been markedly successful in pushing his denomination further than it was anyway prepared to go. In the Church of Scotland, especially, the heated debates between Dr MacLeod and his opponents have tended to polarise opinion and inhibit the conservatives from seeing the radical newness of the problem posed by nuclear weapons.

The Methodist Church in Britain, which possesses both a strong Christian Citizenship Department and also a long tradition of Leftish inclination in political matters, has taken throughout the last seven years a stronger line against nuclear weapons than any other ecclesiastical body in this country. Its *Declaration on Peace and War*, published in 1957,* doubts whether nuclear weapons in the megaton range can possibly satisfy the criteria of a "just war":

"The dreadful devastation caused by such weapons and the possibly more dreadful consequent and persistent effects of radioactive contamination, make it extremely doubtful if a war so

* Epworth Press.

waged could achieve a good outweighing the evil it would involve. If the result of such a war is to make the world a desert and call it peace, it can no longer be presumed that there is a reasonable hope of victory for justice. Nor can it be argued that the extinction of a nation or a continent is in accordance with man's nature as a rational being or with Christian moral principles."

The Declaration did, however, suggest that war waged with "a limited range of graduated and controllable nuclear weapons" might be "just".

Also in 1957 the Methodist Conference passed a resolution saying that there was "a clear moral obligation upon HMG to discontinue the further testing of nuclear weapons and to urge that course upon the other Governments concerned". By 1959 the Methodist Conference was overtly unilateralist, and the resolution adopted by Conference in July 1963 ran:

"Convinced that a defence policy for the United Kingdom based on the maintenance and development of an independent nuclear deterrent cannot be justified on grounds of Christian morality and cannot, in the contemporary situation, offer a reasonably effective defence to the people of this country, the Methodist Conference urges that, as a first step to the intelligent reappraisal of national and international security in an age of nuclear weapons, HMG should now begin to disengage from the attempt to maintain an independent nuclear deterrent."

To examine the position of the Roman Catholic hierarchy on this problem, it is necessary to move outside the frontiers of this country. The Catholic unilateralist authors of *Nuclear Weapons and the Christian Conscience** place on their title page a sentence from Pope Pius XII's address to the World Medical Association in 1954:

"Should the evil consequences of adopting this method of warfare ever become so extensive as to pass utterly beyond the control of man, then indeed its use must be rejected as immoral. In that event, it would no longer be a question of 'defence' against injustice and necessary 'protection' of legitimate possessions, but of the annihilation, pure and simple, of all human life within the affected area. That is not lawful on any title."

The same writers are also able to adduce statements by the French hierarchy in 1950:

"No one who has a true sense of humanity can fail to censure the use of all those modern weapons which strike indiscriminately

* Merlin Press, 1961.

201

at combatants and civilian populations and which scatter death blindly over areas more widespread in proportion as the scientific power of man increases. For our part, we condemn them with all our strength, as we did not hesitate to condemn during the last war the mass bombardments which, in attacking military objectives, struck down at the same time old men, women and children" (p. 113).

By Cardinal Godfrey of Westminster in 1958:

"Nobody can subscribe to the thesis that it would ever be morally lawful to use indiscriminate nuclear weapons on centres of population which are predominantly civilian" (p. 115).

And by Cardinal Ottaviani, arguing in his *Institutiones Juris Publici Ecclesiastici* that the conditions for a just war no longer exist:

"Leaving aside the question of a defensive war (and even this under fixed conditions), fought in the defence of the state against actual and unjust attack by another state, there can no longer be a just war which a state may undertake to retrieve its rights" (p. 111).

It is noteworthy that two of these pronouncements were made by men who in the climate of the Vatican Council have been regarded as extreme conservatives. Pope John XXIII, of course, secured through his famous encyclical *Pacem in Terris* (April 1963) a status among unilateralists roughly equivalent to that of patron saint. Writing about this encyclical the Protestant theologian Karl Barth recalled that the World Council of Churches had already said many "proper, important, and to certain ears, offensive" things about atomic and general disarmament, but he added:

"Why is it that the voice of Rome made such a far greater impression than the voice of Geneva on the world (from the editor's desk of *Pravda* all the way to that of the *Basler National-zeitung*)? Was it only because of the obviously greater historical and political halo which Rome possesses? Is the reason not also the fact that in the encyclical the same things were not only talked about but also *proclaimed*, that Christianity and the world were not only taught but also summoned unreservedly and bindingly with an appeal to the highest authority, that they received not only advice and admonition but also *directives*, in short, that the encyclical had more the character of a *message* than our previous ecumenical publications, in spite of its extensive use of terms and concepts taken from natural law?"*

* "Thoughts on the Second Vatican Council", *Ecumenical Review*, July 1963.

There is no doubt that Karl Barth's verdict gave expression to a deeply felt popular yearning for a proclamation to be made by whichever section of the Church the yearner stayed away from. It is less certain that the yearning was legitimate. It implied a view of Christianity and the Church which many Christians did not accept, and which, at least in mid-20th century England, had become anachronistic. In this country, the time has long since passed since bishops spoke and politicians trembled. This is not merely because the bishops are, by and large, quite ordinary Christians with uncomplicated minds, far too busy to be fully aware what an upset nuclear weapons have caused to moral and theological, as well as to political and strategic, categories. It is also because the first question a politician asks about a hostile orator is not "What did he say?" but "Whom does he speak for?" In sub-Christian countries, ecclesiastical pronouncements only count if they stand for a corpus of churchgoers who are prepared to adjust their weekday behaviour and opinions on the advice of their bishops and curates, or who have been taught how to arrive for themselves at theological judgements on contemporary problems. Neither community exists in the English Church, except as a small minority force, and in its absence, strong words by church leaders or even church assemblies on controversial issues tend only to confirm the prejudices of some churchgoers, irritate others, and reassure the unchurched masses that someone believes in moral absolutes, even if they themselves do not.

Is there, then, nothing that the Church can usefully say about nuclear weapons? It would be intolerable if there were not, and it is to the possible alternative ways for the Christian conscience on this question to evolve that I now turn.

By at once strengthening and modifying the traditional pacifist element in Christian thought, the Campaign for Nuclear Disarmament has undoubtedly contributed to this evolution. This is especially true at the level of the local church, where CND has sometimes been able to provoke a dialogue by virtue of its character as a mass movement, and of the influence which it has exerted on young people. At a higher level of theological and technical argument CND has with one or two distinguished exceptions failed to match the work done by non-pacifist Christians who share its concern, but have worked within an organisational framework provided by the British Council of Churches, the Christian Frontier Council, and the Institute of Strategic Studies. But this body of work, by its very nature, can less easily be simplified and popularised than CND propaganda. Moreover, its messages are seldom clear-cut, and often uninspiring. It is asking a great deal, for example, to expect Christians to go out into the streets shouting, not "Ban the Bomb", but "Limited nuclear war" or "Spend more on conventional forces". Indeed, the very suggestion makes it clear that objectives of this sort, even if the Church could agree that they were the right ones, cannot be forwarded by mass action, but only by private pressure on the decision-makers.

However, now that CND has itself largely abandoned hope of achieving its aims by mass demonstration, and accepted that technically informed presentation of both short-term and long-term proposals represents its only real prospect of influencing the actual decisions of government, a limited degree of reconciliation between the dominant and recessive theological traditions, between the "involvement" of the Christian soldier and the "separation" of the unilateralist or pacifist citizen, looks more possible.

Ironically, this reconciliation seemed closer in 1946 than at any time since. In that year the British Council of Churches published *The Era of Atomic Power*, which was the first attempt in this country to arrive by agreement in committee at an intelligent Christian judgement of the problems posed by nuclear weapons. It is a distinguished document, unfortunately out of print, which would require surprisingly little rewriting today. The Commission which produced it included the Bishop of Chichester and Professor (then Mr) Donald MacKinnon, both of whom were subsequently identified with a CND position.

On the narrow issue (whether or not to manufacture, use, or threaten the use of nuclear weapons) the Commission was not surprisingly unable to do more than state the dilemma sharply and sympathetically: On the one hand:

"It is clear that in so far as war becomes 'total', in the sense that every means may be adopted that appears conducive to victory, and that the attack is directed not against armies but against nations by methods of mass destruction, the restraints in waging war which have been regarded by the Christian tradition as essential to a 'just' war disappear . . . Atomic warfare, if it does not present us with a new ethical problem, introduces at least a new element into the problem . . .

"The possibility that an uncalculating refusal to have anything to do with methods of warfare involving wholesale massacre, and the acceptance of the political consequences arising out of such a refusal, is a duty demanded of us by the present historical crisis, is one which every serious mind must weigh. Some members of the Commission take the view that in no circumstances whatever should a Christian approve the use of the atomic bomb or similar weapon of wholesale massacre" (pp. 51–3).

On the other hand:

"It is a serious question whether it is right for Christians to weaken the hands of their government by announcing in advance that, if hostilities take place, they will have no part in them. Such an attitude, if adopted on a large scale, might have the effect of encouraging an aggressor and thus of precipitating the catastrophe which it is hoped to avert. Christians are no more immune than others from the operation of the element of frustration in human affairs by which actions, however well meant, may have results the very opposite of what was intended" (p. 56).

The Commission as a whole refused to follow the authors of a report* to the Federal Council of Churches of Christ in America, which condemned as morally indefensible the dropping by the Allies of atomic bombs on Hiroshima and Nagasaki. Those members of the British Commission who shrank from this condemnation were not sure that the facts in the possession of those who took this decision were sufficiently known. (They are known now, and those who resolutely declined to express a hostile judgement in 1946 may since have changed their minds. Even in 1946 the Commission thought that the burden of proof rested on those who decided to use the atomic bomb, and at the time of writing the authors were evidently unaware of, for example, the genetic implications of nuclear warfare.) They add (p. 50):

"The argument that on balance the use of the atomic bomb saved hundreds of thousands of lives, both in the forces of the United Nations and in Japan itself, undoubtedly has weight. But it is one of peculiar danger, since it can be used to justify any kind of barbarity . . . It may also be maintained that the destruction at Hiroshima was not in fact greater than the wholesale devastation caused by thousand-bomber raids on German and Japanese cities. But apart from the fact that the atomic bomb was a new *type* of weapon, capable in its full development of immeasurably greater devastation than any previous weapons, the comparison appears to us not so much a justification of the use of the atomic bomb as a ground for questioning the policy of indiscriminate bombing."

An even less dated part of the report is its discussion, the more valuable for having been generated within months of the explosion itself, of the inner significance of atomic power, and of the transformed relation between science and the humanities. The authors wondered what effect a prolonged period of nuclear angst might have on a society's birth-rate, when for the first time lack of faith in the continuity of life was accompanied by the power to prevent the birth of children. (They need not have

* *Atomic Warfare and the Christian Faith*, 1946.

worried, but that is not the point.) They also foresaw one of the main elements in the social situation which gave rise to CND:

"The mere discovery of the atomic bomb itself, even if it is never used, might well create such strains in our society as to destroy it. If human experience counts for anything we can only conclude that in such a state of insecurity most men and women would be forced back into a life that accepted impermanence as something inevitable, and would live only for the present. No more powerful solvent of any society can be imagined. It would be blindness to ignore the presence already in the minds of many young men and women of a feeling in some ways akin to despair, a belief that for them political action is futile, for they are helpless in the grip of forces quite beyond their control" (p. 17).

It is a pity that so much of this ground had to be gone over again between Christians, often in an atmosphere of public acrimony and ignorance, when CND came to be formed. But it is perhaps not surprising for, as already stated, discussion lapsed for several years after 1946. Then in 1953 the Catholic symposium *Morals and Missiles* made it clear—for the first time, as far as many British Christians were concerned—that there was a serious body of Roman Catholic thought demanding a radical repudiation of types of war which could no longer earn the title "just". In 1954 the World Council of Churches at Evanston, after declaring that "Christian pacifism and Christian participation in war are two ways in which the individual Christian can serve peace", went on to make various recommendations, of which one at least carried precise political implications: "Governments should discipline themselves not to begin with atomic weapons if they have not already got them."

The ensuing years saw a spate of books and reports, by individuals and committees, from several ecclesiastical sources, but especially from people associated with the British and the World Council of Churches. There are, in fact, far too many to analyse in detail, and now that they have gathered dust on the shelf one does not have to be a pacifist or a member of CND to perceive their imperfections. But the importance of these studies may lie less in their practical conclusions than in the method and presuppositions by which these conclusions were reached, in the audience to which they were addressed, and in the kind of reaction which they have evoked from their critics.

It should be remembered that in the early days of CND its moral drive was more powerful, its Quaker content probably rather higher, and its intellectual analysis less fully worked out, than is the case today. Presentations of "the Christian case against nuclear weapons" resembled in form if not in content the manifestoes of traditional pacifism, and tended to discount altogether the possibility that there might be a Christian case for the nuclear deterrent in some form or other. Consequently, "orthodox" theologians usually countered these arguments by restating, in various forms, the classical Christian doctrine of the "just war". In its contemporary versions this doctrine requires, for instance, that war should be fought by "proper means", that it should offer reasonable hope that justice should be victorious, and that the good achieved would outweigh the evils which the war would involve. By the late fifties, however, many theologians who had in 1939 found themselves able to regard the Allies' cause as just on criteria such as these became convinced that nuclear war, if it occurred, would violate all or most of the necessary conditions. The point was succinctly expressed by Fr John Ford, one of the leading Catholic moralists in the U.S., in an article published in 1957:

"It is my contention that the civil and military leaders who would plan and execute the dropping of a series of high megaton H-bombs on an area like Moscow or New York (1) would not in practice avoid the direct intention of violence to the innocent; (2) could not if they would; and (3) even if they would and could avoid it, would have no proportionate justifying reason for permitting the evils which this type of all-out nuclear warfare would let loose."*

The logic of this kind of analysis drove some to become "nuclear pacifists" (that is, people who accepted war providing nuclear weapons were not used) and others to become pacifists for nuclear reasons (that is, people who regarded nuclear weapons as imposing a kind of retrospective ban on all kinds of violence capable of leading to their use). Others, again, looked for ways to reduce nuclear war to acceptable proportions by limiting it, or to be more precise, by suggesting to their readers that the Church could tolerate it if it were limited, both in its scale and in its targets. The last distinction is important. Theologians discussing this topic have sometimes forgotten that they are not concerned with some "ideal" nuclear war which exists only as a useful counter in debate, but with the actual kind of war for which the Ministry of Defence or the Pentagon is preparing. Since Mr McNamara's reshaping of American defence policy, military actuality has approximated a little more closely to the theologians' ideal, but there is no guarantee that this situation will be permanent. The Catholic unilateralists quoted above put beside their title page quotation from Pius XII a remark

* "The Hydrogen Bombing of cities", reprinted in the symposium, *Morality and Modern Warfare* (Helicon Press, Baltimore, 1960), pp. 98–103.

of Mr Roswell Gilpatric, U.S. Deputy Defence Secretary, in 1961:

"We are not going to reduce our nuclear capability. Personally, I have never believed in nuclear limited war. I do not know how you could build a limit into it when you use any kind of nuclear bang."

Out of the desire to forswear utopianism, to preserve the period of peace provided since the war by the nuclear power balance, and to restore to war if it broke out the controllability and discrimination which in theory if not always in practice belonged to "conventional" battles, there evolved the theological and political approach which is today still dominant in, for example, the British Council of Churches and the Christian Frontier Council. This approach is both in content and in tone a good way from CND's outraged moral protest. It allies a technically sophisticated strategical analysis (prepared in collaboration with some distinguished members of the Institute of Strategic Studies) with an "immanentist" description of God's ways with men, summed up as follows by the authors of the 1963 British Council of Churches report on the British independent deterrent:*

"Our concern is to find God's will in this given situation—the will of a God of whom it may not be said that he does certain things in general but nothing in particular. His particular will for this country in these circumstances at this time can be recognised only when we have apprehended the real situation in which we find ourselves, and the possibilities open to us in it . . . Only then can we determine how the revelation of the Gospel requires of our country a greater self-denial, more adventurous faith, a deeper trust in the power of God, and in what concrete actions these are to be expressed."

Similarly the World Council of Churches Report *Christians and the Prevention of War in an Atomic Age*† written by Sir Thomas Taylor and Dr Robert S. Bilheimer for the international commission appointed in 1955 by the World Council of Churches, rejects all attempts to argue directly from theological categories to our contemporary problems. The Commission made three attempts to do this, with regard to the doctrine of creation, the last things, and the just war, and gave up each time. Taylor and Bilheimer comment (pp. 12–13):

"The attempt to deduce from the Gospel isolated principles and then to apply them immediately and directly to specific situations is too simple an approach . . . God in Christ is the

* *The British Independent Deterrent* (SCM Press, 1963). † SCM Press, 1961.

Lord of history, and summons us to obedience within the situations of our life."

Nuclear war is wrong because it is uncontrollable and indiscriminate and "in any realm of human endeavour the uncontrollable and the indiscriminate are in contradiction to the will of God for us" (p. 20).

A variant of the same argument is (p. 24) that technological civilisation must develop a spiritual discipline capable of using technological achievements responsibly. We must never reach a stage where "things are in the saddle and ride mankind".*

The practical conclusions to which these considerations of theological principle have led these intelligent, subtle, and indubitably concerned men deserve more notice than they have received, either from secular journals or from CND itself. Even the U.S. State Department, it is said, was rather worried by the World Council of Churches report, which said that Christians must never consent to the use of nuclear weapons in all-out war, and must openly make their views known on this question; and that if all-out war should occur, Christians should urge a cease-fire, if necessary on the enemy's terms, and resort to non-violent resistance.

Similarly in the British context, last year's report on the British Independent Deterrent, compiled by a committee ranging from the Chairman of the Conservative Party Foreign Affairs Committee to a Vice-President of CND, concluded (with one or two individual reservations) that there was no case for British independent nuclear action in any part of the world. It allowed that some might see "an element of sacrifice" in abandoning the independent deterrent, but "party differences should not be exaggerated for electoral purposes". It rejected the view, much canvassed by Sir Alec Douglas-Home in his election campaign, that British representation at top level international conferences depended on this country's possession of her own nuclear weapons and urged that the operational control of these weapons should be vested solely in the hands of the Americans as far as the West was concerned, in return for a greater British share in the planning and targeting of the NATO deterrent as a whole.

There are two great practical objections to commissions and

* Mr Thomas E. Murray of the U.S. Atomic Energy Commission has pointed out that when the first atomic bomb was being manufactured, the politicians and strategists did not tell the scientists and engineers that "so much fire power was needed to accomplish such and such an objective". Only one "limiting item of information" was furnished them: the size of the bomb bay into which the device had to fit. The controlling factor was not a policy, but a mechanism. Presumably if in 1945 20 megatons could have fitted the space as easily as 20 kilotons, 20 megatons would have been used.

reports of this nature. The first is that the clergymen who generally comprise a high proportion of their membership (50 p.c. in the case of the British study just discussed) are extraordinarily vulnerable to whatever military doctrine happens at the time to be fashionable among that minority of strategists, not necessarily the best or most influential strategists, who make a Christian profession or are willing to participate with Christians in studies based on Christian assumptions. Christian strategists, in the phraseology made famous in Washington at the time of Cuba, may tend (indeed, one hopes that they do tend) to be "doves" rather than "hawks". But in so far as such strategists are depended upon by theologians for up-to-date technical knowledge about the world and its armoury, their dovelike harmlessness is a less useful commodity than serpentine wisdom, even ruthlessness. Many of the strategic concepts which have inserted themselves into theological thinking are still in dispute. The viability of "limited nuclear war" is a case in point. Dr John Vincent, whose *Christ in a Nuclear World** is one of the few worthy contributions to this discussion to have been written from inside the CND, effectively quotes Sir Solly Zuckerman:

"My experience of the way commanders worked in the Second World War does not lead me to suppose that, if unlimited force were available, less rather than more would be used in order to secure some objective, whether on the defensive or offensive . . .

"In a war game involving just three NATO Corps, nuclear weapons were 'used' against military targets only, in an area of 10,000 square miles which contained no large towns or cities. In this 'battle', lasting only a few days, it was assumed that the two sides together used a total of between 20 and 25 megatons in not fewer than 500 and not more than 1,000 strokes. It turned out that $3\frac{1}{2}$m. people would have had their homes destroyed, if the weapons were air burst, and $1\frac{1}{2}$m. if ground burst. In the former case, at least half the people concerned would have been fatally or seriously injured. In the case of ground burst weapons, all $1\frac{1}{2}$m. would have been exposed to a lethal radiological hazard, and a further 5m. to serious danger from radiation."

Dr Vincent—who in this passage is criticising earlier British Council of Churches documents—comments: "Such is the slaughter the British Council of Churches has courageously set its seal to."

The other practical objection to such documents is that while they have to some extent succeeded in establishing a common

* Crux Press, Manchester, 1962, p. 114.

ground and language through which Christians of widely varying political and theological positions can meet and acknowledge each other's good faith, they have not so far had more than a marginal effect on the Church as a whole. Documentary evidence for this assertion is recently available in a survey of 1,850 American Protestant ministers conducted by the Fellowship of Reconciliation.* Questionnaires were sent to a scientifically selected sample of 12,000 ministers, so the response itself was poor. But the conclusion of the survey was that the average American Protestant minister, although he believes that war is contrary to the will of God: (1) would accept military service if drafted; (2) is likely to believe that the Christian approach is inappropriate for "atheist" Communists; (3) would rather be "dead" than "Red"; (4) does not feel that the present nuclear crisis (the survey was conducted in the summer of 1962) is the most important problem of the day. The most popular estimate for the probable American casualties in a future all-out nuclear war was 50 million or below (that is, between a quarter and a third of the population).

The survey report also states:

"In matters of peace and war, more than half the clergy believe that the Church is obligated to 'formulate a position and advocate it vigorously'; one-third feel the Church should 'stimulate concern and discussion among its members without itself taking a position on the issues'; and the remainder 'recognise that religion and not politics is its specialty, and thus to refrain from any involvement in such issues'. When asked to 'agree or disagree' with each of a series of statements developed by the World Council of Churches"—(these are, in fact, the conclusions of the Taylor–Bilheimer report already referred to)—"85 p.c. of the clergy agreed that war is contrary to the will of God, that Christians should openly declare that all-out use of nuclear weapons should never be resorted to, and that Christians must oppose all policies which give evidence of leading to all-out war. But only about 15 p.c. agreed with the more radical statement: 'If all-out war should occur, Christians should urge cease-fire, if necessary on the enemy's terms, and resort to non-violent resistance.'

"About 20 p.c. of the clergy were in favour of total unilateral disarmament, and another 40 p.c. that the United States should give up its nuclear weapons only if other nations agreed to give up theirs. About 20 p.c. were against nuclear disarmament on any terms."

* *Fellowship* (Journal of the Fellowship of Reconciliation), September 1, 1963, Box 271, Nyack, New York. Single copy 30 cents.

It can thus be seen that the differences between American clergy and their congregations and the American public at large are perceptible but not exactly dramatic; and though the actual opinions voiced might vary, the same would in all probability be the case if a similar survey were conducted in this country. The Christian unilateralists and pacifists, both in this country and in America, consequently feel a strong sense of isolation from the rest of the Christian community. It is this that has encouraged them so consistently to underrate both the intelligence and the good faith of their opponents on this issue. There has been a similar tendency on the non-unilateralist side to underrate the intelligence, though not in this case the good faith, of articulate Christians in CND; and in this cloud of mutual misunderstanding, it has sometimes been hard to discern what precisely the argument was about.

On the unilateralist side Dr Vincent's book and Professor Donald MacKinnon's recent essay "Ethical Problems of Nuclear Warfare"* suggest that the real division of opinion between Christian unilateralists and the more sensitive of their multi-lateralist brethren is less about the issues themselves—whether the issues are regarded as strategic, political or even moral—than about the methods by which the Church is competent to decide upon the issues, and act upon its conclusions. Dr Vincent has expressed this clearly:

"The decisive question is whether there is something unique and specific which the Christian has to offer, which arises organically out of Christian faith. This I believe to be quite basic. If one is to choose between third-rate theology written by lay 'experts' in this and that, on the one hand, and fourth-rate comment on politics by theologians who are at least aware of what they are saying from a Christian point of view, on the other, then I for one would opt for the latter. Our theological frustration turns us ever more and more to the 'experts', but the only way to avoid purely arbitrary choice between the various positions is to have an adequate theology."†

Professor MacKinnon, though much more "radical" in his general theological standpoint than Dr Vincent, makes a similar point when he protests against Christian acceptance of the way in which the deterrent, and the unacceptable type of warfare to which it points, have been built into our culture as part of the whole context of international relations—a context which up to the present time has always depended on the use, as well as the threat, of force. He adds:

* Reprinted in *God, Sex and War* (Fontana, 1963).   † *Frontier*, winter 1962/3.

"Caiaphas in his supreme hour showed himself powerless to distinguish the substance of the Jewish inheritance from a particular stabilisation of the situation of the Jewish state. We must, if we are Christians, be careful we do not confuse the substance and core of Christian fidelity with the forms in which we have received the same. What we believe is something which demands not that we cast all scruples to the wind in concern to preserve its outward embodiment; rather it is something that bids us fearlessly seek, in situations relatively novel in the demands they make upon us, new ways of fidelity to the order of Christ."

Dr Vincent derives his contingent proposals for making the world safer and happier—proposals which are themselves part of the general unilateralist case—from certain freshly interpreted but familiar theological principles: for example, that man is the steward of God's creation, and may not contemplate using, let alone use, weapons which are capable of destroying this creation. Dr Vincent also rejects a "dual standard" which he identifies in the British Council of Churches documents. To him, these seem to divide Christians into the many and the few: the few who can follow the commands of Jesus in all their stringency, and the many (including the Church as a whole) who do not attempt to abdicate from their human and worldly situation. On the contrary, Dr Vincent says, Christians are called to live the life of the few without abdicating the duties of the many.*

Similarly, for Professor MacKinnon "the spirit of protest is not Luddite . . . it is the expression of a temper at once humanist and Christian, which refuses to acquiesce in what we are told cannot be otherwise than it is, because that in which we are bidden to acquiesce is something which men have fashioned. *And what men have fashioned men can change*"† (cf. the World Council of Churches report's rejection of a state of affairs where "things are in the saddle and ride mankind").

Thus, it seems as if one of the chief differences between unilateralist and multilateralist Christians is that the former will not be excessively dismayed if their analyses of the contemporary situation and "the next step before us" can be shown, either by argument or events, to be erroneous. They can quietly retire to prepared positions, assuring us that what really has to be changed before reliable results can be seen is the whole context of international relations, which must now no longer rest, as it has always done up to now, on the threat of force.

(It is only in recent months that unilateralists have adopted an originally multilateralist interest in the formation of a world

* *Christ in a Nuclear World*, p. 55.   † *Op. cit.*, p. 67.

police force equipped with coercive, perhaps even nuclear power.)

On the other hand, non-unilateralist thinkers, who are normally prepared to underwrite particular solutions of current problems, expose themselves to more serious dismay when these solutions are outpaced by technological or political change, or simply shown to be wrong. Distrusting absolutism, they have no firm base to fall back on.

It is not difficult to see in this controversy an echo of that other controversy which has recently been resounding round the Christian parts of the world, and which concerns our images of God: whether God intervenes in power in human affairs or whether he is characterised precisely by his powerlessness to do anything but suffer what men do to him by their behaviour towards each other; whether Christianity is to be regarded as a religion, an area of experience "over against" the area of ordinary secular experience, or whether Christianity exists in the present age only to give a dimension of depth and trust and hope to this secular experience of life. Christian unilateralists would normally regard themselves as "radicals" among believers, but in their attempts to persuade the Church that it ought to espouse their cause they have tended to use categories of argument which are, as it were, pre-Bonhoeffer, pre-Robinson. They have assumed that the Church ought to be, in this connection at least, an authoritative, autonomous institution, capable of deciding what the "law" of Christ is and enforcing it. They treat New Testament passages, such as the Sermon on the Mount, as mandatory commandments rather than as parabolic and paradeigmatic "illustrations of what love may at any time require of anyone". There are obvious difficulties about applying to modern warfare the system of "situational ethics" which progressive theologians think appropriate for relations between the sexes, but it is equally obvious that traditional systems, seen at their most coherent in Roman Catholic teaching about the "just war", are no less difficult to apply in an age which has outgrown the longbow.

If peace in our time is to be negotiated between the opposing factions of Christendom on the issues arising out of modern weapons it may well be through a common realisation of the vocational and existential element in Christian decision on these issues, and through a simultaneous abandonment of the belief—held with equal conviction on both sides—that the Church as a whole ought to say one thing to the State and say it loudly and clearly. For ironically it is this belief, and the polarisation of churchgoers' attitudes which is a consequence of it, that have since the First World War deterred most Christian communities from daring to raise the problem at all, for fear of disrupting the fellowship. CND, though it has contributed something to the polarisation of attitudes, has at least broken the numbing silence which only a decade ago was the most obvious characteristic of the English Church as it appeared, say, to a National Serviceman about to receive his call-up papers. Perhaps the Church needs to recognise more dynamically than hitherto that vocations and decisions on this matter may legitimately take different forms for different people in different social situations. The peace-making which is expressed through CND or conscientious objection or works of international reconstruction may at any time for any Christian individual, group or even denomination be a full-time overriding summons which neither State nor Church must block or belittle. Granted the fixed institutional structure and conservative traditions of Western Christendom, now being sapped by the extraordinary fluidity of the times in which we live, the chances are that this kind of summons is not heard or heeded in our society nearly as often as we ought to expect.

But equally, it may at any time be right for groups of Christians, while remaining both individually and collectively moral agents, to immerse themselves in the institutions and power structures of "immoral society", which in the 20th century expresses its inevitable and characteristic secularity by depending for stability on the inordinate force which the created order has now made available. By thus immersing themselves, such individuals or groups necessarily find themselves devising policies or condoning actions which they cannot in conscience describe as Christian, only as somewhat more Christian than the alternatives might have been, had the world been left entirely to the guidance of men who lacked the Christian faith and hope. In these circumstances, Christians may well find uses for the codes of military conduct and patterns of ethical reasoning which their forbears have evolved over nearly 2,000 years, but they will find them useful as walking-sticks rather than as crutches. In an essay on "Power" written shortly after the founding of CND (five years, that is, before the publication of *Honest to God*) Dr J. A. T. Robinson described CND to an American audience as "a much more profound reappraisal than anything I detect going on in public thinking over here in the States" and added:

"The case for the Christian's participation in the power struggle is increasingly becoming the more difficult case to sustain. I still accept it, but I am in danger of being persuaded by events."*

It is precisely this willingness to be persuaded by events—the

* Reprinted in *On Being the Church in the World* (SCM Press, cheap edition, 1963), p. 54.

hallmark, incidentally, of the great politician—which the extremists on both sides of this argument have lacked. Dr Robinson's own conclusion is—as Dr Vincent has complained*—scarcely conclusive, but most Christians will surely recognise it as a fruitful starting-point for an ongoing practical debate in the world, a debate to which they will certainly have something to contribute, but whose course they can no longer expect to dictate.

"God's self-definition of power is terrifyingly simple—as simple and as terrifying as the Cross. He has exposed the strong right arm by which he wills to curb the nations, and it is pierced with nails, stained with blood and riveted in impotence. That is still an almost insurmountable offence to our political thinking. In consequence, we either transfer our worldly conceptions of power into our Christian moral judgements or we try to resolve the complexities of the political situation by texts from the Sermon on the Mount. The great man, the true prophet, is the man who can see the moral issue as simple as it is—as simple as Jesus always saw it—and the political issue as complex as it is."†

* *Op. cit.* (Vincent), p. 147.   † *Op. cit.* (Robinson), p. 56.

CHAPTER NINE

ART IN A COLD CLIMATE

"If scientists, intimidated by self-seeking people in power, are content to amass knowledge for the sake of knowledge, then science can become crippled, and your new machines will represent nothing but new means of oppression. With time you may discover all that is to be discovered, and your progress will only be a progression away from mankind. The gulf between you and them can one day become so great that your cry of jubilation over some new achievement may be answered by a universal cry of horror."

Bertolt Brecht,
The Life of Galileo, Sc. 14 (Methuen, 1963)

NOTHING signifies more plainly both the horizontal spread and the vertical penetration of Bomb-consciousness in British society than the response of creative artists to the theme. Yet paradoxically, the significance of this response lies as much in eloquent silences and omissions as in direct utterances. During the high noon of the Committee of 100, it almost seemed that the entire younger generation in the theatre—John Osborne, Arnold Wesker, Robert Bolt, Shelagh Delaney, Vanessa Redgrave, John Neville, and others—were strewn around the pavements of London in flat rejection of everything which the political leadership of the country was trying to do in the world; and indeed, this was precisely the impression that their impresario, Ralph Schoenman, wished to create.

Unilateralism and commitment had long since become a critical orthodoxy. By another of those strange half-coincidences of the late fifties, the stirring of anti-Bomb feeling had been narrowly anticipated by a theatrical revolution. It was in the spring of 1956 that Jimmy Porter complained that there were none of the good, brave old causes left. By the following year there were two new ones, Suez and the Bomb, and commitment reigned supreme thereafter in Sloane Square and Stratford, E. Vanessa Redgrave herself admitted to the *Sunday Times* in September 1961 that at the time of the Hungarian revolution she had been belligerently inclined, but had changed her mind through reading John Hersey's *Hiroshima* and then playing the part of Stella in Robert Bolt's *The Tiger and the Horse*. (This play was staged in London in August 1960, at the time of the Committee of 100's formation. Stella's anti-nuclear lover, Louis, circulates a petition in the university against tests, and her mother, a biologist, worries herself over the edge of insanity wondering whether or not to sign it.)

Some of the Campaign's writers and artists were highly effective pamphleteers. Mr Bolt, for example, wrote at least one of the large Committee of 100 advertisements which appeared in the national press in the autumn of 1961. Much of Christopher Logue's poetry has a polemical content. Nevertheless, in their professional work they tended to approach the fundamental problems of nuclear weapons and their use tangentially, if at all. Bolt in *The Tiger and the Horse* and Doris Lessing in *Each His Own Wilderness* both wrote plays which have as a main or subsidiary theme the impact of an anti-nuclear campaigner's enthusiasm on his or her own domestic circle. (It is interesting to note that Miss Lessing's play was first performed in March 1958, and was thus evidently written out of acquaintance with the NCANWT rather than with the CND.)

But the Bomb, in these plays, is little more than a topical vehicle for what are essentially clashes of temperament and personal backgrounds rather than of ideas and schemes of values. Mr Bolt's play is vastly superior to Miss Lessing's because its characters are more actable, because it develops where the other play gyrates, and because it leaves the spectator feeling that a particular quality of donnish evasiveness and self-deceit has been skilfully held up for his critical inspection and censure. But the Spanish Civil War would have done almost as well as the Bomb for these authors' purposes.

One senses a feeling not only of political helplessness before the fact of nuclear weapons but of imaginative helplessness also. The impression is if anything confirmed by comparisons of the written word with the visual and auditory arts. I speak with diffidence here: moreover, the transmutation of feeling into forms other than words makes it hard to identify with any reliability a particular social or political theme in a man's work, even if one suspects its presence. There is no reason to suppose that modern British painters and musicians have been any less touched by the concern of the CND than have poets and playwrights. The names of John Bratby, Henry Moore, Benjamin Britten, and Michael Tippett strongly suggest the contrary. The last two named were both Second World War conscientious objectors and Tippett was gaoled for his beliefs. But the nuclear age has not found its visual image as the Spitfire age did in Paul Nash's *Totes Meer*; and it is surely suggestive that one of the very few British musical works of the past 150 years which have been seriously acclaimed as great, Britten's *War Requiem* (1963), goes to the First World War for a text and mingles the sublime impersonality of the Requiem Mass with the intimate, haunting assonances of Wilfred Owen.

Are we, then, being told by our artists that nuclear weapons by their very nature are so obscene, so incomprehensibly destructive, that the creative imagination cannot well assimilate them?

"It is like a deep-seated neurosis; some try to repress it altogether; some try to alleviate its symptoms; a few try to understand the condition which created it. But under the surface of life it is always there. Perhaps it always will be until some writer or artist at last succeeds in creating the great tragic masterpiece which the subject calls for."*

Thus Goronwy Rees, writing not of the British nor of the Bomb, but of the Germans and their responsibility for the

* *Encounter*, April 1964.

liquidation of the Jews. Both themes, by their terrifying impersonality as much as by their hugeness of scale, require distance as well as genius before they can be satisfactorily treated.

Nevertheless, the attempt has been made by British dramatists, at least, to do something with the Bomb theme, and even in these last 10 years, the attempts seem to fall into three distinct genres or phases. The first, taking up the position announced by Brecht's *Galileo* in 1947, was Charles Morgan's Christian-philosophical approach to the responsibility of the scientists, worked out in *The Burning Glass** (1954). The second was the New Wave drama's commentary on the responsibility of the common man to get on the streets and *do* something—one thinks here of Bolt and Doris Lessing, and on television of David Mercer. (This categorisation omits two earlier television plays, more overtly polemical, written by well-known Campaigners: J. B. Priestley's *Doomsday for Dyson* (1958) and Marghanita Laski's *The Offshore Island* (1959).†) The third, and in many ways the most promising, phase is the attempt made by the young dramatist David Campton to say something serious about the Bomb through the self-distancing technique of farce—or what he himself calls "comedy of menace".

Charles Morgan's *The Burning Glass* is a marginal note on the history of 20th-century physics. In its naïvetés as much as in its complexities, it reflects the long debate described by Robert Jungk in *Brighter than a Thousand Suns*,‡ and if the play had a text it might have been Robert Oppenheimer's reminiscence:

"It is my judgement that when you see something that is technically sweet you go ahead and do it and you argue about what to do about it only after you have had your technical success. That is the way it was with the atomic bomb. I do not think anybody opposed making it; there were some debates about what to do with it after it was made."§

In "knowing sin", as Oppenheimer has also described the making of the bomb, the scientists after 1945 also saw their cherished traditions of free international exchange of information swept away by political mistrust, their small self-contained community transformed into departments of State, and their respect for evidence corrupted to suit the requirements of partisan lobbies. Morgan, writing out of a "civilised" English tradition which preferred, at least until the advent of Sir Charles Snow, not to recognise the existence of these forces, only nibbled at the theme. His characterisation is flat and conventional (young man with nothing to live for gives away secret to transparent enemy

* Macmillan.   † Cresset Press.   ‡ Gollancz and Hart-Davis, 1958.
§ Quoted in Jungk, *op. cit.*, p. 266 (Pelican edition).

agent of mittel-European origin) and the plot is crude, though after some recent security scandals no one could accuse it of being far-fetched. Yet in its very fumbling, the play indicates the arrested development, the limited social awareness, which a decade ago could pass muster on an English stage.

Morgan's scientist, Sir Christopher Terriford, working on weather control, discovers a means of using the upper atmosphere of the earth as a lens to focus the rays of the sun with complete accuracy on any part of the earth and burn it up. The plot rests upon his decision not to communicate this knowledge, nor to make it available for civilian use, but to reserve it for military use in supreme national emergency. The emergency occurs. Terriford is kidnapped, and to get him back, the Prime Minister is obliged to incinerate a forest and make a lake boil over in the enemy country. But the secret itself remains with Terriford.

Morgan's scientist is a creative, imaginative man, not a mere technician. He describes his stumbling upon the "burning-glass" setting of his weather machine as though it were a kind of anti-religious experience (knowing sin). Terriford's first instinct, the author assures us in his preface to the play, was to destroy all memory of the discovery; his second, to preclude its military and allow its peaceful use; his third, to forbid all uses except in certain circumstances the military, on the grounds that man's power over nature, even if beneficently employed, had become disproportionate and hubristic. Morgan oddly concludes:

"History moves in phases; the power-phase may be drawing to its close; there may be a halt for many centuries in all but the minor developments of technology ... We need time in which to shake off the nightmare of the absence of God. Christopher Terriford's decision is no more than a refusal to plunge us deeper into it.

"Of his decision to allow, nevertheless, the use of the Burning Glass in extreme military emergency against a totalitarian enemy, little more need be said than is said in the play itself. It is consistent with his resolve to give the world time to shake off the nightmare which totalitarianism would fasten upon it, for totalitarianism is a daemonic forbidding of the spirit of man to open its eyes."

The Burning Glass, in fact, represents the liberal–conservative reaction to nuclear weapons. Nostalgic for a vanished age of innocence, helpless without entirely recognising itself to be so, this school viewed totalitarian systems of government as a temporary aberration of a world which would eventually return to "civilised", pre-1914 values. It could afford to be indifferent to the fate of the peoples unfortunate enough to live, and even enjoy living, under totalitarian systems. For them—the

Gentiles or the barbarians of the 20th century—were reserved those ultimate weapons which would be considered inappropriate for use within the circle of civilised, democratic states. While Stalin still lived and Hitler was vividly remembered, it was, perhaps, a natural reaction. But in the years after *The Burning Glass* the totalitarian regimes became less absolute and the weapons devised against them became more so. Considerations alike of morality, prudence, and political realism began to forbid simple adherence to that "nation-hero—nation-villain ideology" which John Foster Dulles had condemned in 1939* and later himself espoused. In England especially, the simultaneous occurrence of Suez and Hungary suggested strongly to a whole generation that muddle and brutality were common to both Eastern and Western systems.

Thus did we enter the dramatic world of a man like David Mercer. The antithesis with Charles Morgan could scarcely be sharper. Television instead of the legitimate theatre, self-conscious Socialism instead of unconscious Conservatism, kitchen sink instead of gracious living, the responsibility of the many instead of the responsibility of the few—the two are as far apart as Nelson on his column from the demonstrators on the steps. Mercer's television trilogy—*Where the Difference Begins, Climate of Fear*, and *Birth of a Private Man*—illustrates the present study not because it is the best play written in celebration of the demonstrative years (far from it) but because it is possibly the most characteristic. It was performed in 1962, and in a few years will surely seem as dated as *The Burning Glass* does now.

The anti-nuclear theme of the trilogy† begins with the second play, *Climate of Fear*. The play begins in court, where Colin Waring, a member of the New Left, is being briskly sentenced to three months for refusing to be bound over after a sit-down. The rest of the play is about the conflict of class, temperament and values within his own family which follows upon Colin's action. Colin's father Leonard, a pitman's son who has eagerly embraced a sedate, Tory existence as an atomic scientist, is totally alienated from both his children (for the daughter, Frances, also sits down). The mother, Frieda, hesitates between them. Eventually, she chooses to demonstrate too and is divorced from her husband, but she still cannot get on with her daughter, a tough egg who later characterises her:

"No other society in the world could have produced my mother. Liberally educated, provincially sub-cultured and morally confused. She has the Lady Almoner approach to life——"

* *War, Peace and Change* (Macmillan, 1939), p. 108 ff.
† Published as *The Generations* (John Calder, 1964).

The new tone is nowhere more clearly defined than in the portrayal of scientists. No longer intellectual and moral giants, in Mercer's play they have become puny suburbanites, cultivating their gardens in between devising better mechanisms for blowing us all up. Frances is choosing a dress to wear at a parental party:

Frances: That one's snazzy. That's the small-talk ensemble. That's my gauche-girl-listening-to-big-masculine-men dress. That's the bosom-crusher. Something for every occasion. That's sexy-rexy. Take your pick. All our models supplied with a piece of sticking-plaster to stretch over the mouth.

Frieda: Oh Frances——

Frances: Well, parties bore me. Especially scientists' parties. Conversation with them is either pi-mesons or disk brakes, with a yawning void in between. If you're a woman you don't get so much of the old pi-mesons, either.

Frieda: You're doing Edgerton an injustice at least. He's very cultured.

(Frances pinches her nose and makes a lavatory-chain pulling gesture with her other hand.)
You're embarrassingly like I was at your age.

Frances: Not to worry. I expect when I conceive I shall mutate, and restore the family honour. (p. 95)

The mind boggles at the thought of attempting to explain this exchange to Charles Morgan. The same dual argument between attitudes and generations reappears in a discussion between Colin and his father in the visiting room at Brixton Prison:

Leonard: You broke the law.
Colin: And that's self-evidently wrong?
Leonard: Yes. Colin: Any law? Leonard: Yes.
Colin: You think apartheid laws are right?
Leonard: I'm not going to sit here and listen to sophistry. This isn't South Africa. We have perfectly legal ways of expressing opposition in this country.
Colin: The legal ways haven't been very effective. And time's short.
Leonard: In a democracy, you must accept it if you can't persuade the others.
Colin: And if the others aren't properly informed about the issue? Oh, let's stop it. Let's just say I'm against democratic suicide for whole nations. Do you think governments always act in the best interests of their peoples? (pp. 124–5)

Leonard goes on to explain what Colin thinks was a betrayal—Leonard's abandonment of his father's Socialism:

"Never mind what he said about politics. He really only understood success in terms of money. Position. He never respected me till I had both. Underneath his talk, I've never known such a bloody old reactionary in all my life . . . In the end he was like everyone else—out for himself. As for being against the bomb, aren't we all? Isn't everybody? Scared out of their wits. And that's why we're still alive and still free, because we've *got* it.

Colin: Free for what? To turn into what you've turned into? Is it worth it? Free to wait until it's too late? Free to twist the meaning of that dedicated old man? You make me want to throw up."

These plays are punctuated by snatches from the folksongs of the anti-nuclear revival—themselves an extraordinarily potential cultural influence, whether borrowed from the American Negroes like:

> "*It's like a tree that's standing by the water,*
> *We shall not be moved.*"

or native like:

> "*Men and women, stand together*
> *Ban the Bomb, for evermore.*"

(Every Aldermaston March—and many local groups also—had their bands and their songsheets, and some of these songs, such as Sydney Carter's "The Crow on the Cradle" and "The Sun is Burning" were highly distinguished examples of their genre.)

Was it all, then, to no purpose? By the last play in Mercer's trilogy, it is beginning to look like it. Colin, who eventually breaks down and gets himself shot on the Berlin Wall in a cinematic closing sequence, explains his resignation from the Committee of 100:

"I've marched. I've been on sit-downs. I've been arrested a dozen times and in prison twice. I've worked in the Labour Party and the New Left until I couldn't stomach the one and the other disintegrated . . . I've read and argued and talked . . . factories, dockyards . . . turned my home into a bloody office . . . refused to give my girl a child, which is what she wants more than me even. I've dropped my Ph.D. I live on handouts from people who are 'sympathetic' to the movement . . . I'm poor, and tired, and rapidly turning nihilistic." (p. 177)

Again, later:

"There are people in every generation who act out some of its hopes and needs. The subjective reasons for their actions hardly matter. In some way they define a generation to itself . . .

224

In times of violent or radical change such people—either as individuals or in a group—can be decisive. In times of stagnation what are they? Articulate phantoms? The self-elected conscience of the nation? They're so much weaker than the forces they oppose." (pp. 202–3)

And when Frances protests that this is not the end of it Colin replies:

"Well isn't it? When the very word 'protest' makes a nation yawn? The middle classes are bored by it, the working class is suspicious of it—and the writers have grown fat on it. Bloody hell when a society reduces a precious idea to a saleable commodity."

These plays, or others like them, might easily have been the end as well as the high point of the Bomb's influence on the contemporary theatre. All but the most "experimental" drama has to reduce problems and immensities to personal terms and terms which make theatrical sense. When the big battalions of demonstrators faded away, the dramatic celebrants of the protestant years might well have faded with them. But already by 1960 there were signs of a new genre emerging. Three of the four playlets from David Campton's *A View from the Brink* were performed in that year at a stop on the Aldermaston March. The three were later put together with a new, more substantial and more mature piece to form the sequence, *Four Minute Warning*, which the author generically entitles "comedy of menace". Though little known outside the Theatre-in-the-Round circuit in the North of England, Campton has been working this seam since 1957, before either CND was founded or Harold Pinter's plays had been professionally performed, and the 1957 playlet sequence, *A Lunatic View*, included a study of Bomb survivors called *Then* . . . Of the plays in *Four-Minute Warning*, only two—*Mutatis Mutandis* and *Little Brother, Little Sister*—are directly concerned with the Bomb, but all of them are triggered off by human vulnerability and salted with sick humour. They emit lethal radiations of social unease. The Bomb, for Campton, is not just a topical peg on which to hang good dramatic material about society, morals, or personality, but an underlying element, a given presupposition, in his whole approach to the business of writing plays in the mid-20th century. E. P. Thompson, in an essay already quoted, noted that the Aldermaston generation was "the first in the history of mankind to experience adolescence within a culture where the possibility of human annihilation has become an after-dinner platitude". Campton became the first person to express this cultural revolution in genuinely dramatic terms. He has himself defined his intentions:

"To my mind the Theatre of the Absurd is a weapon against complacency (which spreads like a malignant fungus). The weapon of complacency is the pigeon-hole. Pigeon-hole an idea, and it becomes harmless. (We have a clean bomb.) It is difficult to be complacent when the roots of one's existence are shaken, which is what the Absurd at its best does. Of course, now, having been given a name, the Theatre of the Absurd is in danger of being popped into a pigeon-hole itself . . ."*

Mutatis Mutandis, though almost as slender as a revue sketch in content and duration, achieves its originality and sense of menace by careful stylisations and repetitions. It is set in a hospital waiting room, where a husband progressively breaks to his wife the news that their baby, just born, has curly green hair, three eyes, and a tail. Neither the man nor the woman are distracted by this intelligence, but they are perturbed; and the delicate, encouraging reiterations of "but he's a lovely baby . . . our baby" lessen their perturbation only at the price of increasing ours. When the child was conceived, reflects the husband casually, "it was late summer, and the early chrysanthemums were already tapping on the window; the swallows were calling to each other and the sky was patterned with rocket trails".

Little Brother, Little Sister is set in a fall-out shelter 20 years after a nuclear war. A brother and sister who have never known any other environment have been brought up in the shelter by the family cook, a tyrannical blend of blubber-and-screech whose two terrors are that Sir and Madam will discover each other's sexuality, Egyptian fashion, and that they will discover the shelter's hidden, forbidden door to the outside world, which neither of them have ever seen, and which may or may not (we are not told) still be lethal to human beings.

Both fears are realised, and the build-up to the moment when Cook brings out her ultimate weapon, the meat-cleaver, to execute her charges and so save them from two fates worse than death is excellently managed. Sir and Madam remain children, even if artificially retarded children, at the very moment when they are breaking into adolescence, and the habit of obedience is strong enough for them to be prepared to submit to their fate. The W. S. Gilbert of *The Mikado* and the *Yarn of the Nancy Bell* seems to be peeping over Campton's shoulder during the preparation for execution, but this serio-farcical scene is interrupted when Sir breaks away like a jazz soloist and launches at

* Quoted in *Anger and After*, by John Russell Taylor (Pelican 1963), p. 165, and cf. pp. 162–9 for a bibliography and discussion of Campton's work to date.

Cook the one attack against which she is not proof—a verbal courtship compiled out of her own sentimental conversation over the years, and out of the fragments of women's magazines and popular newspapers which have been the survivors' only reading matter. Cook has a heart attack from excitement, and the pair tiptoe out into whatever awaits them on the far side of the shelter door. Only when the play is over does one realise that as well as saying something about the obvious troubles of the modern world, Campton has contributed in purely theatrical terms a parable of freedom, authority, and sanctions. Sir and Madam cannot gain by violence the freedom to which as adults they are entitled, even though what prevents them is habit rather than the force ranged against them. Yet their imprisonment under Cook's tutelage has, presumably, been necessary for their own safety up till the time when their own physical and mental development provides them with the wherewithal for escaping from it. Our larger world too, perhaps Mr Campton is saying, is like a shelterful of childish or adolescent nation-states, kept in control only by the fact of the meat-cleaver in the hands of the super-powers. What happens when their flank is turned as neatly as was Cook's?

In the theatre, as elsewhere, the decade which followed *The Burning Glass* has been an eventful one, and the popular acceptance of social realism, then of the theatre of the Absurd and the Theatre of Cruelty, was revolutionary. Crudely speaking, nuclear weapons as a theme may well be almost played out. To their other horrors, they add a barrenness. Flanders mud was rich by comparison, and indeed is still yielding, not merely helmets and guns turned up by the ploughshare, but the slowly-gestated commentaries of great artists and writers. But with the Bomb, the further we depart from the superficial aspects of the theme, the more it is still with us. The "climate of fear" has descended, and we can no more banish it than turn back an Ice Age. No play has yet been staged, poem written, picture painted or composition performed which sums up our response to this knowledge, though in short compass Edwin Muir's *The Horses*,* with its haunting reversal of the Genesis creation myth ("On the second day the radios failed . . ."), begins to reveal its imaginative possibilities.

* *Collected Poems* (Faber & Faber, 1963), p. 246.

CHAPTER TEN

AN ALTERNATIVE TO ARMAGEDDON?

"No longer hosts encountering hosts
Their millions slain deplore
They hang the trumpet in the hall
And study war no more."

(Isaiah II. 4—in *Scottish Paraphrases*, 1781)

It would be absurd to end this book, which has been concerned with one European country's still-incomplete response to the great new fact of our time, without inquiring whether we are better, wiser, or safer as a result of all the mental and emotional effort which at least a section of the British public has expended on the Bomb over the past 10 years. Temporarily at least, the Aldermaston marchers have hung up their boots. Are they entitled to hope that the nations of the world will, in return, "hang the trumpet in the hall"? And if there is room for hope, what practical steps can ordinary people take to prevent their hopes from being dashed and their fears from being realised?

Clearly, even after Cuba and the Test-Ban Treaty, the world is only a slightly less dangerous place than it was in 1957, when Mr Duncan Sandys laid the foundations for CND by saddling Britain with a defence policy no more useful than a bee's sting. The probability of war by accident, or by one side mistaking the other side's intentions, has been reduced by more highly sophisticated fail-safe procedures, by tighter civilian control in the Pentagon, and by the Cuban near-miss which seemed to set the two Great Powers wondering how they came to misread each other so alarmingly. Yet over us all, as the late President Kennedy told the United Nations, there still hangs "the nuclear sword of Damocles, suspended by the slenderest of threads". For Britain, if the threads broke, the scale of the execution might not be much greater than it would have been seven years ago: you can't be deader than dead. But for the world at large, if all-out nuclear war is waiting in the wings of history, the sooner she makes her entrance the better. The difference in war potential between 1957 and 1964 might be the difference between the life and the death of a hemisphere. Between 1964 and 1974, according to Herman Kahn, the difference might be between the life or death of earth, if a nation rich enough to build a Doomsday Machine wanted it that way.*

At this level of destruction, even quite hard-headed people think that natural human restraints might begin to operate. "Almost no one," says Dr Kahn, "wants to be the first man to kill a hundred million people." But in 1964 the world has begun to recognise more clearly than before that there will soon, barring an unforeseen coup by the disarmament negotiators, be two leagues of nuclear powers; and that if the top league is safely deadlocked by mutual awareness of destructiveness and destructibility, the clubs of the second league may begin to play

* *Op. cit.*, p. 500.

chicken with each other and ducks-and-drakes with non-nuclear rivals. Indeed, the history of the last five years has done much to bear out Mr Wayland Young's forecast in 1959, when he defined three distinct phases in the "natural history" of a demo-cratic state which develops thermo-nuclear weapons: the Gesta-tion, the Excalibur, and the Damocles period.* France was then in the Gestation phase, cutting down her engagements to NATO and uttering only veiled hints of the marvellous birth to come. Britain was still brandishing the all-powerful sword of Excalibur, not noticing as yet that "the ants were still free to walk in and out of the holes in her shoes". America was passing into the phase of doubt when Excalibur began to look like the sword of Damocles.

So it has developed. America has passed, and Russia seems to be passing, into the Damocles phase, which President Kennedy even borrowed Mr Young's imagery to describe. Britain, thanks to the Arthurian romanticism of the party in power, remained in the Excalibur phase longer than any reasonable person would have expected, and boasted about it so much that Excalibur became more and more widely coveted. France is just plucking Excalibur from the stone, and behaving accordingly. China is now in Gestation, and Britain, which has built great pretensions on the strength of being the only second-rank power with nuclear weapons, will soon be back as one of the crowd without having anything tangible to show for her temporary singularity. Galloping nuclear proliferation is dangerously close.†

Morally, the Campaign's case is unaltered: indeed, it is even strengthened, for now that Britain is visibly dependent on the United States for the greater part of her deterrent power, it is less easy for Right-wing critics of the Campaign to pretend with conviction that it would be somehow immoral to "shelter behind the Americans". But politically, the nuclear world has become vastly more complex than it was in the simple, straightforward days of "Ban the Bomb" and "Get out of NATO"; and the complexities, on the whole, are better understood. NATO itself, though still an odious, doomed institution in the minds of most Campaigners, has come to be valued by Centre-Left politicians in Britain not for itself, but as the kind of embryonic supra-nationalist grouping which alone seems to offer some hope of limiting the spread of nuclear weapons, and preserving for Britain a share in their operational control. The Common Market offered—in the distant future—something of the same hope. But Macmillan's hope was de Gaulle's apprehension, and to the Labour Party, especially its Leftward members, the Com-mon Market was on other grounds distasteful. Nor could anyone

* *Strategy for Survival* (Penguin, 1959), p. 29. † Cf. *The Spread of Nuclear Weapons*, by Leonard Beaton and John Maddox (Chatto & Windus, 1962).

pretend that the Commonwealth was a viable combination for defence purposes, whatever its real or imaginary economic advantages. After Brussels, therefore, the Atlantic alternative began to attract, or ceased to repel, an important section of British political opinion.

All in all, nationalism was by 1964 a dying force in Britain, whether it was the traditional nationalism revived by General de Gaulle and imitated by Sir Alec Douglas-Home, or the nationalism turned inside out which characterised the Campaign. Neither type of nationalism could solve the pressing practical problem of limiting nuclear proliferation, still less the ultimate aim of building a world authority. The Campaign recognised this change by speaking less of unilateralism *tout court* and more of "unilateral initiatives", but the changed approach was less satisfying to the emotions. Milton's "Let not England forget her precedence of teaching nations how to live" was always one of the Campaign's favourite quotations, and the thought that even precedence of this beneficent kind might be beyond England's grasp was as unpleasant to the followers of Lord Russell as it was to the followers of Lord Salisbury.

In a narrower sense, the Campaign's case has over the past few years become part of conventional wisdom in Britain. Few people of significance now believe that nuclear war is something which Britain as a society, or they themselves personally, could reasonably expect to survive; and even Sir Alec Douglas-Home conceded, once the Test-Ban Treaty was safely signed, that nuclear bomb tests represented a danger "to generations yet unborn". But Wayland Young's "natural history of thermo-nuclear states" is at least as likely as the activities of CND to have brought about this more realistic public appraisal by British statesmen of the facts of modern life. Politicians as a class can be myopic or cowardly or both, but at Cabinet level, if not on the back benches, they are usually too well-informed to let the need for public drum-beating affect unduly their private judgement of what the country is able to do or survive. And at the lower level of Parliamentary debate and pressure, it is even arguable that the existence and activity of CND actually prevented the nation from passing as swiftly as it should have done from the Excalibur to the Damocles phase in its attitude to nuclear weapons. On the Conservative side there was a natural tendency to assume that any cause advocated by Canon Collins, Kingsley Martin, and Michael Foot must be, if not wholly mis-guided, at least seriously over-stated. Many Conservative MPs who might have had some sympathy with the objects of the Campaign, and who certainly shared its misgivings about the Sandys Defence White Papers, balked at the personalities of the leading Campaigners, and were later confirmed in their distaste by the phenomenon which Peter Simple of the *Daily Telegraph* cruelly christened "Rentacrowd": London's instantly available progressive claque, ready at the drop of a leaflet to demonstrate on a whole range of causes from South Africa to capital punishment to nuclear weapons. Rentacrowd is, perhaps, a more interesting and less menacing development than Conservative politicians and newspapers are apt to believe, but as an instrument of persuasion it was undoubtedly deficient.

In the Parliamentary Labour Party, the Campaign evoked broadly similar feelings of hostility quite early on, though since the Labour Party is not itself averse to public demonstration, on May Day and other occasions, it was until the disturbances of 1961 and 1962 less impressed than its rivals by the terrors of mob-rule. Among Labour MPs, the Campaign made in the first few weeks almost all the converts that it was ever going to make, and of the basic 70-odd sympathisers, the majority would willingly have joined much less sensible and well-founded movements than CND. The 1959 Election dealt harshly with unilateralist MPs—Mr Frank Beswick and Mr Ian Mikardo, for example, were both defeated—and in the 1959 Parliament, by the time that Labour began winning seats at by-elections in 1962–63, Transport House had established a tight control over the selection of "unreliable" candidates. Apart from Mr Michael Foot, who returned to Parliament as Member for Ebbw Vale in 1960, Mr Neil Carmichael, who won Glasgow Woodside from the Tories in November 1962 was the first whole-hogging CND recruit to the Labour back benches. Consequently, whereas in the country the Campaign was able to break out of the restricted stereotype of peace movements and Left-wing ginger groups, within the Labour Party itself it was too closely involved with the long-drawn-out battle between Left and Right, between constituency parties and unions, to constitute the sub-political persuasive force that it might otherwise have done. As early as September 1958 Sir Richard Acland submitted a revealing and characteristic memorandum to the CND Executive on "the future of the Campaign":

"Instead of spending time at local meetings, our National Names should give an equivalent number of evenings to long, quiet conversations with four or five carefully chosen and carefully invited key people. The purpose of this would be twofold:

"(*a*) Every now and then we should win one key person.
"(*b*) We should begin to find out something about our own arguments. In this connection I am almost sure that the Conservative Party is employing top-level psychologists (Prostitute

233

Psychologists, if anyone would care to describe them so) to advise on public relations. It seems mere nineteenth-century obscurantism if we do not do the same. Surely we can find first class men who would sit in on our quiet conversation and write us a series of notes on what wins and what doesn't?"

Later, with tens of thousands of people gathered in Trafalgar Square and a great political party converted (or rather baptised with a hose, like the Chinese general's army) Sir Richard's idiosyncratic viewpoint disappeared from sight. Anyway, Sir Richard's was not the kind of Campaign that Canon Collins and Mrs Duff would have been equipped or anxious to wage. But when the big battalions slipped away back to their humdrum jobs and family circles, tucking their badges at the back of a drawer, the argument for concentrating, like the late Dr Buchman, on the key men became stronger. Hence the Campaign's intellectual quarterly, *War and Peace* and its factual digest *The Month* (both first published in 1963), and hence the emergence of a small CND caucus in Chatham House and among the members of the Institute for Strategic Studies. But it was a belated development, and in retrospect it seems extraordinary that Lord Russell, whose initiation of the Pugwash Conferences led to the building of numerous invaluable bridges between Eastern and Western scientists, strategists and economists, should apparently have failed to perceive the possible benefits to be derived from an internal counterpart to Pugwash in British politics, and should have surrounded himself with young men who seem to have been more interested in uprooting than in manipulating the decision-making processes of British society.

This is not to belittle what must, on a dispassionate analysis, be reckoned the main achievement of the Campaign and its offshoots over the past seven years: the creation in Britain of an educated minority public opinion on the subject of nuclear weapons. This is signified not merely by the acceptance of jargon words like megaton, counter-force, and half-life into the conversation and reading matter of a far wider circle than the small clique of experts who would have understood them in 1957. It is rather that in Britain—more than in America, despite the possibly superior generalship of American peace movements —ordinary, non-specialised people have come to feel passionately that modern war is too serious a subject to be left either to the soldiers or to the politicians; and that just as the consequences of a war, if it now occurred, would be totally evil and unacceptable, so the problem of preventing the occurrence can fairly be expected to engage a considerable proportion of a thinking man's time and mental energy. This feeling, stimulated no doubt by awareness of this island's extreme vulnerability, has undoubtedly been diffused among sections of British opinion which are neither soft-headed nor soft-hearted; and which have never been persuaded that the actual policies urged on the Government by CND are necessarily prudent ones. It would be hard to find a young Englishman in his twenties who could have said after the Cuban crisis, as an American airman of that age said to me in East Anglia: "We should have gone to war." (He was a pleasant young man and clearly, he had not the faintest idea what he was saying.) CND has often been justly rebuked for its anti-American tone, and its leaders are in no position to claim that they have done even as much as their American counterparts to conduct a dialogue with the disposers of this final, unimaginable power. But your average Aldermaston marcher, at least before the March became a predominantly teenage jaunt, could fairly pride himself with knowing more about the ills of the world and their causes than most of his peers and coevals in Detroit or Denver.

Is it sufficient, though, to assess CND as a mildly educative force? Even some of the Campaign's most vociferous enemies would go much farther than this. Mr John Mander:

"The Campaign for Nuclear Disarmament seems to me the most spontaneous, virile, and sincere political movement Britain has seen since the thirties . . . by far the most significant political movement Britain has produced since the war . . . Today the greater part of public opinion rejects the independent deterrent as an expensive and dangerous chimera . . . Would such a volte-face have come about without six years of agitation by CND?"*

Perhaps it would, but this does not invalidate Mr Mander's main judgement. "The strength of unilateralism," as he says, "was that those who were not for it did not care to speak against it." This was a quality which CND shared with the cause of Spain and anti-Fascism during the thirties, when a book like George Orwell's *Homage to Catalonia* could make enemies on the Left simply by telling honestly what the writer saw. At the same time the Campaign provided what the anti-Fascists never had, outside the limited context of the Peace Ballot, and that was an organisational framework with which decent, non-political people could identify themselves, locally as well as nationally. By uniting these two attributes the Campaign surpassed its predecessors. The "unilateralist case", as it was presented, seems to have been supported thoughtfully or thoughtlessly by some 10 million British adults, and it would be absurd to underestimate this kind of pressure. But the vast majority of the 10 million held

* *Great Britain or Little England*, pp. 44, 47. "Virile", it will be noticed, was also Canon Collins' epithet for his Campaign.

the same views at the beginning of the Campaign, at least in latent form, as they did at the end. The importance of CND—and in this respect it remains "open-ended"—lay in the half million or so people (no one will ever know the exact figure) who were at different times persuaded that it was worth their while to take action, legal or illegal, ambulatory or argumentative, in excess of their normal civic duty to vote at elections and do what they were told in between them. It is from here that any discussion of the future must start.

At the time of writing it is an open question whether the CND as such will wind peacefully to its close, continue in fossilised form like one of the extinct religious revival movements which it in some ways resembles, or lie low, initiating small-scale activities, some useful, some mischievous, until some fresh political twist or an actual nuclear catastrophe revives the feelings which gave birth to the Campaign. On the whole, the second possibility seems more likely than the first, and the third possibility more likely than the second. On the penultimate page of *On the Prevention of War*—his last major book—the late John Strachey wrote:

"Some readers may be disappointed that it is not suggested that we should found societies for this or demonstrate for that. Let them be reassured. Occasions will arise when it will be vitally important to exercise every possibility of pressure, by voting, by talking, by writing, by 'joining', by demonstrating, for or against particular courses of action on the part of the Governments of our respective nation-states . . . Only, none of this kind of activity is likely to be useful or effective unless it is founded upon a comprehension of what is at issue and of the general direction in which a solution may be found."*

For Mr Strachey the "general direction" was, first, short-term staving-off measures to make the balance of terror more stable; second, careful attention to every measure of mutual disarmament and *détente* proposed by either side; and third, concentration on the ultimate goal of unification under a world authority, evolved out of the collective nuclear monopoly of the existing super-powers, whether two or several.

It is obvious that between Mr Strachey and the unilateralists, there is a large area of common ground. Reviewing his book in *War and Peace†* Mr Mervyn Jones, one of the Campaign's spokesmen, remarked: "I agree that the two great objectives of our age—disarmament and world government—are far more likely to be achieved by the enlightened self-interest of the super-powers than by the efforts of idealists." Shorn of idealistic

* Macmillan, 1962.   † January–March 1963, p. 59.

considerations on one side, and nationalistic considerations on the other, the debate between unilateralists and multilateralists had narrowed by this time to a straightforward argument about the best use to make of the leverage supplied by British nuclear power and military alliances. The unilateralists believed that the foundations for agreement between America and Russia—"the bridge across which the giants may walk", in Mr Jones' words—would be built by the minor powers, and built more quickly if Britain abandoned her nuclear pretensions and "special relationship" with America, and joined the bridge-builders. The multilateralists believed that Britain's stabilising influence depended upon her power, both military and geo-political; and that power, while it might usefully one day be transferred by stages to a world authority, should never be un-conditionally renounced, lest worse forms of power entered the vacuum created. Indeed, for this very reason, at least one highly sophisticated multilateralist rejected the whole concept and goal of "general and complete disarmament":

"Quite apart from the permanent prospect of a secret stock of nuclear weapons (which could always be carried in unorthodox delivery systems, like airliners) the potentiality of power can never be abolished ... The problem in the world as in individual nations is not to abolish power but to organise it to serve the causes of peace and justice. General and complete disarmament would give power to those who had been most successful at deception or to those who were most ready for recovery and rearmament. It is a strange comment on public affairs that so much genuine moral energy should be expended on an objective which would be dangerous and undesirable."*

Mr Beaton suggested that the basis of a world force could be provided if the nuclear powers would commit missile-firing submarines to a common command and training structure, preserving their own forces meanwhile; and that the inter-national force thus created should go on to recruit its own men, and perhaps even build its own nuclear force. He drew the parallel of the American West, where the right of personal self-defence was regularly used for many years until the rule of law rendered the habit largely obsolete. It was, perhaps, a more uncomfortable parallel than Mr Beaton realised, for the assas-sination of President Kennedy and then of his murderer, attri-butable on one level of causation to the American tradition of freely available firearms, can be read as a parable of the prospect before us if nations continue for long to insist upon their in-dividual right to defend themselves by indefensible means. As

* Leonard Beaton in The *Guardian*, January 21, 1964.

Mr Robert McNamara said in his Ann Arbor speech on June 16, 1962: "The mere fact that no nation could rationally take steps leading to a nuclear war does not guarantee that a nuclear war cannot take place."

Here it is perhaps appropriate to mention a slight but significant shift which has recently taken place in the concerns, not only of members of CND, but of some of the Campaign's multi-lateralist critics. The National Council for the Registration of Volunteers for a World Police Force, formed in the United Kingdom in 1963, includes among its twelve members four (Mr James Cameron, Group Captain Leonard Cheshire, Captain B. H. Liddell Hart, and the Revd. Dr Donald Soper) who have from different points of view been associated with a CND position. But three members (Major-General W. A. Dimoline, the chairman, Field-Marshal Sir Claude Auchinleck, and Rear-Admiral Sir Anthony Buzzard) belong to a very different stable. The Council has chosen to press for individual recruitment to a World Police Force rather than for national contingents, and has registered as volunteers enough intelligent MPs and opinion-formers of the centre band of British politics to make its demand for a British initiative not altogether remote from attainment. At the same time CND itself, especially its younger members, is seriously alarmed about the hints officially dropped during 1964 that the over-extended British forces abroad might have to be relieved by selective conscription. The wheel has thus come full circle, for in the late forties and early fifties, opposition to conscription was one of the chief preoccupations of the peace movement and the Labour Left. At that time, however, this pacifist concern was never reflected to any great extent in the figures for conscientious objection to military service. The proportion of conscientious objectors in the National Service intake did, however, rise to 0·45 p.c. in 1960, the last year for which figures were published, and if this trend has been projected through, and accelerated by, the years of mass civil disobedience and youthful revolt, CND observers may well be right in thinking that by now it will have reached embarrassing proportions. It would, at least, be interesting to learn what proportion of young Englishmen today would be prepared to fight for the United Nations but not "for Queen and Country", and what proportion of conscientious objectors to all forms of military service would refuse to recognise the authority of CO Tribunals.

If I am correct in supposing that the Campaign is in process of breaking down into its original constituent parts—gradualists and radicals, constitutionalists and anarchists, power-manipulators and power-renouncers—it is important to inquire whether the second of all these pairs are going to be able to contribute in separation anything as distinctive and influential as they contributed while in fusion with the gradualists. It does not seem impossible. Suez and the Bomb, followed by the Campaign itself, lifted British radical pacifism over a hump composed of a lost generation and a moribund corpus of ideas, into a social and intellectual atmosphere which may or may not have been misguided, but is at least contemporary. In the years since Sir Stephen King-Hall first lent respectability to the traditional pacifist case by advocating a Royal Commission to study the possibility of non-violent resistance, a significant number of people in Britain have had both practical and theoretical experience of "non-violent action". It has not been on the scale of Gandhi's operations in British India. It has not demanded as much of its participants (with a few exceptions) as the Norwegian teachers' passive resistance to the Gestapo, the sit-ins and bus boycotts of Mississippi and Alabama, or the boycotts, marches and pass-burnings of South Africa. But it has been native to Britain. It has used these other instances of non-violent action as sources of inspiration or instruction, but not as artificial models. No one could have predicted or invented the Aldermaston March or the Polaris sit-downs. And it is entirely characteristic of this country that one of the most suggestive and wide-ranging studies to have been initiated in this field is—as Sir Stephen has himself admitted—a symposium which arose out of a couple of local peace conferences in Colchester early in 1961, convened by the local CND and other peace organisations and entitled "A Search for an Alternative to War and Violence".* Such a phenomenon itself partially contradicts any attempt to interpret CND and its offshoots in the terms used by Kornhauser in his *The Politics of Mass Society*, as a form of mass manipulation, made possible by the destruction of the institutional and communal ties which once bound people together in small "publics" and other groups. London's "Rentacrowd" may be explicable in these terms, but the Campaign as a whole, in its local aspects, is if anything a testimony to the surviving strength, in Britain, of subsidiary political "publics" and groupings.

However, despite the efforts of the nuclear disarmers over the past few years, it cannot be pretended that non-violent action, and the range of options which it presents, is at all widely understood in this country, let alone by those newspapers which themselves might well be described in Kornhauserian terms as manipulators of mass society. This is not the place for a full discussion but it is important that we should understand, firstly what majorities or minorities who passionately dissent from

Alternatives to War and Violence—a Search, edited by Ted Dunn (James Clarke, 1963).

239

decisions of their Governments are liable to do, and secondly what a nation, forced by nuclear blackmail or other forms of superior power to submit to the will of another State, might usefully teach its own people beforehand. Miss April Carter, the first Secretary of the Direct Action Committee, has classified the methods of non-violent action in the following way:

From *Direct Action* (*Peace News* pamphlet, 1960):

Resistance Methods	*Constructive Counterparts*
CONSTITUTIONAL ACTION AND PROPAGANDA	
Petitions, deputations, lobbies, letters to press, leaflets, pamphlets, canvassing, public meetings, exhibitions.	Negotiations. Investigation of facts in conflict situation. Journals, briefings, conferences.
SYMBOLIC ACTION	
Parades, marches, vigils, silence, fasts. Supplementary aspects: slogans, songs, symbols, badges, salutes.	Rallies, prayer meetings, purificatory acts, pledges, Hartal.
ECONOMIC ACTION	
Strikes: token, go-slow, sit-in, stay-at-home.	Reverse strike, strike funds, union organisation, workers' control.
Boycott: of goods, services, business, military sites; social boycott.	Creation of alternative goods and services.
Labour boycott: of goods, services, sites. Pickets to obtain strikes or boycotts.	Setting up alternative industry.
CIVIL DISOBEDIENCE AND PHYSICAL INTERVENTION	
Open contravention of unjust laws through acts of omission or commission. Trespass, occupation, raids, obstruction, sit-downs, sit-ins, stand-ins, "rides".	Working for constructive legislation.
ACTION AGAINST THE STATE	
Revenue refusal.	Diverting revenue constructively.
Conscientious objection, mutiny.	Fraternising troops and police.
Non-co-operation with State, including boycott of Government or official departments, organisations, institutions. Resignation of offices and titles and boycott of Government employment. Disobedience to Government decrees. Mass revolutionary civil disobedience (may involve breaking "neutral" laws).	Creating alternative organisations and institutions, or continuing to operate existing ones which the Government is trying to replace.
Occupation and take-over of Government buildings and police stations.	Parallel Government.
General Strike.	Organisation of economy.

The CND explored most orthodox methods of constitutional action within its first year, though its confidence about what it expected to achieve was not, perhaps, borne out even by the available precedents, let alone by the nature of the cause. Miss Carter herself shrewdly points out that while under a totalitarian regime, which suppresses everything, a single speech may be dynamite, in Britain it is possible to wage a vigorous and intellectually convincing conventional campaign for years, and even to attract some support in Parliament, but achieve abstract sympathy rather than remedial action. The classic case is the Women's Suffrage Movement from 1866 to 1903.

During 1958, too, symbolic action in the shape of the Aldermaston March probably did more in the end than any other action of the Campaign during the year to bring the cause of nuclear disarmament into the public consciousness. There is a monograph to be written on marches as an expression of spontaneous public emotion. The Hungarian revolt began in this way. Suez evoked a similar demonstration in London. Among prearranged marches, the Washington Civil Rights March of August 28, 1963, stands out as an unprecedentedly effective political gesture.

More specifically Gandhian forms of symbolic action were borrowed only with caution by Campaigners. It was extremely rare to hear of a significant public fast being undertaken (though two men did do this in Swansea during the Cuban crisis); and Dr Rachel Pinney's "silent Wednesdays" were one of the few examples I know of, as it were, the offensive use of silence by nuclear disarmers. Too many, indeed, expected to be heard for their much speaking. But like the Suffragettes, the Campaign yielded at least one suicide in the cause, though Miss Malpas, of Halstead, who killed herself and left explanatory notes when the Great Powers resumed testing in 1962, received little publicity by comparison with Emily Davison.

Industrial action in Britain against the Bomb has been very limited in extent, despite the thousands of woman-hours that Miss Pat Arrowsmith must have put into encouraging it. One of the most significant examples ante-dated the founding of CND, for it was in 1957 in NE Scotland that meetings of the Aberdeen Plumbing Trades Union, the Aberdeen Trades Council, and the National Federation of Building Trades Operatives passed motions against the construction of rocket bases in the area. "Not a pick, not a spade, not a trowel will be used for the establishment of rocket sites in the area," said the builders at Dundee, and they were quite correct: the rocket sites went elsewhere. Cause and effect, however, has not been established. The one-hour token stoppage at Stevenage in protest against the town's reliance on the missile industry has already been noted. This and other industrial campaigns by the Direct Action Committee were allied to "constructive" efforts to find alternative employment or financial resources for workers who were persuaded to leave their military jobs.

Civil disobedience has been in evidence throughout this book on the British nuclear disarmers, though it cannot be pretended that they ever found a form of it which satisfied Miss Carter's ideal synthesis of "symbolic action" and "economic action". ("The classic example," she wrote, "is Gandhi's Salt March, which culminated in his picking up a handful of salt from the sea, thus asserting the right of all men to take salt from the sea and demonstrating the absurdity of the salt monopoly and the tax laws. Thus a handful of salt became a symbol of Indian independence.") "Constructive counterparts" discovered were equally rare, apart from the collections on sit-downs for causes like the Freedom from Hunger Campaign, and the instances of young ladies marrying with the Metropolitan policemen who carted their limp and pliant forms away from the Square.

As for mass revolutionary civil disobedience, this was never really much more than a gleam in Ralph Schoenman's eye. Similarly, the "Voter's Veto" campaign, which called upon the electorate to vote only for candidates pledged to unilateral nuclear disarmament, was firmly rejected on several occasions by Campaigners themselves. This, according to Miss Carter, was because Voter's Veto was seen as a boycott of the polls, and hence of the whole Parliamentary system, and as a threat to the only "constitutional" hope of the Campaign, namely the Labour Party. "The Voter's Veto was seen as essentially negative and destructive of institutions which were deeply respected and depended upon, without posing more dynamic or convincing alternatives."

The same words apply even more strongly to most of the Committee of 100's activities in the days of its power. To connect with the British public as a whole, the Committee would have had first to demonstrate by rational or at least by persuasive argument that British democratic institutions were no longer, or had never been, what in theory and in the public mind they were: reliable channels for the general will of the people to be communicated to the country's leaders. Only then could the Committee have profitably gone on to by-pass these institutions in the name of its cause. But within its own assumptions, the Committee was, of course, entirely justified in acting as it did. We are brought up to regard with awed admiration acts of civil disobedience against totalitarian regimes which commit genocide or violate human rights; and there is no law of God or man which lays down that a majority of people at a free election, or a democratically elected Government between elections, will not endorse or pursue policies which history will later adjudge to have been crimes against humanity.

The most striking feature of Miss Carter's classification, drawn from many different countries at many different periods, is the number of the techniques mentioned which have been used, however inadequately, in Britain by the nuclear disarmers. Indeed, a compilation in this form puts into perspective some of the horrified reactions which greeted these people when they resorted to illegal actions to press their case. Like the line between nuclear and conventional weapons, the line between legality and illegality is sharp, and not to be crossed inadvisedly. Some think it should never be crossed at all. Yet on both sides of these particular lines there may be entrenched at any given moment people with identical attitudes and philosophies. In destructiveness and criminality, nothing divided the bombing of Dresden from that of Hiroshima. Conscientious objection to military service has been legal in some time and place, illegal in others. The types of non-violent action listed by Miss Carter fall some one side, some the other side of the legality line. They share, when properly conducted, the characteristic of non-violence. But the violence line and the legality line do not necessarily coincide. It is as easy to be violent but legal—for instance, by beating one's children or raping one's wife in the privacy of one's own home—as it is to be non-violent but illegal, by sitting down in the road outside a missile base. But of course, non-violent action is not always properly conducted. Nor is it always easy to enable the participants in the action to participate also in the decision to undertake the action. Pickets, trespass, obstruction, occupation of Government buildings, and mass revolutionary civil disobedience require, if they are to be non-violent, an extraordinary degree of collective self-discipline in the participants; and even if this self-discipline is present, it is always likely that the tensions and social upheavals induced by the non-violent action will of themselves generate violence in other people.

Nothing useful can be said or learnt about non-violent action unless its essentially coercive and potentially subversive content is recognised at the outset. It is at the opposite extreme from "passivism". It is an alternative, if embryonic, source of power. When men and women tap this source, they do so out of expediency rather than principle, when they have become conscious that the violent weapons at their disposal are insufficient to ward off the damage that others are capable of inflicting. It was not as pacifists but as patriots that over a thousand Norwegian teachers in 1941 resisted collectively and totally the attempts of Quisling and the Gestapo to Nazify the Norwegian school system. Hundreds were imprisoned, transported to forced labour camps, bullied and maltreated to persuade them to sign satisfactory declarations. But the teachers stood out and won, and eventually, Hitler himself ordered the abandonment of the whole project of setting up a corporate State in Norway. Describing to Gene Sharp the discussions which preceded the teachers' resistance, one of the participants said: "Nowhere did the *idea* of non-violent resistance come in. Instead of an idea, it developed as a way to work, a way to do something. I don't think we realised the theoretical point at all. We just felt that something must be done and that we must do it."*

For obvious reasons, most of the people in Britain who have expressed an interest in this source of power have themselves been pacifists. After all, simply in terms of destructive capability Britain is still the third power in the world, and it is difficult for the wielders of such power to recognise its built-in limitations. But it is certainly arguable today that the citizens of any power, even of a minor nuclear power, would be better employed equipping themselves with some elementary history and practice in the field of non-violent action than in learning the extremely primitive civil defence drills which Governments think more suitable for their populations.

There would appear to be four main possibilities for the world's future: (1) The emergence of a world authority; (2) an enormously destructive nuclear (or bacteriological or toxicological) war; (3) an indefinite continuance of the present uneasy peace, with the deterrent continuing to deter; (4) the withering away of the deterrent, as states discover new ways of fighting both hot and cold wars without bringing the sword of Damocles down on their heads. It would be a bold man who said which of these possibilities was most likely to be realised, but three of them leave obvious openings for the development of non-violence as a weapon of coercion for states as well as for groups and individuals. And if the fourth possibility—total war—is realised it is certain that any descendants of its survivors, if they are able to examine the records of their forebears, will praise the 20th century not for its politicians or its generals but for its individuals, however cranky, who were beginning the belated search for an alternative to violence at the point where domestic politics or external diplomacy breaks down.

CND and the Committee of 100 represented very primitive experiments in this field. Exposed first to the facility of Collins and then to the apocalyptic of Russell, the two organisations were excessively preoccupied with time, and with the imminence of doom. Both were vulnerable to Richard Hauser's criticism: "The Peace Movement makes the grave mistake of frightening people—the more they panic, the more emotional they become and the harder it is for them to think. People who want quick

* *Tyranny Could Not Quell Them, Peace News* pamphlet.

action in peace are like those who go to the doctor and want to become well immediately."* Seldom were these organisations' members sufficiently united over aims and methods to give serious thought to the different problems presented to the Campaign by different social categories, of which Hauser identifies six: the leaders, scientists, and experts who have a direct impact upon events; people who both accept and prepare for war, including nuclear war; active and responsible people emotionally willing to make protest gestures in the cause of peace; people who want peace but "put their country first"; people who are aware of the situation and anxious about it, but have suppressed their feelings in cynicism or day-to-day routine; and finally "the huge mass of people who do not wish to think". Hauser's categories are neither definitive nor exhaustive, but they serve to call in question much of what the Campaign was trying to do.

The cry, in this as in so many other fields, is for more research. There is now not much about war that is not known to somebody—though certainly, the pathological secretiveness of governments, Western as well as Eastern, ensures that comparatively little is known to the general public. But about peace, almost nothing is known. This is as true at the level of disarmament and arms control as it is at the level of "peace psychology" and radical group action. Mr Leonard Beaton has suggested for Britain the formation of a "Royal Disarmament Establishment", a technically qualified body on the lines of the Royal Aircraft Establishment, Farnborough, with a budget of £1–2 million a year and a long-term commitment to maintain a certain size of organisation and to offer careers to a certain type of man.† Up to the time of writing, proposals of this nature, costing about a thousandth of Britain's annual defence budget, have always been rejected by the Government.

Curiously enough, the same figure of £1 million per annum has been mentioned as the sum needed for a serious programme of academic research into the history and applicability of non-violent action as a political substitute for war. The author of the suggestion, Mr Gene Sharp, is a young American whose 280,000-word attempt to provide a conceptual framework for non-violent action, and at the same time indicate the areas where further inquiry is most urgently needed, is regrettably still awaiting a publisher. In essence, of course, this proposal is similar to Sir Stephen King-Hall's request for a Royal Commission on Unarmed Defence, which over seven years ago was one of the lead-ins to the Campaign for Nuclear Disarmament.‡ At the time, Sir Stephen had a better hearing from military men than from

* In *Alternatives to War and Violence* (*op. cit.*), p. 120. † The *Guardian*, January 22, 1964. ‡ Cf. p. 36.

politicians and political journalists, who were (and are) taken up with the much more utopian goal of "general and complete disarmament". Mr Sharp himself is explicitly setting out to solve the problem posed in different terms by Mr Beaton: what forms of coercion do you use as an extension of diplomacy when traditional forms have become self-destructive? Both men, in contra-distinction to the main pacifist stream in Anglo-Saxon thought, take the existence of power and conflict as a given and irreducible fact about human relations. Mr Beaton, it may be thought, is concentrating (as indeed, needs must) on the world of the next decade or two, which must find a way of controlling conflict situations internationally or, quite probably, die. Mr Sharp, although he looks to immediate situations to extend both the knowledge and practice of conflict resolution by coercive non-violence, and although he expects to find in the totalitarian-isms of today and tomorrow ample scope for the exercise of this technique, is also looking beyond any degree of world unification and power centralisation that may be achieved. "International leagues, etc. still need some sanction, and some means of struggle might be needed against them should they become a tool of oppression."* Instead of, with William James, looking for "the moral equivalent to war" (though this, too, enters into it) Mr Sharp is looking for its socio-political equivalent—what the sociologist Talcott Parsons would call its "functional alter-native" as an ultimate sanction.

The interest which contemporary strategists and academic analysts are prepared to take in these ideas was signalled in the spring of this year by the Director of the Institute for Strategic Studies, Mr Alastair Buchan, contributing a foreword to a *Peace News* pamphlet on *Civilian Defence*, containing essays by Mr Sharp, Professor Jerome D. Frank, Professor Arne Naess, and Mr Adam Roberts of *Peace News* staff. Mr Buchan writes of "the particular relevance of non-violent resistance to warding off Communist and especially Chinese pressure":

"The whole of Mao's strategy theory—and he is undoubtedly the greatest strategist of our day—is based on the economy of resources through indirect pressure. In other words, force must never be used nor battle offered until the opponent has been demoralised, penetrated from within, internally divided, the people separated from their government. Internal violence in a free state, especially in the multi-racial societies of Asia, plays straight into Mao's hands, but if techniques of non-violent persuasion and resistance can be developed, then the oppor-tunity for external violence may not present itself."

* Essay in *Pathogenesis of War*, ed.

And again:

"Disarmament can never remove the residual potentiality of force . . . But if the disarming of states were accompanied by a similar build-up of non-violent defence techniques in the countries concerned, then at the level of force which aggressor states could mount, invasion and subjection of other countries would not seem a profitable or attractive policy. (Especially if, as I personally think would be necessary, there were a world security authority still fully armed.)"

One would not be justified in directly attributing to CND as an institution, or even to the British as a whole, this slowly burgeoning interest in ideas which seven years ago were almost as strange to the peace movement as to the war party in this country. Most of what little research has so far been done in this area has been done in America and Norway—the one the most powerful State on earth, with resources enough and to spare for this further, marginal-seeming quest; the other a small, pacific country dependent almost entirely upon external allies for military defence against totalitarian incursions. Britain, which over the past decade has oscillated distressingly from extremes of jingoism to agonies of self-doubt, has hardly been prepared psychologically for cool reflection on these possible alternatives to her historic postures.

And yet what now seems to be a national progress towards a calmer frame of mind and a more exploratory temper would surely have been slower to arrive without the nuclear disarmers' belated but none the less intense concentration on the brute fact of the Bomb. Under the light "brighter than a thousand suns", so many generally admirable national traditions, ranging from seasoned statecraft and spontaneous patriotism to international idealism and a highly developed capacity for moral outrage, have all been scrutinised and discovered to be more or less inadequate. Our statecraft, already found wanting at Suez and at Brussels, was in Cuba Week proved superfluous, and the point was rubbed home symbolically last December when we realised that an assassin's bullet could have killed a British Prime Minister or reigning Monarch without affecting our minds and hearts as nearly as did the death of President Kennedy. Our patriotism is now a domesticated emotion, concerned with preserving the countryside rather than with patrolling the frontiers, for the arrival of push-button massacre has taken from any major conflict everything that once gave war some shreds of nobility, and has left our soldiery with a range of minor operations which, necessary though they be to the peace of the world, no more redound to the glory of Britain than a good month's trade returns or a gold medal at the Olympic games. Our international idealism has been in danger of slipping between the two stools of romantic neutralism and big-league pretensions—both equally foolish responses to the nuclear capability which we possess—and it has been given a further push under the table by our economic weakness and selfishness, which has often prevented us from doing for the developing countries even of our own Commonwealth as much as our commercial and political rivals have been willing to do instead. And lastly our sense of moral outrage, though aroused by the Bomb as once it was by the slave traffic or the Bulgarian atrocities, in the end failed to connect because it lacked both intellectual rigour and practical reference points. Much of it belonged to an ethical and theological tradition which was itself being called in question when the Bomb confronted it with its greatest and most complex challenge. The result was a squeal of pain, largely unaccompanied by any suggestions for extricating ourselves from the particular situation in which we happened, not wholly through our own fault, to have landed.

All this protest is now—perhaps prematurely—assumed to be past. In schools and colleges and places where fashion reigns, one is told that the years of anti-nuclear commitment have given place to a new brand of detachment, cynicism, and garden-cultivation. Such a phase was doubtless inevitable, and it will perhaps do us no harm to enter a period when the question "Will it work?" is heard more often than "Is it moral?", "Is it visionary enough?" or even "Is it sufficiently Socialist?" We live in an age, after all, when academic students of inter-national relations are ceasing to view their subject in terms of power, but are borrowing from the cool discipline of cybernetics to erect "self-steering models" for the dealings of States with each other. It may well seem now that there are no "good, brave old causes" left—only new, complex, and unglamorous problems.

For after nuclear weapons, what bogy remains for children to frighten their parents with? What other cause can get demonstrators out on to the streets? Nevertheless, now that banning the Bomb has run the gamut from skiffle group to study group, sooner or later a new cause will be found. May its leaders learn something from the experience of their pre-decessors.

SHORT BIBLIOGRAPHY

J. Hersey, *Hiroshima* (Penguin Special, 1946)

P. M. S. Blackett, *Military and Political Consequences of Atomic Energy* (Turnstile Press, 1948) and *Atomic Weapons and East–West Relations* (CUP, 1956)

G. K. A. Bell, *The Church and Humanity*, 1939–1946 (Longmans, 1946)

H. Kahn, *On Thermonuclear War* (OUP, 1960)

J. Strachey, *On the Prevention of War* (Macmillan, 1962)

P. Noel-Baker, *The Arms Race* (Calder, 1960)

S. King-Hall, *Defence in the Nuclear Age* (Gollancz, 1958) and *Power Politics in the Nuclear Age* (Gollancz, 1962)

R. Jungk, *Brighter Than A Thousand Suns* (Gollancz, 1958)

G. F. Kennan, *Russia, the Atom, and the West* (OUP, 1958)

P. Toynbee (ed.), *The Fearful Choice* (Gollancz, 1958)

B. Russell, *Common Sense and Nuclear Warfare* (Allen & Unwin, 1959) and *Unarmed Victory* (Penguin, 1963)

W. Young, *Strategy for Survival* (Penguin, 1959)

J. Mander, *Great Britain or Little England?* (Penguin, 1963)

L. Mumford and others, *Breakthrough to Peace* (New Directions, Norfolk, Connecticut, 1962)

C. Urquhart (ed.), *A Matter of Life* (Cape, 1963)

T. Dunn (ed.), *Alternatives to War and Violence* (James Clarke, 1963)

J. C. Bennett (ed.), *Nuclear Weapons and the Conflict of Conscience* (Lutterworth Press, 1962)

P. Ramsey, *War and the Christian Conscience* (Duke University Press and CUP, 1961)

D. L. Edwards, *Withdrawing from the Brink* (SCM Press, 1963)

J. Vincent, *Christ in a Nuclear World* (Crux Press, 1962) and *Christian Nuclear Perspective* (Epworth, 1964)

W. Stein (ed.), *Nuclear Weapons and Christian Conscience* (Merlin Press, 1961)

D. M. MacKinnon and others, *God, Sex and War* (Fontana, 1963)

A. Pirie (ed.), *Fall-out* (MacGibbon & Kee, 1958)

R. F. Kornhauser, *The Politics of Mass Society* (Routledge, 1960)

M. Harrison, *Trade Unions and the Labour Party since 1945* (Allen & Unwin, 1960)

H. Street, *Freedom, the Individual and the Law* (Pelican, 1963)

J. Buxton and M. Turner, *Gate Fever* (Cresset Press, 1962) and *Inside Story* (Prison Reform Council, 1963)

J. R. Taylor, *Anger and After* (revised ed. Pelican, 1963)

C. Morgan, *The Burning Glass* (Macmillan, 1954)

R. Bolt, *The Tiger and the Horse* (French's Acting Edition, 1961)

D. Lessing, *Each His Own Wilderness* (Penguin New English Dramatists, No. 1)

D. Mercer, *The Generations* (Calder, 1964)
E. de Kadt, *British Defence Policy and Nuclear War* (Frank Cass, 1964)
T. Stonier, *Nuclear Disaster* (Penguin 1964)

Unpublished

R. A. Exley, *The Campaign for Nuclear Disarmament: Its organisation, personnel and methods in its first year* (thesis presented to the University of Manchester, 1959)
D. V. Edwards, *The Movement for Unilateral Nuclear Disarmament in Britain* (Swarthmore College, 1962)
D. Campton, *Four Minute Warning* (plays)

Periodicals, etc.

The *Guardian, The Times,* The *Observer, New Statesman, Peace News, Anarchy, Encounter, CND Bulletin* (monthly) 1958–60 and *Sanity* 1961–64, *War and Peace, New Left Review.*

Minutes, leaflets, and pamphlets of the Campaign for Nuclear Disarmament, the Direct Action Committee Against Nuclear War, and the Committee of 100.

Hansard, Labour Party and TUC Conference Reports, Defence White Papers.

INDEX

251

253